Charles Coppens

A Practical Introduction to English Rhetoric

precepts and exercises

Charles Coppens

A Practical Introduction to English Rhetoric
precepts and exercises

ISBN/EAN: 9783337300845

Printed in Europe, USA, Canada, Australia, Japan

Cover: Foto ©Paul-Georg Meister /pixelio.de

More available books at **www.hansebooks.com**

A

PRACTICAL INTRODUCTION

TO

ENGLISH RHETORIC:

PRECEPTS AND EXERCISES.

BY

REV. CHARLES COPPENS, S.J.,

Author of "The Art of Oratorical Composition."

NEW YORK:
SCHWARTZ, KIRWIN & FAUSS,
42 BARCLAY STREET.

CONTENTS.

Contents.

BOOK II.—THE ORNAMENTS OF COMPOSITION.

BOOK III.—STYLE IN LITERARY COMPOSITION.

BOOK IV.—SPECIES OF PROSE COMPOSITION.

BOOK VI.—NATURE AND VARIETIES OF POETRY.

PREFACE.

AFTER devoting nearly thirty years of his life to the sacred cause of education, the author of this volume has been requested by many of his friends to arrange for publication the notes on Rhetoric and Poetry which he had gradually accumulated. These consisted partly of precepts carefully selected from the works of the best critics, ancient and modern, partly of choice models gathered from the ·works of the most distinguished writers, to which were added the results of his own observation and experience.

He began his task by publishing, last year, *The Art of Oratorical Composition*, for the benefit of those who aim at success in public speaking. Encouraged by the readiness with which that treatise has already been adopted in many leading colleges, and urged by his superiors and others to undertake a work of still wider usefulness, he has now written this *Practical Introduction to English Rhetoric* as a general text-book on Composition for the use of Colleges and Academies.

He rests his claims to the patronage of such nstitu- tions on the following points:

1. The work is so comprehensive as to embrace all the precepts of Rhetoric usually explained to the pupils of academies. In conjunction with *The Art of Oratori-*

cal Composition it contains the entire course of Rhetoric as studied in colleges and universities.

2. It is very practical, as will appear from even a cursory glance at the numerous exercises suggested in its pages. In the first part of the work many matters are explained and exercises suggested, which the teacher may utilize for the improvement of even young children in the lowest classes.

3. It contains a copious collection of choice quotations in prose and verse, to serve as models for the imitation of pupils. But it does not contain long lists of faulty sentences, etc., because the author thinks that students, in their daily exercises, supply the professor with a sufficient amount of such matter for criticism.

4. Lastly, the work pretends to do what many text-books on Rhetoric neglect, and what is really the most important task of all—namely, to educate the heart as well as the head of the student; or, as Southey expresses it, "to throw his affections aright": to guide the steps of the young through the pleasant paths of literature, without exposing them to the danger of losing what is far more precious than all the literature of the world—the purity of their Faith and the innocence of their hearts.

The treatise on "Versification" which forms part of this work is from the able pen of Rev. Eugene H. Brady, S.J., of St. Xavier College, Cincinnati, O. It is highly appreciated by the author of this volume; and he does not doubt that it will prove most acceptable to those for whose benefit it is now published.

ST. LOUIS UNIVERSITY, April 13, 1886.

INTRODUCTORY.

1. The foundation of all literary excellence is **common sense.**

> " Scribendi recte sapere est et principium et fons,"

says Horace. His translator, Francis, applies this rule to Poetry,

> " Good sense, the fountain of the Muse's art ";

but it holds for all kinds of composition. Now, one of the first dictates of common sense is that an exercise be **not above the power of the writer.** The same critic remarks :

> " Examine well, ye writers, weigh with care
> What suits your genius, what your strength will bear.
> To him who shall his task with judgment choose
> Nor words nor method shall their aid refuse."

School-exercises should therefore be carefully adapted to the capacity of the pupils. A boy may be taught to compose a natural and interesting narration of an excursion a favorite game, a festive celebration, a distressing accident, etc. ; but he is as yet incapable of handling intricate or abstract subjects. He will only write nonsense and acquire a faulty taste and style, if his first theme is the descriptive of an ancient or modern battle, an essay on ' The spirit of progress,' or even on ' The Declaration of Independence.'

2. The first requisite for success in any composition is that the writer have **clear and correct ideas** on the matter

to be treated.   Therefore, before speaking of style or the expression of thought, we shall premise a few exercises on the acquisition of thought.   Children acquire knowledge readily and naturally by observing what is presented to their senses.   We shall follow nature's guidance, and begin with such exercises as will promote or direct this habit of observation, as a preparation for original composition.

BOOK I.

THE ELEMENTS OF COMPOSITION.

CHAPTER I.

OBJECT-LESSONS.

3. **Object-Lessons** are exercises on objects that fall under
the senses. In these lessons children are trained to notice
such objects with care, to observe their parts, their qualities, their actions; the sources whence they come, the
means by which they may be obtained, the uses to which
they may be applied, and so forth.

4. The **chief advantages** derived from object-lessons are :

  1. They cultivate habits of attention ;

  2. They lead to greater distinctness of perception ;

  3. They store the mind with useful knowledge ;

  4. They cultivate a taste for what is real ;

  5. They develop the habit of tracing effects to their
causes, and following out causes to their effects ;

  6. They make the child acquainted with numerous
words, not learned at random and vaguely understood, but exactly suited to the clear ideas thus
acquired ;

  7. The spelling of those same words can easily be
learned in connection with the objects studied.

8. The exercises may be so conducted as to introduce various portions of grammar; for instance, the distinctions between nouns, adjectives, verbs; proper and common nouns; gender, number, and case; etc.

9. They afford the teacher opportunities to introduce, in a natural and interesting way, information concerning plants, animals, countries, nations, historical facts; above all, moral and religious maxims and principles, and to point out the evident marks in all things of the wisdom and love of the Creator.

10. They may easily be directed to the cultivation of good taste.

ARTICLE I. NAMES OF OBJECTS.

5. The **name** of anything which exists or of which we have any notion is a noun or substantive.

6. **1st Exercise.**—Write the names of all the objects you notice in this class-room, in the school-yard, in a dining-room, in a garden, in the church, at a picnic, at a funeral, in a sick-room, at a college exhibition, etc., etc.

7. **2d Exercise.**—Point out the agreeable objects collected by Goldsmith to describe a happy village:

> " Sweet Auburn, loveliest village of the plain,
>   Where health and plenty cheered the laboring swain,
>   Where smiling spring its earliest visit paid,
>   And parting summer's lingering blooms delayed :
>   Dear lovely bowers of innocence and ease,
>   Seats of my youth where every sport could please,
>   How often have I loitered o'er thy green,
>   Where humble happiness endeared each scene !
>   How often have I paused on every charm,
>   The sheltered cot, the cultivated farm,
>   The never-failing brook, the busy mill,
>   The decent church that topped the neighboring hill !"

8. **3d Exercise.**—Point out separately the gloomy and the pleasing objects in the following lines of the same poem, "The Deserted Village":

> " Amid thy bowers the tyrant's hand is seen,
> And desolation saddens all thy green :
> One only master grasps the whole domain,
> And half a village stints the smiling plain.
> No more the glassy brook reflects the day,
> But choked with sedges works its weary way ;
> Along the glades, a solitary guest,
> The hollow-sounding bittern guards its nest ;
> Amidst thy desert walks the lapwing flies,
> And tires their echoes with unvaried cries.
> Sunk are thy bowers in shapeless ruin all,
> And the long grass o'ertops the mouldering wall ;
> And trembling, shrinking from the spoiler's hand,
> Far, far away thy children leave the land."

9. **4th Exercise.**—Mention the objects peculiar to morn. ing, to noon, to evening, to night, to winter, to summer, to spring, to autumn, a graveyard, a Sunday, a solemn feast, etc.

Example of an evening scene.

> " Or when the plowman leaves the task of day,
> And trudging homeward whistles on the way ;
> When the big-uddered cows with patience stand,
> Waiting the strokings of the damsel's hand.
> No warbling cheers the wood : the feathered choir,
> To court kind slumbers, to the sprays retire,
> Where no rude gale disturbs the sleeping trees,
> No aspen leaves confess the gentlest breeze.
> Engaged in thought, to Neptune's bounds I stray,
> To take my farewell of the parting day ;
> Far in the deep the sun his glory hides,
> A streak of gold the sea and sky divides ;
> The purple clouds their amber linings show,
> And edged with flame rolls every wave below :
> Here pensive I behold the fading light,
> And o'er the distant billows lose my sight."—*Gay.*

It must be remembered that object-lessons properly apply to such objects only as are actually presented to the senses of the learners. The exercises here set down enlarge this field, so as to include other objects not actually observed, but known to exist under given circumstances. Great fidelity in describing things as they really are is earnestly recommended: exactness is one of the chief qualities of good writing.

ARTICLE II. PARTS OF OBJECTS.

10. **Exercise.**—Examine with care and mention the different parts of the following objects: A pear, a rose, a cherry-tree, a desk, a stove, a furnace, a carriage, a book, a newspaper, a bookcase, a map, an engine, etc. This exercise is treated in detail and with great variety of illustration in many books on Object-Lessons; its main purpose is the promotion of close observation in the learner. It will be sufficient to add here a few **examples.**

> *An apple* has stem, peel, pulp, juice, veins, eye, dimples, core, seeds, seed-case.
>
> *A pocket-knife* has handle, pivot, blade.
>
> *The handle* has rivets, frame, heel, sides, back, spring, grooves, plate.
>
> *The blade* has edge, point, back, notch, sides, maker's name.

ARTICLE III. QUALITIES OF OBJECTS.

A quality of an object is expressed by an adjective; as 'new,' 'old,' 'gentle,' etc.

11. **1st Exercise.**—Write the names of the objects in this room, and add to each name a suitable adjective; as, 'a new chair,' 'a square table,' 'a hot stove,' 'a gentle voice,' 'a harsh tone,' etc.

12. **2d Exercise.**—Point out the adjectives occurring in the verses quoted in Nos. 7, 8, 9, distinguishing those that make the objects more pleasing from those that produce the opposite effect.

13. **3d Exercise.**—Mention all the adjectives you know which denote color, figure, size, place, time.

Example of size : Large, big, great, voluminous, bulky, ample, capacious, huge, immense, enormous, vast, monstrous, gigantic, giant-like, colossal, Cyclopean, infinite, boundless; middling, mediocre, moderate, ordinary, average; little, small, minute, diminutive, inconsiderable, tiny, puny. petty, dwarfed, dwarfish, stunted, Liliputian.

ARTICLE IV. ACTIONS DONE BY OR TO OBJECTS.

An **action** done by a person or thing is expressed by an active verb ; as, 'to run,' 'to read,' 'to honor,' 'to love,' etc. An action suffered by a person or object is expressed by a passive verb ; as, 'to be seen,' 'to be loved,' 'to be rebuked,' etc.

14. **Exercise.**—Mention various actions which can be done by or to flame, rain, air, steam ; the eyes, hands, feet, tongue ; by or to birds, fishes, paper, pen, ink, etc.

15. **Example** of actions done by and to water ("The Cataract of Lodore ") :

" The Cataract strong	Showering and springing,
Then plunges along,	Flying and flinging,
Striking and raging	Writhing and ringing,
As if a war waging	Eddying and whisking,
Its caverns and rocks among ;	Spouting and frisking,
Rising and leaping,	Turning and twisting
Sinking and creeping,	Around and around
Swelling and sweeping,	With endless rebound;

<table>
<tr><td>And pouring and roaring,</td><td>And working and jerking,</td></tr>
<tr><td>And waving and raving,</td><td>And guggling and struggling,</td></tr>
<tr><td>And tossing and crossing,</td><td>And curling and whirling,</td></tr>
<tr><td>And flowing and going,</td><td>And purling and twirling,</td></tr>
<tr><td>And running and stunning,</td><td>And thumping and plumping,</td></tr>
<tr><td>And foaming and roaming,</td><td>And bumping and jumping,</td></tr>
<tr><td>And dinning and spinning,</td><td>And dashing and flashing,</td></tr>
<tr><td>And dropping and hopping,</td><td>And splashing and clashing,"</td></tr>
</table>

Etc.

ARTICLE V. USES OF OBJECTS.

16. **1st Exercise.**—Mention the uses of every article to be seen in a school-room, a parlor, a kitchen, a cloak-room, a dining-room, a church, a street-car, a sitting-room.

17. **2d Exercise.**—Mention the purposes served by the various parts of a tree, a stove, an umbrella. a bridge, a wagon, a trunk, a door, an apple.

Example: The parts of a hat.

Body: To cover the sides of the head and give shape to the hat.

Brim: To protect the neck and the face from sun and rain.

Crown: To protect the top of the head.

Band: To keep the hat in shape.

Binding: To keep the edge of the brim from wearing out.

Lining: To keep the sweat from soiling the material of the hat.

Trimming: To give the hat an attractive appearance.

ARTICLE VI. COMPOSITION.

18. **1st Exercise.**—Write a connected description of a fruit, a plaything, a plant, or an article of furniture which you have carefully examined, noting: (*a*) What kind of a

thing it is, what it resembles, how it differs from other things ; (*b*) What qualities it has ; (*c*) What uses it serves ; (*d*) Whence it comes and how it is obtained ; (*e*) Its parts and their relations, so as to give a full and clear idea of the whole object.

19. **Example: Description of the Cocoa-nut** in the *Encyclopædia Americana :*

" The cocoa-nut is a woody fruit, of an oval shape, from three or four to six or eight inches in length, covered with a fibrous husk, and lined internally with a white, firm, and fleshy kernel. The tree (cocos nucifera) which produces the cocoa-nut is a kind of palm, from 40 to 60 feet high, having on its summit only leaves or branches, appearing almost like immense feathers, each 14 or 15 feet long, 3 feet broad, and winged. Of these the upper ones are erect, the middle ones horizontal, and the lower ones drooping. The trunk is straight, naked, and marked with the scars of the fallen leaves. The nuts hang from the summit of the tree in clusters of a dozen or more together. The external rind of the nuts has a smooth surface, and is of a triangular shape. This encloses an extremely fibrous substance of considerable thickness which immediately surrounds the nut. The latter has a thick and hard shell, with three holes at the base, each closed with a black membrane," etc.

20. In writing these exercises be **sure of every statement** you make. It is no shame for one to acknowledge himself ignorant of many things, but it is a shame to pretend to know that of which he is ignorant. Attention to this rule forms an upright character, besides imparting clearness to the knowledge acquired.

21. *Remark* 1.—Object-lessons may be **indefinitely multiplied** and diversified with judicious applications to Botany, Mineralogy, Geology, and other natural sciences. But care should be taken not to attach undue importance to the study of these subjects.

22. *Remark* 2.—A man's own observation is necessarily

limited to a small number of objects, and even about these he generally needs instruction from other persons. **Reading** opens up a wide field of knowledge; but in this field many wander and lose much precious time by reading what is of little or no use. Young people should accustom themselves early to seek for books that are instructive rather than trifling. They may read to advantage books of travel, books on natural history, the lives of great men, the histories of various lands. But even among such works they should be guided to select the most truthful and reliable. Works of fiction readily fill the mind with false notions of men and things; still, when judiciously selected, they may serve a useful purpose.

, CHAPTER II.

OF WORDS.

23. **Language** is articulate sound expressive of thought. Children learn it from their parents and from other persons with whom they associate. But it is evident that the first man, Adam, did not learn it in this manner. How did he acquire language? He was not created a child, but a man with all his faculties fully developed ; far from being a savage, he was possessed of a much higher intellect before his fall than any man has possessed since. We are not left to conjecture how **he formed a language,** since the Holy Scripture explains what happened :

" The Lord having formed out of the ground all the beasts of the earth, and all the fowls of the air, brought them to Adam to see what he would call them ; for whatsoever Adam called any living creature, the same is its name. And Adam called all the beasts by their names, and all the fowls of the air, and all the cattle of the field " (Genesis ii. 19, 20).

A Christian acts very absurdly if he sets aside this teaching for idle theories, such as Dr. Blair explains in his *Rhetoric* (Lect. vi.)

24. Object-Lessons, while giving the learner ideas of a multitude of things, supply him at the same time with the words or terms by which those ideas are to be expressed. This way of learning words, in connection with the objects signified, imparts clearness to knowledge ; but it cannot extend to a great variety of things. Most **words in a language** are to be acquired by reading and conversation. As

terms stand for ideas, an enlarged familiarity with words and their meanings extends the limits of our knowledge, and is thus an important part of education. It would not, however, be correct to say that a man's **knowledge is valuable** in proportion to the multitude of words which he has learned to understand; for some matters are far more worthy of knowledge than others.

25. From all this it follows that the **exercises selected for the young** should—

    1. Make them familiar with a large number of words;

    2. Aid them to understand those words clearly in their various meanings;

    3. Fix their attention by preference on those words which represent the most valuable ideas.

It must also be remarked that words found in print or heard in conversation are not all equally fit for use; precepts and exercises will train the pupil to make a proper choice.

26. **To acquire a copious supply of proper words—**

    1. Children should **converse** frequently with persons whose knowledge is sound and whose language is correct and elegant.

    2. Their **reading** should be confined to the choicest productions of the best writers, suited, however, to their age and their circumstances. The text-books which they use for reading and for models of composition should be selected with the greatest care. Such selection being made, the following exercises are recommended:

27. **1st Exercise.**—Write in one column all the nouns occurring in the First Lesson of your Reader, all the adjectives in a second column, the verbs in a third, and the adverbs in a fourth.

28. **2d Exercise.**—Write, in the same manner, all such words of the Second Lesson as did not occur in the first, or occur in a different meaning.

29. **3d Exercise.**—Point out the new words of the Third Lesson, of the Fourth, of the Fifth, etc.

Similar exercises may be written on passages in text-books of History, Geography, etc., to familiarize pupils with numerous good English words, and with the different meanings which each may bear.

In selecting words for actual use pupils must attend to the rules of Purity, Propriety, and Precision.

ARTICLE I. PURITY.

30. **Purity** requires that all our expressions belong to the idiom of our language. It forbids the use of words and phrases which are (*a*) foreign, (*b*) obsolete or no longer in use, (*c*) newly coined or not yet adopted into the language. A violation of purity is called a *barbarism.*

31. The **standard of purity** is the practice of the best writers and speakers. This standard is thus explained by Campbell in his *Rhetoric.* To judge whether a word is pure he bids us consult : 1 *Reputable use*—that is, the usage of the best writers and speakers, as opposed to that of the uneducated ; 2. *National use*, as opposed to provincial and foreign ; 3. *Present use*, as opposed to obsolete.

32. We may add this special **rule regarding foreign words**: When our own language has a good word to express a certain idea it is pedantry to borrow a word from another tongue, as those persons are fond of doing who wish to show that they know a little French, Italian, etc. We need not, for instance, talk of a 'coup d'œil,' a 'chef-d'œuvre,' or a 'faux pas,' etc., when we have such words as a 'glance,' a 'masterpiece,' a 'false step,' etc.

33. Pope, in his "Essay on Criticism," lays down this rule regarding **obsolete and newly-coined words:**

> " In words, as fashions, the same rule will hold,
>   Alike fantastic if too new or old :
>   Be not the first by whom the new are tried,
>   Nor yet the last to lay the old aside."

In conformity with this rule we should avoid in prose composition words which were at one time in general use, but which are now confined by our best writers to the language of poetry.   Such are: 'Sheen,' 'swain,' 'ween,' 'wist,' 'wot,' 'quoth,' etc.

34. Even among such words as are conformable to the standard of purity **a further selection** may often be advisable, for which Campbell lays down these rules :

1. Choose the word or phrase which has but **one meaning** in preference to that which has more than one ; *e.g.,* say 'The weapons dropped from the hands of his soldiers,' not 'The arms dropped from the hands of his soldiers.'

2. Prefer the word that conforms to the **analogy** of the language ; hence use 'contemporary' rather than 'cotemporary,' since the 'n' in 'con' is usually retained before a consonant and dropped before a vowel.

3. Prefer the word **more agreeable** to the ear ; hence rather say 'kindness' than 'graciousness,' if either will suit the sense.

4. Prefer the **simpler expression**: 'to approve' is better than 'to approve of,' to 'subtract' than to 'substract.'

5. Prefer what **savors less of innovation,** unless there be a special reason to the contrary.

35. **Exercise.**—Substitute English words and phrases for

the following barbarisms: à la mode, incertain, resurrect-
ed, docible, preventative, sang-froid, enthused, rampage,
amour propre, parvenu, soi-disant, skedaddle, vamose,
patois, instanter, fête, absquatulate, fixings, walking-pa-
pers, sine qua non, comme il faut; to get into a scrape,
to acknowledge the corn, to pitch into, to cut shines, to
clear out.

ARTICLE II. PROPRIETY.

36. **Propriety** means suitableness. Words should be
suited: 1. To the expression of a given idea; 2. To the
usage of polite society; 3. To the understanding of the
reader or hearer; 4. To the subject treated.

§ 1. *Proper to express a given idea.*

37. Propriety should make us choose those words of our
language which most exactly express our ideas. This
choice of **the right word for every idea** is in itself a source
of pleasure to the intelligent reader; it is one of the chief
beauties of style, and it is necessary in all species of compositions. There are many words in English which express the same idea; such words are called **synonyms.**
If they present the same idea somewhat differently they
are *imperfect* synonyms. There are few *perfect* synonyms; and negligence in discriminating between imperfect ones leads to many violations of propriety.

38. **Exercise.**—Point out the meanings which the following synonyms have in common, and the differences between them. Write brief sentences in which these differences appear.

Austerity, severity, rigor. Custom, habit. Surprised,
astonished, amazed, confounded. Desist, renounce, quit,
leave off. Pride, vanity. Haughtiness, disdain. To distinguish, to separate. To weary, to fatigue. To abhor,

to detest. To invent, to discover. Only, alone. Entire, complete. Tranquillity, peace, calm. A difficulty, an obstacle. Wisdom, prudence. Enough, sufficient. To avow, to acknowledge, to confess. To remark, to observe. Equivocal, ambiguous. With, by. (See Blair's *Rhetoric,* Lect. x.)

39. Even ordinary conversation cannot dispense with this propriety in the choice of words. A foolish **habit of exaggeration** leads some people to commit gross mistakes in this matter. To signify that an object is very pleasing they will say that it is 'awfully nice' or 'perfectly splendid'; they express themselves to be 'delighted,' when they mean 'pleased'; they 'love' poetry, flowers, and fine clothes, instead of 'liking' them.

40. **To select the proper synonym** the following hints may help:

1. Some words are *more comprehensive* than others: every 'river' is a 'stream,' but every 'stream' is not a 'river.' 2. Some relate more to *action,* others to a state: 'force' effects, while 'strength' sustains; 'reasonable' men use reason, 'rational' men have reason. 3. Some are *positive,* others negative: a 'fault' is positively bad, a 'defect' is a want of something needed. 4. Some differ in *degree:* 'damp,' 'moist,' 'wet'; 'angry,' 'furious.' 5. Some relate more *to nature,* others to art: a 'gentle,' a 'tame' animal. 6. Some regard more what is *inward,* others what is outward: 'dignity,' 'decorum,' 'form,' 'feature'; 'detract,' 'disparage.' (See Kerl's *Treatise on the English Language,* p. 460.)

§ 2. *Proper to be used in polite society.*

41. The Latins called every object by the name which most directly recalled it to the mind. Shakspeare and most of his contemporaries often made their characters

discourse in similar language. But in our days there are many words and phrases that are universally banished from polite conversation, and others that are often used familiarly, but are considered out of place in dignified composition. The former are called **vulgar**; they should always be avoided : the latter are familiar or **colloquial**, and may be used on proper occasions.

" Be thou familiar, but by no means vulgar."—*Shakspeare.*

Some young people contract the habit of using vulgar words and slang phrases to such an extent that they are ignorant of the proper terms. Others go to the opposite extreme, and, through a false notion of propriety, fastidiously avoid excellent English words used by the best writers. They would think it vulgar to name 'arms,' 'legs,' and 'knees,' calling all these 'limbs.' This is not propriety, but prudery.

42. Some writers on Rhetoric give the name of "low expressions" to such terms as hurly-burly, topsy-turvy, currying favor, dancing attendance, left to shift for one's self, had as lief, not a whit better, half an eye, self-same, it irks me, etc. All these, however, are **good old English idioms**, which it would be a pity to lose from our language, as they are more expressive than any substitutes yet proposed for them. (See *Every-Day English*, by Richard Grant White, c. xxx.) Some would even discard our good Saxon 'women' and 'mothers,' and give us 'ladies' and 'mammas' instead.

§ 3. *Proper or suited to the intelligence of readers and hearers.*

43. Many terms are appropriate before a learned audience and in books written for educated men and women which would be unintelligible to children and to the unedu-

cated. Words of **Saxon origin** are the simplest and the most likely to be generally understood. Scientific terms should be confined to scientific audiences.

44. In addressing persons of slow mind, or in addressing any person on abstruse matters, it is well to express the same idea, whenever it recurs, by the same word, so as not to confuse; but with more intelligent readers, and on easier topics, such repetitions would convey the impression of poverty of language in the writer, except when special beauty results from the repetition, as will be explained further on. It is never proper to use the same word in different meanings in the same sentence. Do not write, "It soon *appeared* that these diplomatic courtesies meant more than *appeared* on the surface"; nor, "Wellington was *anxious* to be relieved from *anxiety* in that quarter."

§ 4. *Proper to the subject.*

45. Language is the dress of thought. As different dress becomes different persons and different occasions, so the language will **vary with the subject.** We shall here consider how this will affect the choice of words.

When the thoughts are remarkably beautiful, smoothness and beauty are desired in the expression. Now, as Blair correctly remarks, words are most agreeable to the ear which are composed of smooth and liquid sounds, in which there is a proper intermixture of vowels and consonants, without too many harsh consonants rubbing against each other. Too many open vowels in succession cause a hiatus or a disagreeable aperture of the mouth. Sounds hard to pronounce are harsh and painful to the ear. Vowels give softness, consonants strength, to the sound of words. The music of language requires a just proportion of both. Of long words those are the most musical in which long and short syllables are properly intermixed, as 'independent,' 'impetuosity,' 'adoration.'

46. Long words bestow dignity upon style ; this is the chief reason why those of Latin and Greek origin are preferred by many writers to the more expressive and forcible, but less harmonious, Saxon.

Still, for sweetness of sound we need not have recourse to the learned languages. Notice the beauty of these Saxon lines :

> " There is sweet music here that softer falls
> Than petals from blown roses on the grass,
> Or night dews on still waters between walls
> Of shadowy granite, in a gleaming pass ;
> Music that gentler on the spirit lies
> Than tir'd eyelids upon tir'd eyes ;
> Music that brings sweet sleep down from the blissful skies.
> Here are cool mosses deep,
> And through the moss the ivies creep,
> And in the stream the long-leaved flowers weep,
> And from the craggy ledge the poppy hangs in sleep."
> —*Tennyson.*

> " How sweet the moonlight sleeps upon this bank !
> Here will we sit and let the sounds of music
> Creep in our ears ; soft stillness and the night
> Become the touches of sweet harmony.
> Sit, Jessica.   Look how the floor of heaven
> Is thick inlaid with patines of bright gold :
> There's not the smallest orb which thou behold'st
> But in his motion like an angel sings,
> Still choiring to the young-eyed cherubins.
> Such harmony is in immortal souls ;
> But, whilst this muddy vesture of decay
> Doth grossly close it in, we cannot hear it."
> —*Shakspeare.*

See also Shenstone's Pastoral, II. " Hope " :

> " My banks they are furnished with bees," etc.

See also the well-known songs of Tom Moore, "Sweet Vale of Avoca" and "'Tis the Last Rose of Summer."

Exercise.—Write in soft and pleasing words a description of a quiet scene, such as 'a boat-ride,' 'an evening scene in autumn,' 'a morning of spring,' 'midnight in summer,' 'the stillness of a city on Sunday,' etc.

ARTICLE III. PRECISION.

47. Precision here means the selection of such words as mean nothing vague, or too much, or too little, but just what we desire to express. For example, we should not say, unless we mean to use a figure, 'The boy broke a *window*,' when he broke a *pane* only; nor, 'The *room* is full of water,' when it is only the *floor* that is covered with water; nor speak of 'courage and fortitude,' when we mean only one of these virtues. Vagueness, as opposed to precision, is exemplified by the use of general instead of particular terms. There are persons whose stock of words appears to be very scanty; every object with them is *great* or *small*, *beautiful* or *ugly*, *good* or *bad*. They should distinguish various degrees of such qualities. We have elsewhere pointed out several terms expressive of size (No. 13); we shall here add some varieties of beauty and ugliness: Beautiful, handsome, fine, pretty, lovely, graceful, elegant, delicate, refined, fair, comely, seemly, bonny, shapely, well-formed, well-proportioned, symmetrical, becoming, neat, spruce, brilliant, splendid, gorgeous, superb, magnificent, sublime, grand; Ugly, gross, homely, unsightly, unseemly, unprepossessing, etc.

48. The use of the general term for a particular one, as 'ugly' for 'clumsy' or 'squalid,' would be a violation of precision; the use of one particular term for another, as of 'gross' instead of 'homely,' offends against propriety.

(See Roget's *Thesaurus of English Words*, a work of great utility in its way to the students of our language.)

49. **Not every subject requires the same attention** to precision ; but all those compositions should excel in it which are intended to instruct the reader. Such are all philosophical and critical works, histories, essays, text-books, etc.

50. That an author may write with precision, he must have a clear and exact **knowledge of his subject**; such knowledge is not as common as many imagine. Besides, he must have a distinct conception of the exact meaning of all his words. But even these two conditions are not sufficient. He must, besides, be so devoted to truth as to select his words with great care and strive to say exactly what he means.

51. Some writers are so given to **habits of exaggeration** as hardly to be able to state the sober truth, even in matters of importance. Such, for instance, is Lord Macaulay, whose style is unusually brilliant, but who is fond of saying more than he means. He deliberately studied a style of exaggeration, on the theory that men will not be impressed except by what is uncommonly striking. For instance, he says of Livy :

" No historian with whom we are acquainted has shown so complete an indifference to truth. He seems to have cared only about the picturesque effect of his book and the honor of his country. On the other hand, we do not know, in the whole range of literature, an instance of a bad thing so well done. The painting of the narrative is beyond description vivid and graceful. The abundance of interesting narratives and splendid imagery is almost miraculous," etc., etc. (" Essay on History ").

Such use of superlatives is injurious to precision ; it does for the understanding what sensational literature does for the imagination and the heart ; it corrupts men's relish for the real and makes them sensible to nothing but what is striking. Macaulay's style is oratorical, and beautiful as such ; but it has not the precision expected in the critic and the historian : it is therefore ill-suited to impart correct knowledge to the young.

52. Precision is of great importance **in the transaction of business** ; in fact, for mercantile transactions it is, perhaps, the most necessary quality of style. It will be useful, therefore, to practise pupils for some time on such familiar exercises as the following :

53. **Exercise 1.**—Write an advertisement for insertion in a newspaper, offering a reward for the return of a lost article.

54. **Exercise 2.**—Write an advertisement of a house to let ; one for a bookkeeper. a gardener, a private tutor.

CHAPTER III.

SENTENCES.

55. A *sentence* is a collection of words making complete sense; as, 'In all climes spring is beautiful.' 'Wisely improve the present hour.' 'Where are the great conquerors now?' 'Hurrah for the Red, White, and Blue!'

The first example contains an assertion; the second, a command; the third is a question; the fourth, an exclamation: each makes complete sense, and is therefore a sentence. But the following words, 'As if the death angel in passing had touched them and made them holy,' do not make complete sense, and therefore they do not form a sentence.

56. **Exercise 1.**—Write a short sentence about every article in the room, every State in the Union, every hour of the day, etc.

57. **Exercise 2.**—Write a sentence of more than twenty words about each of the four seasons, about the soul, about angels, flowers, birds, fishes, a river, a mountain, the ocean, eternity, time, England, Ireland, France, Italy.

58. Both Grammar and Rhetoric lay down laws for sentences: **Grammar** considers the form and the position of the words with a view to the correct expression of the thought; **Rhetoric**, the choice and the position of the words with a view to clearness, beauty, and power of expression. The rhetorical arrangement may be quite different from the grammatical. 'The order of the

world around us is indeed glorious,' is a sentence grammatically arranged. Irving puts it thus, rhetorically: "Glorious indeed is the order of the world around us."

59. We are here concerned with the rhetorical laws of a sentence. Of the choice of words we have already treated. It remains for us to explain the proper arrangement of a sentence with a view to clearness, beauty, and power of expression. This arrangement requires attention to five points: *Clearness, Precision, Unity, Strength,* and *Harmony.*

ARTICLE I. CLEARNESS.

60. **Clearness** in a sentence enables the reader to seize at once, without effort or hesitation, the meaning intended to be conveyed. It excludes two faults: (*a*) *Ambiguity,* which leaves a doubt between two possible meanings ; and (*b*) *Obscurity,* which fails to exhibit the true meaning at the first glance.

Both faults are exemplified in the following sentence of J. R. Lowell: "The relation of Dante to literature is monumental [what does this mean ? — Obscure], and marks the era at which the modern begins." [The modern what ? relation ? literature ? era ? Dante ?—Ambiguous.]

61. **General rules** to secure clearness :

Rule 1.—As a man cannot express clearly what he does not clearly understand, let every writer begin by **studying his subject thoroughly,** and let him not attempt to write till he knows well what he wishes to say. This is the most important rule of all.

Rule 2.—Let him express his thoughts with care, striving to make everything he says so clear to his readers that **they cannot help understanding him.** In particular, let the words and phrases related in sense be so disposed that this relation may at once appear.

62. **Special Rules**: 1. Let **adverbs** obviously qualify the right words. The adverb 'only' is often misplaced, as in this very defective sentence of Addison (*Tatler*, 133): "When one considers this subject only in its sublimity, this great instance could not but occur to me ; and since I only make use of it to show the highest example of it, I hope I do not offend in it." Does the first 'only' qualify 'subject' or 'sublimity'? and the second, 'I' or 'make use'?

63. Blair judiciously remarks :

"In regard to such adverbs as '*only*,' '*wholly*,' '*at least*,' the fact is that in common discourse the tone and emphasis we use in pronouncing them generally serve to show their reference and to make the meaning clear ; and hence we acquire a habit of throwing them in loosely in the course of a period. But in writing, where a man speaks to the eye and not to the ear, he ought to be more accurate, and so to connect those adverbs with the words which they qualify as to put his meaning out of doubt upon the first inspection."

64. 2. **Circumstances**, and all kinds of clauses and adjuncts, should be so placed that the reader cannot fail to see at first sight where they belong. The following sentence violates this rule : "Say to him, if he is in the wrong, he should retrace his steps." Does the clause, 'If he is in the wrong,' qualify what precedes or what follows it? "Meanwhile the children in the house had been making themselves happy also in their manner."—*Ruskin.* Does 'also' refer to children, or to happy, or to manner? Ruskin means it for children.

65. 3. **Pronouns** should at once present to the mind the nouns for which they stand. The relative pronoun is misplaced in this sentence of Dean Swift: "Many, from a habit of saving time and paper, which they acquire at the

university, write in so diminutive a manner that they can hardly read what they have written."

66. 4. **Participles** should be obviously connected with the words to which they refer. Edward Everett violates this rule when he writes:

" By this [the aristocratic] system we mean the aggregate of all the institutions which a people, supposing them to be virtuous and well informed, and meeting together free from all prejudices, to organize themselves into a political community, and capable of foreseeing consequences, would reject as not tending to the greatest happiness of the greatest number."

Who is 'supposing'? 'meeting'? 'tending'? who is 'capable'?

ARTICLE II. PRECISION.

67. **Precision** in sentences requires that we strike out all words and phrases which do not contribute to the clearness, the strength, or the beauty of the sentence. It is, as Blair remarks, the proper opposite to a loose style, which, he says, generally arises from using a superfluity of words.

68. **Avoid in particular**: 1. *Useless relative pronouns:* " The queen, who by this time had entered the hall, proceeded to seat herself upon a throne, which had been prepared for the occasion," may be shortened to " The queen now entered the hall, and seated herself on a throne prepared for the occasion."

69. 2. *Lengthy verbal forms:* " The soldiers of Hannibal, having been enervated by their luxurious winter-quarters in Capua, were no longer able to cope with the Romans." 'Having been' is superfluous.

70. 3. **Tautology**, or the useless repetition of an idea in different terms. A common form of this fault is the coupling of synonyms ; as, ' They mutually disliked one another.' ' The Romans sustained a terrible and fearful de-

feat at Cannæ.' 'The consul Paulus Æmilius had fought bravely and courageously.' 'Plain and evident,' 'clear and obvious,' 'joy and satisfaction,' etc.

Another form of tautology consists in repeating a thought in different words for the mere sake of sound ; as, "It is impossible for us to behold the divine works with coldness or indifference, or to survey so many beauties without a secret satisfaction and complacency."—*Addison.*

71. Precision is necessary in all kinds of composition ; the opposite quality of style, **prolixity**, is always a fault, whether it results from the use of superfluous words or the statement of superfluous details. But precision should not be confounded with **conciseness**, or great brevity of detail and expression. Conciseness is appropriate in certain species of writing, but not 'n others ; its opposite is diffuseness or copiousness of st· .e, which is often a source of great beauty.

72. **Example.**—*Concise :*

" Great actions and striking occurrences, having excited a temporary admiration, often pass away and are forgotten, because they leave no lasting results affecting the prosperity of communities."
—*Webster.*

Copious :

" Of the ten thousand battles which have been fought ; of all the fields fertilized with carnage ; of the banners which have been bathed in blood ; of the warriors who had hoped that they had risen from the field of conquest to a glory as bright and as durable as the stars, how few that continue long to interest mankind ! The victory of yesterday is reversed by the defeat of to-day ; the star of military glory, rising like a meteor, like a meteor has fallen ; disgrace and disaster hang on the heels of conquest and renown ; victor and vanquished presently pass away to oblivion, and the world holds on its course with the loss only of so many lives and so much treasure."—*Id.*

ARTICLE III. UNITY.

73. A sentence has **unity** if it presents to the mind a single thought with or without attendant circumstances; as, 'God alone is great.' 'Why do little children remind us of angels but on account of their innocence?'

> "Hail, mildly pleasing solitude,
> Companion of the wise and good,
> But from whose holy, piercing eye
> The herd of fools and villains fly."--*Thomson.*

*I*n the last sentence the main thought expressed is a greet-ing to solitude; and the reason of this greeting is added—namely, the fact that solitude is the companion of the wise and good on the one hand, and the dread of fools and villains on the other. A sentence may thus run through many lines and be clearly the development of a single thought. And, on the other hand, even a short sentence may be wanting in unity by containing two or more thoughts not properly united: as "Washington is the father of his country, and the story of the hatchet is a mere invention."

74. Rules: 1. Do not unite in one sentence things which do not combine to present *one main thought.*

2. Avoid *parentheses*, unless they be short and have evi-dently a happy effect.

3. When the sense is complete and the ear expects a full stop, do not append a remark by way of *a tail to the sen-tence.* Do not write: " May is the month in which nature appears most enjoyable, on a fine day at least."

4. As the *subject* is the ruling word in a sentence, it should be changed as little as possible. Do not write: " After *we* came to anchor, *they* put me on shore, where *I* was welcomed by all my friends, *who* received me with the greatest kindness." But rather write: " Having come to

anchor, I was put on shore, where I was welcomed by all my friends and received with the greatest kindness."

ARTICLE IV. STRENGTH.

75. **Strength** is that quality which gives to a sentence its due weight and force. When the rules regarding clearness, precision, and unity are well observed, a certain strength of expression will result. How this strength may be further promoted is the question to be now considered.

76. *Rule* 1.—Conceive a **strong conviction** of the truth and the real importance of all you write. For as water cannot flow higher than its source, so the expression of thought will not be either clearer or stronger than is the conception of it in the mind. To attain to the firm conviction here spoken of, be ever thoroughly honest with yourself and with your readers; do not advocate what you do not sincerely believe; do not pretend to understand fully what you see only in part; do not urge as necessary what is only advisable; put forth your firm convictions with becoming firmness, and your probable speculations with modest reserve. This earnestness of mind is. the fundamental rule for strength of style; without it no, other rules will be of great utility.

77. *Rule* 2.—Keep ever before your mind the **purpose** for which you write, and direct all your efforts to its attainment. If your object is to instruct your readers on any point, stick to that point, and study how you can make it clear to them; choose your words, your arrangement, your figures with a view to promote this instruction. If your object is to move your hearers, aim in everything at the exciting of the proper passions. If your object is to please, use freely all the ornaments of style which the subject admits; but remember that good sense is indispensa-

ble. Language, no matter how musical, is worthless if
sound sense does not pervade it.

78. *Rule* 3.—Place **the important words** where they will
make the most marked impression. The beginning and
the end of a sentence, and of any considerable portion of
it, are places favorable to emphasis ; unusualness of position makes a word most emphatic. Edward Everett taste-
fully writes :

" On this frozen soil—driven from the ivy-clad churches of their
motherland, escaped at last from loathsome prisons—the meek fathers . . . will lay the spiritual basement of their temple."

The natural order would be :

" The meek fathers, . . . driven from the ivy-clad churches
of their motherland, escaped at last from loathsome prisons, will
lay the spiritual basement of their temple on this frozen soil."

79. The Latin and Greek writers were enabled by the genius of their languages to make extensive use of such **inversions,** and thus to write with uncommon beauty and power.
Many earlier English writers imitated their constructions ;
but gradually this practice has been abandoned as not
suited to our idiom and to our turn of thought. Still,
within certain limits, inversions may be used to great
advantage. Even so easy a writer as Longfellow has frequent recourse to them with very pleasing effect. He
says :

" Throughout this beautiful and wonderful creation there is never-
ceasing motion, without rest by night or day, ever waving to and fro.
Swifter than a weaver's shuttle it flies from birth to death, from death
to birth. . . . Of all these forms the highest and most perfect in its
God-likeness is the human soul. . . . Into this vast cathedral comes
the human soul seeking its Creator. . . . But in the soul of man
alone is this longing changed to certainty and fulfilled. . . . Thus
is the glory of God made visible. . . . Thus then stands man—a

mountain on the boundary between two worlds—its foot in one, its summit far-rising into the other," etc.

80. *Rule* 4.—More necessary still than the preceding rule is that which directs us to **simplify our thoughts**, to rid them of all useless details, and then propose them one by one without intricacy or confusion.

81. *Rule* 5.—Let there be **no falling off** in sense or sound towards the end of the sentence. For this reason—

(*a*) A *stronger assertion* or a nobler thought should never be followed by a weaker member of the sentence; and of two members the longer should come last. Longfellow writes: "It has become a common saying that men of genius are always in advance of their age; which is true." Speaking generally, the following construction will be better: "It has become a common saying, and it is true, that men of genius are always in advance of their age."

(*b*) Get rid of *less important details* and circumstances in a sentence as soon as possible.

(*c*) Avoid *concluding* it with an insignificant word. Do not say, "It is a mystery which we firmly believe the truth of and humbly adore the depth of"; but rather, "It is a mystery the truth of which we firmly believe, and the depth of which we humbly adore."

82. *Rule* 6.—When there is **a correspondence or an opposition** in meaning between two sentences or two members, this fact will be brought out more strikingly by a similarity in the construction. Thus Giles, in his "Essay on True Manhood," contrasts the characters of Lord Bacon and of More, the martyr-chancellor of Henry VIII.:

"More was incorruptible; Bacon was venal. Both More and Bacon served each a great purpose for the world. More illustrated the beauty of holiness; Bacon expounded the infinitude of science. Bacon became the prophet of intellect: More the martyr of conscience. The one pours over our understanding the light of knowledge ; but the other inflames our hearts with the love of virtue."

83. Exercise 1.—Select from any good writer six sentences, each containing two or more members, and expressing a beautiful or useful thought in faultless and elegant language.

84. Exercise 2.—Compose an elegant sentence of at least forty words on each of the following subjects : Air, water, earth, sky ; the sun, the moon ; railroads, steamboats ; patriotism, painting, poetry, music ; a lake, a river ; ice, snow ; a city, an island, a flower.

85. Exercise 3.—Strive to surpass each other in finding or composing a sentence that unites the most perfect clearness, precision, unity, and strength with the noblest thought and the most pleasing harmony.

ARTICLE V. HARMONY.

86. By harmony in a sentence we mean agreeableness of sound. We are now to treat of this agreeableness as produced by well-constructed sentences in prose.

§ 1. *Sources of Harmony in a sentence.*

87. We shall begin by carefully considering **a harmonious sentence**, examining what elements combine to make it harmonious. Milton writes in his " Treatise on Education " ·

"We shall conduct you to a hillside, laborious indeed at the first ascent, but else so smooth, so green, so full of goodly prospects and melodious sounds on every side, that the harp of Orpheus was not more charming."

88. *Notice :* 1. The liquid and soft sounds in the *words* 'laborious,' 'smooth,' 'green,' 'goodly,' 'melodious,' 'harp,' 'Orpheus,' 'charming.'

2. The division of the sentence into *clauses* of moderate length.

3. The *climax*, or gradation, by which each member rises in harmony above the preceding member : 'We shall conduct you to a hillside'—'laborious indeed at the first ascent'—'but else so smooth, so green'—'so full of goodly prospects and melodious sounds on every side.'

4. The *most harmonious member* preserved for the close : 'that the harp of Orpheus was not more charming.'

5. The *last word*, whose sound, of course, remains longest on the ear. Blair remarks that a musical close in our language requires either the last syllable or the last but one to be a long syllable. But it will be found that even two very short syllables may follow such a sound without impairing the harmony, as in the words agreeable, period, harmonious, victorious, etc.

6. The binding together of the sentence by the *periodic construction*. The word 'indeed' suggests that we may soon expect an opposite reflection, which is next introduced by 'but'; at once the word 'so' prepares our ear for the 'that' which opens the concluding member; and the sense is not full till we reach the last word of the sentence.

The periodic construction contributes so much to harmony, and even to power of expression, that it requires a fuller explanation.

§ 2. *The Periodic Construction.*

89. The word **period** is often used as synonymous with sentence; at other times it means the punctuation mark, called the full-stop, at the end of a sentence. But its radical meaning is different, and this is the meaning we are now to consider. And it will be found that, as the practice of dancing, that of gymnastic exercises and military

drill, impart grace to a person's ordinary motions, so practice in periodic composition improves the whole tone of
a student's literary style. On the other hand, it has been
remarked by attentive observers that the only reason why
some public speakers failed to gain that applause which
the beauty of their thoughts and their elocution deserved,
was the evident absence of the periodic construction from
their sentences.

90. What, then, is **the periodic construction?** It is that
peculiar turn given to a sentence which closely binds
together all its members by suspending the sense for a
while, in order to bring it afterwards to a satisfactory
close. The following sentence has the ordinary or *loose*
construction :

"Woman performs her part towards the preservation of a free
government by the promulgation of sound morals in the community,
and more especially by the training and instruction of the young."

Notice the increased harmony when Webster combines
these words into a *period:*

" It is by the promulgation of sound morals in the community,
and more especially by the training and instruction of the young, |
that woman performs her part towards the preservation of a free
government."

91. To form a period **the sense may be suspended** in
various ways :

1. *By an inversion,* as in the period just quoted.
2. *By a prepositional phrase :*

" In the highly rarefied atmosphere of these upper regions, | even
remote objects have a brilliancy of coloring and a distinctness of
outline which seem to annihilate distance."—*Prescott.*

3. *By a dependent clause :*

" When my eyes shall be turned to behold, for the last time, the sun in heaven, | may I not see him shining on the broken and dishonored fragments of a once glorious Union."—*Webster.*

4. *By a participial clause :*

" We wish that this column, rising towards heaven among the pointed spires of so many temples dedicated to God, | may contribute also to produce in all minds a pious feeling of dependence and gratitude."—*Id.*

5. *By an accumulation* of subjects or predicates :

" A bright, cheerful, happy soul ; a sensitive heart, a temperament open to emotion and impulse ; and all this elevated, refined by the touch of heaven | —such was St. John Chrysostom, winning followers, riveting affections, by his sweetness, frankness, and neglect of self."—*Cardinal Newman.*

92. In every period there are necessarily two parts : the former, called the **protasis,** keeps the meaning in suspense ; the latter, the **apodosis,** brings the sentence to a harmonious close.

These two parts are naturally separated by the fullest pause which occurs in the course of the sentence ; in the examples quoted we have marked the separation.

93. When the protasis or the apodosis admits of one or more considerable stops, these stops divide it into **members,** which are themselves often subdivided into clauses. When no such stops occur the protasis is one member and the apodosis another.

94. A **well-balanced period** supposes that the protasis and apodosis are of nearly the same length. When the apodosis is the shorter of the two, it should be richer in thought or in sound than any single preceding member.

95. The following period, taken from Irving's reflections on Christmas in his *Sketch-Book,* will illustrate these details (the semi-colon marks the members, and the colon the protasis and apodosis) :

" The preparations making on every side for the social board that is again to unite friends and kindred; the presents of good cheer passing and repassing, those tokens of regard and quickeners of kind feelings; the evergreens distributed about houses and churches, emblems of peace and gladness: all these have the most pleasing effects in producing fond associations, kindling benevolent sympathies."

96. As periods are sentences of peculiar splendor, they are not **appropriate** on all occasions. They are suited to subjects of dignity, and to the region of the gentler emotions and the moderate passions. When used they must be mingled with loose sentences—that is, with such as do not suspend the sense—and with partial periods, which are now to be explained.

97. Between the regular period and the loose sentence there is a third species, which embraces perhaps the largest number of sentences in the works of elegant English writers. Some rhetoricians have called such sentences periods in a wider sense of the word. They may well be called **partial periods**; for they partake of the nature of a period inasmuch as they contain some suspension of the sense and some rounding of the expression, without, however, suspending the sense from the beginning to the end. They differ very much among themselves. These are the **most common varieties**:

98. 1. Some of them contain *a part* which, if separated from the rest, would make a period; *e.g.*:

" Yet even in the sixteenth century a considerable number of those who quitted the old religion followed the first confident and plausible guide who offered himself, and were soon led into errors far more serious than they had renounced."—*Macaulay.*

99. 2. Some comprise *two parts* independent of each other, but analogous in construction and of parallel or antithetical meaning; as the second of the following sentences:

"The Christian faith is a grand cathedral, with divinely-pictured windows. Standing without, you see no glory, nor can possibly imagine any; standing within, every ray of light reveals a harmony of unspeakable splendor."—*Hawthorne.*

100. 3. Other partial periods contain *several independent rounded clauses* strung together to develop one central thought; e.g. :

"Whatever I have tried to do in life I have tried with all my heart to do well; whatever I have devoted myself to I have devoted myself to completely; in great aims and in small I have always been thoroughly in earnest."—*Scott.*

101. 4. Others, again, unite various *parts of clauses* with one part common to them all; as :

"The greatest man is he who chooses the right with invincible resolution; who resists the sorest temptations from within and from without; who bears the heaviest burdens cheerfully; who is calmest and most cheerful under menaces and frowns; whose reliance on truth, on virtue, on God is most unfaltering."—*Channing.*

Facility in writing partial periods is acquired by practice in the use of the perfect period. To the latter we should mainly devote our attention.

§ 3. *Period-Building.*

102. We have stated that the unity required in a sentence consists in its presenting to the mind a single thought, with or without attending circumstances. We shall now explain how such thought may be developed into a period, without loss of unity and with increase of harmony.

103. Besides the ways of suspending the sense which were explained in the preceding paragraph, the following **modes of development** are of frequent use.

104. 1. By *paraphrase*—that is, by explaining more fully

the different parts of the given sentence. The simple sentence, "Man has no better friend than his Creator," may
be thus paraphrased :

"Every member of the human family, no matter how dear he
may be to parents or relatives, or to his own children, has no one
who is so earnestly concerned about his real and lasting happiness
as the infinitely good God who has given him existence."

105. 2. By *enumeration.* The thought, "We were once
what the Africans are now," is thus developed by William
Pitt :

"We were once as obscure among the nations of the earth, as
savage in our manners, as debased in our morals, as degraded in
our understandings, as these unhappy Africans are at present."

106. 3. By adducing *proof or reason* of our assertion.
Pitt thus develops the thought, "We should not keep the
Africans in bondage" :

"If, then, we feel that this perpetual confinement in the fetters of
brutal ignorance would have been the greatest calamity which could
have befallen us ; if we view with gratitude and exultation the contrast between the peculiar blessings we enjoy and the wretchedness
of the ancient inhabitants of Britain ; if we shudder to think of the
misery which would still have overwhelmed us had Great Britain
continued to the present time to be a mart for slaves to the most
civilized nations of the world, through some cruel policy of theirs :
God forbid that we should any longer subject Africa to the same
dreadful scourge, and preclude the light of knowledge, which has
reached every other quarter of the globe, from having access to her
coasts."

107. 4. By *circumstances* of time, place, persons, etc.
Curran, evidently imitating Cicero's oration for Milo, begins his plea in behalf of Rowan as follows :

"When I consider the period at which this prosecution is brought
forward ; when I behold the extraordinary safeguard of armed soldiers, resorted to, no doubt, for the preservation of peace and order ;

when I catch, as I cannot but do, the throb of public anxiety which beats from one end to the other of this hall ; when I reflect on what may be the fate of a man of the most beloved personal character, of one of the most respected families in our country, himself the only individual of that family—I may almost say of that country—who can look on that possible fate without concern "; etc.

108. 5. By *comparison* or *contrast.* The thought, " Every form of life bears an impress of God's love," is thus de- veloped by Longfellow :

" As the ice upon the mountain, when the warm breath of the summer's sun breathes upon it, melts and divides into drops, each of which reflects an image of the sun ; so life in the smile of God's love divides itself into separate forms, each bearing in it and re- flecting an image of God's love."

109. **Caution.**—Great care, of course, should be taken that every phrase introduced for the sake of development be really significant and appropriate, that the words be noble and well chosen, without redundancy ; else an exer- cise, in itself most beneficial, might become by abuse a source of empty declamation.

110. **Exercise.**—Develop the following simple thoughts into elegant periods of at least three members each : Mur- der will out. There is no peace for the wicked. Every season has its blessings. Life passes away. God is every- where. Imitate the best writers. Evil associations corrupt good manners. Youth is like spring. Manhood is like summer. Autumn is like old age. Winter is like the grave.

§ 4. *Model Sentences to be learned by heart.*

Periods.

111. 1. " I am dissatisfied with all the metaphors and similes that have been used by poets and philosophers to illustrate the futile and miserable state of man upon the earth. The fly upon the wheel ;

the insect of a day (perhaps a sunny day for the insect); the generations of swiftly crumpling, withering, rotting leaves; the flower that
buds, and grows, and falls away, petal by petal, delicately in the
breeze; the smoke that rises, seen for a moment, and that, dissipat-
ing, goes no man knows whither; the noxious vapor that soon
vanishes away—are all of them too favorable emblems of the state
of erring, short-lived, misguided, miserable man."—*Sir Arthur
Helps.*

2. "Ye who listen with credulity to the whispers of fancy, and
pursue with eagerness the phantoms of hope ; who expect that age
will fulfil the promises of youth, and that the deficiencies of the present day will be supplied by the morrow—attend to the history of
Rasselas, Prince of Abyssinia."—*Dr. Johnson.*

3. "If ever there was a power on earth who had an eye for the
times, who has confined himself to the practicable and has been
happy in his anticipations, whose words have been facts and whose
commands prophecies, such is he, in the history of ages, who sits
from generation to generation in the chair of the Apostles as the
Vicar of Christ and the Doctor of his Church."—*Cardinal Newman.*

4.   "I held it truth with him who sings
                To one clear harp in divers tones,
                That men may rise on stepping-stones
            Of their dead selves to higher things."—*Tennyson.*

5. "The older I grow—and I now stand upon the brink of eternity—the more comes back to me the sentence in the catechism
which I learned when a child, and the fuller and deeper becomes its
meaning : 'What is the chief end of man? To glorify God and to
enjoy him forever.'"—*Thomas Carlyle.*

6. "The Sacred Humanity of the Eternal Son, beaming in the
very central heart of the Ever-blessed Trinity—that is the type, the
meaning, the accomplishment of the creature."—*Rev. F. W. Faber.*

7. "All that is good, all that is true, all that is beautiful, all that
is beneficent, be it great or small, be it perfect or fragmentary, natural as well as supernatural, moral as well as material, comes from
God."—*John Henry Newman.*

8. "There is not a moment of any day of our lives when Nature
is not producing scene after scene, picture after picture, glory after
glory, and working still upon such exquisite and constant principles
of the most perfect beauty, that it is quite certain it is all done for
us and intended for our perpetual pleasure."—*John Ruskin.*

Partial Periods.

112. 1.   " The spacious firmament on high,
With all the blue, ethereal sky,
And spangled heavens, a shining frame,
Their great Original proclaim ;
The unwearied sun, from day to day,
Doth his Creator's power display,
And publishes to every land
The work of an Almighty hand."—*Joseph Addison.*

2. " If one should give me a dish of sand, and tell me there were particles of iron in it, I might look for them with my eyes and search for them with my clumsy fingers, and be unable to detect them ; but let me take a magnet and sweep through it, and how would it draw to itself the almost invisible particles by the mere power of attrac·tion ! The unthankful heart, like my finger in the sand, discovers no mercies ; but let the thankful heart sweep through the day, and, as the magnet finds the iron, so it will find in every hour some heavenly blessings—only, the iron in God's sand is gold."—*Oliver Wendell Holmes.*

3. " Intelligent intercourse with the angelic choirs, and the incessant transmission of the divine splendors through them to our minds, cannot be thought of without our perceiving that the keen pleasures and deep sensibilities of the intellectual world on earth are but poor, thin, unsubstantial shadows of the exulting, immortal life of our glorified minds above."—*Rev. F. W. Faber.*

Loose Sentences.

113. 1. " Some books are to be tasted, others to be swallowed, and some few to be chewed and digested—that is, some books are to be read only in part ; others to be read, but not curiously ; and some few to be read wholly, and with diligence and attention."—*Francis Bacon.*

2. " Reading maketh a full man, conference a ready man, and writing an exact man ; and therefore, if a man write little, he had need have a great memory ; if he confer little, he had need have a present wit ; and if he read little, he had need have much cunning, to seem to know what he doth not."—*Id.*

3. " Every individual has a place to fill in the world, and is im·

portant in some respect, whether he chooses to be so or not."—*Haw-thorne.*

4. "The talent of success is nothing more than doing what you can do well, and doing well whatever you do, without a thought of fame."—*Longfellow.*

5. "Life bears us on like the stream of a mighty river. Our boat, at first, glides down the narrow channel, through the playful murmuring of the little brook and the winding of its grassy border. The trees shed their blossoms over our young heads, the flowers on the brinks seem to offer themselves to our young hands ; we are happy in hope, and we grasp eagerly at the beauties around us, but the stream hurries on, and still our hands are empty."—*Heber.*

6. "Live for something. Do good and leave behind you a monument of virtue that the storm of time can never destroy. Write your name in kindness, love, and mercy on the hearts of thousands you come in contact with, year by year : you will never be forgotten. Your name, your deeds, will be as legible on the hearts you leave behind as the stars on the brow of evening. Good deeds will shine as the stars of heaven."—*Chalmers.*

7. "Beneath us is that beautiful rolling plain, with its dark masses of summer foliage sleeping in the sun for miles and miles away, in the varying shades of blue and green, according to the distance of the clouds."—*Rev. F. W. Faber.*

CHAPTER IV.

COMBINATION AND PUNCTUATION OF SENTENCES.

ARTICLE I. COMBINATION OF SENTENCES—THE PARA-
GRAPH.

114. As words are combined into sentences to express thoughts, so sentences are combined into paragraphs to express fuller developments of thought. A **paragraph** is defined to be such a portion of a composition as develops one thought or consideration. It is usually marked by a break in the composition, and the beginning of a new line.

115. The division of writings into paragraphs is less important than the division into sentences; still, it has great **advantages**: it pleases the eye, it relieves the attention of the reader, it presents to him distinct groups bearing on the same thought, and it accustoms young writers to arrange their sentences in an orderly manner.

From the explanation so far given the rules for paragraphs are obvious.

116. *The 1st Rule* is that of **unity**. Separate into distinct paragraphs sentences that develop distinct considerations. Thus, for instance, in an essay, one paragraph may be introductory, another may define the subject treated, a third may compare it with a similar subject, a fourth contrast it with its opposite, a fifth assign its causes or origin, a sixth its effects or consequence, etc. (See Book IV. Ch. V. Art. II. § 1, School Essays.) If the paragraph thus formed appear rather long, subdivide it; for instance, para-

graph each of the causes, or each class of causes or effects, etc.

117. *The 2d Rule* is that of **completeness.** Do not separate into distinct paragraphs sentences which must be read in connection to be properly understood, or which obviously belong to the same consideration.

118. *The 3d Rule* is that of **clearness.** Usually the beginning of the paragraph should clearly indicate what portion of thought it proposes to develop ; and throughout the whole paragraph the leading word, subject, or idea should be kept prominently before the reader. Thus Cardinal Newman, in developing the definition of a gentleman as "a man who never inflicts pain," opens the subject by laying down this definition, and then, throughout a long paragraph, keeps the 'gentleman' as the prominent word in every sentence (*Characteristics*, p. 93). In a preceding paragraph 'pride' is made the leading word throughout (*Id.* p. 92).

119. When a thought is sufficiently developed in one sentence, the sentence itself then constitutes a paragraph. We even find that one long period of a special kind is often divided into several portions printed separately after the manner of paragraphs. This occurs in **solemn resolutions** drawn up in the form of an elaborate period, as is the memorable "Declaration of Rights" adopted by the First Continental Congress in 1774. In such documents it is usual to assign a distinct paragraph to every clause beginning with the conjunction 'whereas,' and to every one of the 'resolutions.'

120. Two points require special attention in the composition of paragraphs—namely, the **connection of the sentences** with one another, and the transition from one paragraph to the next.

The connection of sentences is usually indicated by conjunctive words and phrases. These are of the *co-ordinate* kind; the *subordinate* ones unite dependent with principal clauses. The chief **co-ordinate** ones may be thus classified :

(*a*) The *cumulative :* and, also, yea, likewise, in like manner, so, first, secondly, etc., again, besides, then, too, further, moreover, furthermore, add to this, yet another, etc.

(*b*) The *alternative :* 'or' and 'nor' (when the ·latter stands for 'and not'); 'neither—nor' are better embraced in one sentence.

(*c*) The *adversative :* else, otherwise, but, still, yet, only, nevertheless, however, at the same time, for all that.

(*d*) The *illative :* therefore, wherefore, hence, whence, consequently, accordingly, thus, so, then.

(*e*) The *causal*, 'for.' But the causal 'because' is always treated as a subordinate conjunction; 'whereas' should be similarly treated.

The phrases used for *returning* are chiefly 'to return,' 'to proceed,' 'to resume'; those for summing up, 'in short,' 'in a word,' 'on the whole,' 'to conclude,' 'in conclusion,' 'to sum up,' 'to recapitulate,' etc. Any of these conjunctional words or phrases may be used to connect paragraphs.

121. When the connection between the sentences is obvious the **tendency in our language** is to omit the connective, on the correct principle that superfluous words are generally worse than useless. But when the connection is not obvious it is a great mistake to neglect such links of thought : many writings are obscure owing to such omissions, because the reader does not know whether a sentence contains an illustration of the preceding sentence, or an exception, or is the beginning of a new consideration.

122. There is one class of connectives which is of spe-

cial importance—namely, those which indicate a **transition** from one portion of our subject to another.   They are like the bolts and hinges that connect the larger portions of a machine.   Sometimes the transition contains two parts, one referring to what precedes by such words as 'hitherto,' 'so far,' 'thus far,' 'we have seen,' 'it has been proved,' etc.; and the other part introducing the new matter by such words as 'next,' 'besides,' 'in the second place,' 'we shall now,' etc.   In reasoning, transitions should not be lightly dispensed with.   In order that the reader may follow us with ease and profit he should at all times see what we are striving to prove, and what particular argument is proposed for his consideration.   But in addresses to the passions transitions are better hidden.   Now, sensational writers are always addressing the passions ; hence they habitually dispense with connectives.   This is one of the ways in which sensational literature is causing style to deteriorate.

123. As a **specimen** of the careful use of connective words and phrases we quote this passage from the writings of Cardinal Newman :

"This practice of asserting simply on authority, with the pretence and without the reality of assent, is what is meant by formalism.   To say, 'I do not understand a proposition, but I accept it on authority,' is not formalism ; it is not a direct assent to the proposition, still it is an assent to the authority which enunciates it ; but what I here speak of is professing to understand without understanding.   It is thus that political and religious watchwords are created ; first one man of name and then another adopts them, till their use becomes popular, and then every one professes them because every one else does.   Such words are 'liberality,' 'progress,' 'light,' 'civilization'; such are 'justification by faith only,' 'vital religion,' 'private judgment,' 'the Bible, and nothing but the Bible.' Such, again, are 'Rationalism,' 'Gallicanism,' 'Jesuitism,' 'Ultramontanism '—all of which, in the mouths of conscientious thinkers, have a definite meaning, but are used by the multitude as war-cries, nicknames, and shibboleths, with scarcely enough of the scantiest grammatical apprehension of them to allow of their being considered really more than assertions."—*Grammar of Assent.*

124. The best kind of **exercises** on the combination of sentences consists in the constant application of these precepts to the compositions of the students. If pupils are made to carry out in practice what they learn in theory, the object of teaching is fully attained.

ARTICLE II. PUNCTUATION.

125. **Punctuation** is the use of artificial marks as aids in making the writer's meaning clear. It does not so much regard the length of the pauses as the grammatical relation of the words, clauses, and members of the sentence. The ancients knew little or nothing of punctuation. St. Jerome appears to have used some signs, which he called commas and colons; but the marks now in use were not generally adopted till after the invention of printing. The present system of punctuation is ascribed to the Manutii, learned printers of Venice at the beginning of the sixteenth century. It has since undergone many minor changes, and even to-day, while its leading principles are generally acknowledged, the application of them by various writers and printers is extremely varied. We shall briefly explain and illustrate the rules most commonly followed.

126. When the formation of the period and the analysis of the sentence have been well understood, a few rules will suffice for training an intelligent pupil to a sensible mode of punctuation, without imposing on him laws which, no matter how ingeniously devised, are not obeyed by the public. There is no more need of **uniformity in punctuation** than of uniformity in style. The general principles of both should be clearly understood; in the application some latitude must be allowed. Some writers introduce as many points or marks as the composition will admit; others con-

fine themselves to such as are absolutely necessary to avoid confusion of sense. One advantage in training pupils to follow the latter course is that they are apt to continue punctuating through life, while many who have been trained to the other system find it so troublesome as soon to abandon punctuation altogether. Besides, easy and elegant constructions, such as all should cultivate, require but little punctuation.

§ 1. *The Period.*

127. **Rules.**—The **period,** or full-stop, is put: 1. At the end of every sentence ; 2. After such headings, addresses, signatures, numbers, letters, etc., as do not belong to any sentence ; 3. After a word that is not written in full.

128. *Note*—The period used after abbreviations does not dispense with any other mark required by the sense, except the period ; as, " He is an LL.D., that is certain ; and he signs all his letters ' H. Smith, Jr., LL.D.' " Short forms of Christian names used in conversation, and such forms as 1st, 2d, etc., do not take the mark of abbreviation; as, ' Ben Jonson,' ' Tom Moore.'

§ 2. *The Colon.*

129. **Rules.**—The **colon** is used : 1. Before a **formal quotation** of some length ; but very short quotations take a comma, and those not formally introduced require no special points. Thus :

> " From the cold grave a hollow murmur flowed :
> ' Time sowed the seed, we reap in this abode.' "
>
> —*Marsden.*

" Away, then, with your expensive follies, and you will not then have so much cause to complain of hard times, heavy taxes, and chargeable families ; for

> *Women and wine, game and deceit,*
> *Make the wealth small and the want great.*

And, further, *What maintains one vice would bring up two children.*
You may think, perhaps, that a little tea, or a little punch now and
then, diet a little more costly, clothes a little finer, and a little en-
tertainment now and then, can be no great matter ; but remember,
Many a little makes a mickle.   Beware of little expenses ; *a small
leak will sink a great ship,* as Poor Richard says ; and again, *Who
dainties love shall beggars prove;* and moreover, *Fools make feasts, and
wise men eat them."—Franklin.*

130. 2. Before a detailed **enumeration** ; while a brief one
takes a semicolon.   Thus :

" There are two questions that grow out of this subject : 1st.
How far is any sort of classical education useful ?   2dly. How far is
that particular classical education adopted in this country useful ?"
—Sydney Smith.
   " Grammar is divided into four parts ; namely, Orthography, Ety-
mology, Syntax, and Prosody."—*Gould Brown.*

131. 3. Before the **details of a description,** narration, etc.
Thus :

" How beautiful is night :
A dewy freshness fills the silent air ;
No mist obscures, nor cloud, nor speck, nor stain
   Breaks the serene of heaven :
In full-orbed glory yonder moon divine
Rolls through the dark-blue depths ;
   Beneath her steady ray
   The desert-circle spreads,
Like the round ocean, girdled with the sky.
   How beautiful is night !"—*Southey.*

132. 4. Before a **new member** of a sentence, complete in
itself and shedding some additional light on the thought so
far expressed ; but if it begins with a conjunction, a semicolon is used.   Thus :

" We have but faith : we cannot know ;
 For knowledge is of things we see ;
 And yet we trust it comes from Thee,
 A beam in darkness : let it grow."—*Tennyson.*

133. 5. To separate the **main divisions** of a sentence when minor divisions are marked by semicolons.   Thus :

" Homer was the greater genius ; Virgil the better artist : in the one we admire the man ; in the other the work."—*Pope.*

§ 3. *The Semicolon.*

134. The **semicolon** separates members having a closer connection than those requiring the colon. It occurs much more frequently than the colon, and less frequently than the comma.

135. **General Rule.**—Use the semicolon for all considerable divisions of a sentence for which the colon is not required by the preceding rules.

136. **Special Rules.**—The semicolon is used to separate :

1. **Co-ordinate clauses,** one or more of which contain a comma ; thus :

" Such, O men of Athens ! were your ancestors : so glorious in the eyes of the world ; so bountiful and munificent to their country ; so sparing, so modest, and so self-relying."—*Demosthenes.*

2. To mark a somewhat **more emphatic pause** when commas precede or follow ; thus :

" Books are needed, but not many books ; a few well read. An open, true, patient, and valiant soul is needed ; that is the one thing needed."—*Carlyle.*

3. To separate the **subdivisions** of members that are marked with a colon ; thus :

" Love thyself last ; cherish those that hate thee :
Corruption wins not more than honesty."—*Shakspeare.*

4. Before an **additional remark** beginning with a conjunction or incomplete in itself ; thus :

" Among the oaks I observed many of the most diminutive size ; some not above a foot high, yet bearing small bunches of acorns."—*Irving.*

137. *Note.*—Many writers use the semicolon, instead of the colon, even though the additional remark makes complete sense and has no conjunction; thus:

> "Speak clearly, if you speak at all;
> Carve every word before you let it fall."—*Holmes.*

§ 4. *The Comma.*

138. In the use of the **comma** considerable diversity exists; most writers, however, observe the following rules:

Rules.—Use commas for any of these three purposes:

1. To indicate the **omission** of such words as are readily suggested to the mind; as:

> "Conversation makes a ready man; writing, an exact man."—*Bacon.*

139. *Note.*—If the place where the word is omitted requires a comma for another reason, a semicolon is usually substituted; if it requires a semicolon, a colon is then used; as, "My comrade, on the contrary, made himself quite one of the family; laughed and chatted with them.' Here the insertion of 'and' before 'laughed' would leave only a comma; while the insertion of 'he' without 'and' would require a colon.

140. 2. To mark off the **members of a series** or enumeration when all are brief; while if any are long, all take the semicolon; thus:

> "He tried each art, reproved each dull delay,
> Allured to brighter worlds, and led the way."
> —*Goldsmith.*

When words are arranged in pairs, each pair takes a comma after it; as:

> "Sink or swim, live or die, survive or perish. I give my hand and my heart to this vote."—*Webster.*

141. 3. To mark **a break** in the grammatical construction :

(*a*) Before and after the *vocative* case ; as :

" Pizarro, hear me !—Hear me, chieftains ! And thou, All-powerful, whose thunder can shiver into fragments the adamantine rock," etc.—*Sheridan.*

(*b*) After *introductory* and before *appended* words, phrases, or clauses ; and both before and after incidental ones ; as :

" Whilst almost the whole of Europe was desolated by war, peaceful Ireland, free from the invasion of external foes, opened to the lovers of learning and piety a welcome asylum. . . . In crowds, numerous as bees, as Aldhelm writes, the English went to Ireland, or the Irish visited England, where the Archbishop Theodore was surrounded by Irish scholars."—*Card. Newman.*

(*c*) After an *inversion ;* as :

" Of the most celebrated Anglo-Saxon scholars and saints, many had studied in Ireland."—*Card. Newman.*

(*d*) Before *appositives*, and

(*e*) Before *relative clauses* when they do not restrict the meaning of the antecedents. Thus :

" Among these were St. Egbert, the author of the first Anglo-Saxon mission to the pagan continent, and the blessed Willibrod, the Apostle of the Frieslanders, who had resided twelve years in Ireland."—*Card. Newman.*

No qualifying word or clause should be separated from the word with which it forms one integral meaning. Thus :

" Though the people who own that language is Protestant, a race pre-eminently Catholic has adopted it, and has a share in its literature ; and this Catholic race is, at this very time, of all tribes of the earth the most fertile in emigrants both to the West and to the South."—*Card. Newman.*

(*f*) Wherever the insertion of a comma may *prevent an*

ambiguity, in the use of such words as 'however,' 'besides,' 'hence,' 'then,' 'only,' 'chiefly,' etc.; as, "Those who seek for pleasure only, defeat their own object."

142. *Note.*—There is much **variety in the practice of writers** with regard to *incidental words and phrases;* some usually mark them by commas, others seldom mark them unless for emphasis or to avoid ambiguity. The same diversity exists in regard to brief clauses united by 'and,' 'or,' and other conjunctions that produce close union. Thus :

> " O what a tangled web we weave
> When first we practise to deceive ! "

admits a comma after 'weave.' "Cicero and Seneca remarked that in their time there was not a single people professing atheism," may be punctuated as follows : "Cicero and Seneca remarked, that, in their time, there was not a single people professing atheism." "The morning stars sang together ; and all the sons of God shouted for joy." Here the semicolon is by many changed into a comma.

§ 5. *The Interrogation and Exclamation.*

143. I. An **exclamation** or wonder mark is placed—

(*a*) After every *interjection* except 'O'; as, 'Fie !' 'Begone !' When words accompany the interjection the mark is placed after them ; as, 'Woe is me !'

(*b*) After words that are *shouted ;* as :

> "To arms ! they come ! the Greek ! the Greek!"—*Halleck.*

(*c*) After words, clauses, or sentences expressive of *strong emotion ;* as, "We must fight !—I repeat it, sir, we must fight !"—*Patrick Henry.*

II. The **interrogation** point marks a direct question, whether asked for information or used as a rhetorical figure ; as, " When shall we be stronger ? Will it be the next week ? or the next year ?"—*Patrick Henry.*

144. *Note.*—The marks of interrogation and exclamation supersede the points with which they may coincide.

§ 6. *The Dash.*

145. The **dash** is a comparatively recent invention, intended to express various modifications of thought not sufficiently expressed by any of the other points.

(*a*) When a speech, a drama, a conversation is written or printed, the dash denotes an accidental or intentional **pause in the discourse.**

(*b*) In a narration, it expresses a sudden pause or **interruption in the action** related.

(*c*) In a document or didactic treatise, it marks an **omission** of a word or phrase, such as 'namely,' 'that is,' 'for example,' etc.

(*d*) In any composition, it denotes the **end** of an enumeration ; omitted names, dates, letters, etc. ; a **sudden change** in the course of the sentence, either parenthetically, to insert a brief remark, or definitively, without resuming the original construction.

(*e*) Besides, printers often use a dash instead of beginning a **new paragraph,** and also before examples and references. But many writers, chiefly in periodicals, abuse the dash by using it for other points of definite meaning.

146. **Rule.**—Do not use the dash except to express something that the other points do not signify.

Note.—The dash need not supersede, but rather follow, any other point that the sense requires ; but many neglect this distinction.

147. The following **examples** will suffice to explain its proper use :

(*a*) *Emphasis :* " Give me liberty, or give me—death."

(*b*) *Hesitation :* "It was to inquire by what title General—but catching himself, Mr. Washington chose to be addressed."—*Irving*.

(*c*) *Pause :* "I pause for a reply.—None? Then none have I offended.—I have done no more to Cæsar than you should do to Brutus."—*Shakspeare*.

(*d*) *Breaking off*, or *Omission :*

> " Here lies the great—false marble, where?
> Nothing but sordid dust lies there."—*Shakspeare*.

"The pulse fluttered—stopped—went on—throbbed—stopped again," etc.—*Sterne*.

"*A man*—one unknown or indefinite ; *the man*—one known and particular."—*Gould Brown*.

(*e*) *Close of enumeration :* "The noble indignation with which Emmet repelled the charge of treason against his country, the eloquent vindication of his name, and his pathetic appeals to posterity—all these entered deeply into every generous breast."—*Irving*.

(*f*) *Unexpected transition :*

> " Whatever is, is right.—This world, 'tis true,
> Was made for Cæsar—but for Titus too."—*Pope*.

(*g*) *A parenthetical remark :* "There was a little picture—excellently done, moreover—of a ragged, bloated New England toper."—*Hawthorne*.

(*h*) *Intended disconnection* of words or sentences : " Traitor !—I go, but I return.—This—trial !—Here I devote your senate ! "—" I've had wrongs," etc.—*Croly*.

§ 7. *Curves, brackets, and quotation marks.*

148. **Curves, or parentheses,** are used to enclose words, phrases, clauses, numbers, letters, points, etc., which are to be kept independent of the main construction. If the

insertion is prompted by emotion, especially if its words fall readily into the construction of the sentence, two dashes are usually preferred.

149. **Brackets, or crotchets,** are chiefly used to insert the words of some one else, by way of explanation, correction, or comment.

Examples:

(*a*) *Emotion :* "I had given all my savings—five pennies —to the poor peddler."

(*b*) *Explanation :* "I had given all my savings (five pennies) to the poor peddler."

(*c*) *Comment :* "I had given all my savings [five pennies] to the poor peddler."

Sometimes, to mark a total want of connection, the dash and the curves are combined; as :

> " Thou idol of thy parents—(Hang the boy !
> There goes my ink)—
> With pure heart newly stamped from nature's mint—
> (Where did he learn that squint ?)"—*Hood.*

As appears from this example, the portion between the curves takes such points as its own meaning requires. The main sentence is **punctuated** as it would be if the whole parenthesis were taken away. If the parenthesis affects more directly the words preceding it, the stop, if any occurs, is marked after the curves or brackets ; if it affects more directly what follows it, the point is placed before the brackets ; if it refers equally to both parts, the point is marked before the first curve and repeated before the second. No parenthesis should occur at the beginning or at the end of a sentence.

150. **Examples:** " *W.*—This letter (which is unmarked) is a consonant."—*Noah Webster.*

" The sound *p* (unmarked), as in pay, page, etc."—*Id.*

"I send you, my dear child, (and you will not doubt) very sincerely the wishes of the season."—*Chesterfield.*

"Hear him with patience, (and at least with seeming attention,) if he is worth obliging."—*Id.*

"By adding *able* or *ible :* (sometimes with a change of the final letters :) as 'perish,' 'perishable.' "—*G. Brown.*

151. **Quotation marks** are double inverted commas put before and after whatever is presented as the identical words of others, or of the same writer on another occasion. A quotation occurring inside of another is included between single points. Either double or single marks enclose words, phrases, etc., mentioned as examples, or pointed out particularly as if underscored. When a quotation runs continuously through several paragraphs, each of these has the double commas at the beginning.

> "The Switzer gazed—the arrow hung,
>   ' My only boy !' sobbed on his tongue ,
>   He could not shoot.
>   ' Ha !' cried the tyrant, ' doth he quail ?
>   Mark how his haughty brow grows pale !'
>   But a clear voice rang on the gale—
>   ' Shoot, in God's name !' "

As **Capital Letters**, the **Hyphen**, the **Apostrophe** belong properly to the spelling of words, they are supposed to be fully known before the study of rhetorical precepts is undertaken.

BOOK II.

ORNAMENTS OF COMPOSITION.

152. "When we have acquired that ease of diction and harmony of numbers which I have explained," says Cicero, "our whole style of oratory is to be adorned and frequently interspersed with brilliant lights, as it were, of thoughts and language" (*De Or.*, iii. 52). The principal of these ornaments are figures. Quintilian thus defines them : "**Figures** are departures from the ordinary mode of expression for the purpose of adorning our style" (*Inst.*, ix. 1). By 'adorning' he means bestowing on style additional clearness, strength, or beauty.

153. Frequently all **three effects** at once are produced by figurative language. For instance, Pope wishes to say that vice is in reality loathsome, and that every one at first shrinks from committing sin ; yet that, by sinning often, a person may lose this horror and become fond of vice. He expresses this more strikingly, pleasingly, and clearly by means of figures :

> " Vice is a monster of so frightful mien,
>   As to be hated needs but to be seen ;
>   Yet seen too oft, familiar with her face,
>   We first endure, then pity, then embrace."

This imagery is beautiful, yet it is not perfect. There is in the whole conception a flaw which might have been avoided. We are said to embrace the monster through pity ; it would have been more correct to say that we are attracted by its deceptive charms, which become more seductive in proportion as familiarity with vice lessens our horror for its guilt. The figure would be far more beautiful without this inaccuracy.

154. Let us take an example in prose. Dr. Johnson writes :

"If he who considers himself as suspended over the abyss of eternal perdition only by the thread of life, which must soon part by its own weakness, and which the wing of every minute may divide, can cast his eyes round him without shuddering with horror, what can he judge of himself but that he is not yet awakened to sufficient conviction ?"

Here are some striking and appropriate images : a man in danger of eternal loss is compared to a man suspended over an abyss ; his life to a thread ; this thread is so frail that it must soon part by its own weakness ; a minute is a winged creature, to denote its swiftness, etc. But these figures are not consistent : we cannot conceive a man as hanging by a mere thread, especially by one so weak that the wing of a little creature, as we necessarily conceive a minute to be, can divide it. Such flaws, and even more serious faults, are not uncommon in the works of brilliant writers, and are very numerous in extempore speeches. To learn how to use figures with as much correctness as brilliancy requires very careful study.

Figures are thus classified :

155. 1. Those which *turn* or change words from their literal meaning ; these are called **tropes** ($\tau\rho\acute{o}\pi o\varsigma$, a turning).

2. Those which leave words in their original meaning ; these are of two kinds :

(*a*) **Figures of words,** also called figures of diction, which consist in the mode of expression ; they depend on the words themselves or on their position.

(*b*) **Figures of thought**, which consist in some peculiarity of the thoughts, independently of any special mode
of expression.

We shall treat: 1. Of *tropes;* 2. Of *figures of words;*
3. Of *figures of thought.*

156. It is well to remark, for the sake of avoiding confusion, that **the ancients** did not include tropes under the
head of figures (*figuræ, σχήματα*), while we do, with moderns generally.   Still, like the ancients (Quintilian, ix. 1).
we consider tropes as neither figures of words nor figures
of thought, but as a distinct kind of figures, subject to special laws, and therefore requiring special treatment.

CHAPTER I.

TROPES.

157. **Tropes may be thus defined:** "Figures in which words are turned or changed from their literal meaning"; or, "Words used in meanings not their own, with a peculiarly happy effect." Thus when Thomson writes:

> "But yonder comes the powerful king of day,
> Rejoicing in the East, . . ."

he uses "king of day" for "sun"; and no one can fail to notice the happy effect produced.

158. **The pleasure arising from the use of figures** is due to two principal causes:

1. **One cause** is **the play of our imagination.** For as children, by a wise dispensation of Providence, rejoice in running and jumping, and other bodily exercises conducive to their health and physical development, so all men find delight in the play of their fancy or imagination ; the exercise of which faculty, if properly directed by reason, becomes a source of great mental development.

159. 2. **The second cause** of pleasure is the introduction into the composition of such **new images** as add special strength or beauty. Thus, in the example quoted, not only the sun is presented to our minds, but also the image of a powerful king. From the consideration of these two sources of pleasure we readily infer that the following rules must direct the use of tropes.

160. *Rule* 1.—The new images introduced must be really **suited to add strength or beauty.** Hence we should not

refer to low or mean objects, as they are offensive to good taste ; but the images selected must be beautiful or dignified.

Burlesque compositions form an exception to this rule : their aim is to render undignified what in itself is noble or grand. Notice the contrast between these two descriptions of morning :

> " The saffron morn, with early blushes spread,
> Now rose refulgent from Tithonus' bed,
> With new-born day to gladden mortal sight,
> And gild the courts of heaven with sacred light."
>
> —*Pope's Homer.*

> " The sun had long since in the lap
> Of Thetis taken out his nap ;
> And, like a lobster boiled, the morn
> From black to red began to turn."
>
> —*Butler's Hudibras.*

161. *Rule 2.*—Figures should not be drawn from **objects insufficiently known** to the reader, for they would thus present no distinct image to the imagination. This rule is violated by Dryden when he writes :

> " From harmony to harmony
> Through all the compass of the notes it ran,
> The *diapason* closing full in man."

162. *Rule 3.*—They should not be drawn from **objects too remotely connected** with the literal meaning ; else there is no play, but a painful straining of the imagination. Some one has called ' dewdrops ' "the tears of the day for the loss of the sun " ; this is forced, far-fetched.

163. *Rule 4.*—Nor should the connection be **too close,** the analogy too great ; else the play of the fancy is too insignificant. Thus a poet may be said to paint a scene to the eye, comparing his art to that of the painter ; but it would not do to compare the art of the sculptor to that

of the painter, the two being too much alike ; we should not say 'a sculptor paints to the eye.'

164. *Rule* 5.—The figures should not be **trite**—that is, too familiar on account of frequent use ; the imagination finds no more pleasure in these ; they are like faded flowers. Such expressions as 'the mantle of charity,' 'a storm of passion,' 'frantic rage,' 'a howling wilderness,' etc , may be used as plain language, but not as ornaments.

165. *Rule* 6.—Tropes should not be so **crowded** together as to confuse the mind : Mr. James Russell Lowell is often regardless of this rule. His style is brilliant, but very different from what classic taste admires. He writes :

"It cannot be denied that in Wordsworth the very highest powers of the poetic mind were associated with a certain tendency to the diffuse and commonplace. It is in the understanding (always prosaic) that the great golden veins of his imagination are embedded. He wrote too much to write always well ; for it is not a great Xerxes-army of words, but a compact Greek ten thousand, that march safely down to posterity. He set tasks to his divine faculty, which is much the same as trying to make Jove's eagle do the service of a clucking hen. Throughout 'The Prelude' and 'The Excursion' he seems striving to bind the wizard Imagination with the sand-ropes of dry disquisition, and to have forgotten the potent spell-word which would make the particles cohere. There is an arenaceous quality in the style which makes progress wearisome. Yet with what splendors as of mountain-sunsets are we rewarded ! what golden rounds of verse do we not see stretching heavenward, with angels ascending and descending ! what haunting harmonies hover around us, deep and eternal like the undying baritone of the sea ! And if we are compelled to fare through sands and desert wildernesses, how often do we not hear airy shapes that syllable our names with a startling personal appeal to our highest consciousness and our noblest aspiration, such as we wait for in vain in any other poet !"

166. *Rule* 7.—Tropes must be **true to nature**. To express the thought that "wisdom is gathered from adversity rather than prosperity," some one has written : "We

gather the honey of earthly wisdom not from flowers but from thorns." This would be correct if any kind of thorns yielded honey.

167. *Rule* 8.—Tropes should be **suited** to the nature of the composition. Many figures appropriate in poetry are inappropriate in prose ; many admissible in oratory are excluded from didactic writings. They should not unduly elevate the subject, nor sink it below its proper dignity. Some persons display very bad taste by frequently violating this rule. They cannot tell a simple story or propose a plain argument without rambling through " earth and sky and ocean's wide abyss" for images and figures. Some one said of a bill presented in Parliament : " At length it floated through both houses on the tide of a great majority, and steered into the safe harbor of royal approbation."

168. It is a violation of this same rule to clothe serious thoughts in **figures taken from mythology** and other unrealities ; this practice was well enough among the ancients, who believed in such follies.

169. That one object expressed may recall another object not expressed, **there must be some connection** between those two objects, some relation so obvious that as soon as one object is conceived the other is sure to be suggested to the mind. Consider the words—

> " But yonder comes the powerful king of day,
>   Rejoicing in the East."

As the king is the most conspicuous, most majestic, and most powerful person in a kingdom, so the sun is the most conspicuous, most majestic, and most powerful body in the heavens. In this case the relation of 'king' with 'sun' is one of *resemblance :* the figure is called a *metaphor.* Thus there is in every trope some relation between what is expressed and what is really meant ; and the figures receive different names from the different relations on which they are founded. **All tropes then agree** in this, that they *turn* ($\tau\rho\acute{\epsilon}\pi\omega$, to turn) a word from its proper meaning, so that a term expressing one idea is put for another idea, owing to some relation existing between those two ideas ; and **they differ in kind** from one another, according to the various *relations* that underlie them. We shall next consider the different kinds.

ARTICLE I. METAPHOR.

170. **A Metaphor** is a trope founded on the relation of *resemblance*. Thus Shakspeare calls a good name "the jewel of the soul"; the sun, "the beauteous eye of heaven." What a good name does for the soul resembles what a jewel does for the body : it adorns or honors it ; here the resemblance is *between the two effects*. Again, as the eyes are the brightest and noblest portion of the human countenance, so the sun is the brightest and noblest object on the face of heaven ; here the resemblance is *between the objects themselves*. In each instance the word expressing resemblance is omitted : every metaphor is thus an abridged comparison, in which the words, 'like,' 'as,' 'similar to,' etc., are omitted. Metaphors enable us to **condense** much beautiful thought into few words, as a jewel presents much beauty in a small compass : we may well call the metaphor a jewel of literature. No wonder, then, that Poetry loves to deck herself with such jewels. Prose is plainer in her attire ; still she, too, loves to adorn herself with the more modest species of metaphors, and even, at times, with the more brilliant kinds, when the occasion invites her to walk forth in all her splendor.

171. A marked **effect of metaphors** is that they spread life and light over all creation. In particular :

1. They **clothe abstract conceptions** and invisible beings in sensible and striking forms : anger is said to 'burn,' remorse to 'gnaw the heart,' baseness to 'shrink from the light,' pride to 'swell,' and modesty to 'retire from notice'; good thoughts become the 'music of the soul,' chastity the 'pearl among the virtues,' the 'garb that angels wear'; etc.

172. 2. **Sensible objects exchange qualities,** putting on more striking or more pleasing forms : the earth is said 'to pour forth its treasures,' the ocean 'roars,' the cataract 'thunders'; a brave man is a 'lion,' a gentle one a 'lamb,' a pure and simple heart a 'dove.' Attila is 'the Scourge of God,' the Scipios are called by Virgil 'duo fulmina belli' —'two thunderbolts of war'; etc.

173. Besides the five rules above given for all tropes, the following rules apply to metaphors in particular :

Rule 1.—The **figurative and the plain meanings** must not be **inconsistently mixed,** as is done in these verses of Pope :

> " Now from my fond embrace by tempest torn
> Our other column of the state is borne,
> Nor took a kind adieu, nor sought consent."

Telemachus is here figuratively called a 'column of the state,' and is said to have been borne off without 'taking leave' of his mother, Penelope : he is at once a 'column' and a 'man.' A late copy of a newspaper contained, printed in large capitals, "Three boys drowned in the Father of the Waters."

174. *Rule* 2.—**Two inconsistent tropes** should not be blended together, as is done by Shakspeare when he says, "To take up arms against a sea of trouble," meaning 'to resist adversity.' Aubrey de Vere says of Alexander :

> " He flung,
> Nighing the shore, his spear, that shook for gladness,
> Rooted in Asia's soil."

It is a very poetic conception that makes the spear by
which Alexander took possession of Asia 'exult for gladness,' like a person ; but a person is not 'rooted in the
soil,' like a plant.　But there is no objection to **different
metaphors succeeding one another**, each presenting a separate image.　Thus the martyr-poet Robert Southwell, S.J.,
describes the martyr-Queen of Scots as saying :

> " Rue not my *death*, rejoice at my *repose ;*
> 　It was not death to me, but *to my woe :*
> The *bud* was opened to let out the rose ;
> 　The *chains* unloosed to let the captive go."

The same poet writes :

> " Not always *fall of leaf*, nor ever spring,
> 　Not *endless night*, nor yet eternal day ;
> The *saddest birds* a season find to sing,
> 　The *roughest storm* a calm may soon allay.
> Thus, with succeeding turns, God *tempereth all*,
> That man may *hope to rise*, yet fear to fall."

175. *Rule* 3.—When the metaphors are of more than
usual length, they should **grow in beauty** and dignity as
they proceed, not descend into lesser details.　Young says
beautifully :

> " Walk thoughtful on the solemn, silent shore
> 　Of that vast ocean it must sail so soon."

But he fails to keep up this elevation of thoughts when he
adds :

> " And put good works on board, and wait the wind
> 　That shortly blows us into worlds unknown."

176. **Exercise 1.**—Point out the metaphors contained in
the extracts from Goldsmith's " Deserted Village " quoted
under Object-Lessons (Nos. 7 and 8), also in Southey's
" Cataract of Lodore " (No. 15) ; and examine with care
whether any of the rules just given are violated in any of
those metaphors.

177. *Note.*—The rules for metaphors most frequently violated, and often the most difficult to apply, are the first and second—namely, those regarding the *mixing of literal and figurative* language, and the blending of *inconsistent metaphors.* The difficulty arises from the fact that it is often not clear whether the meaning given to a word should be considered as literal or figurative. All discourse abounds in words that are not taken in their original or primitive meaning. Even in common conversation we constantly borrow the names of sensible objects or qualities to denote what is insensible. Thus we speak of a ' piercing judgment,' ' a clear head,' ' a soft or hard heart,' ' a rough or smooth behavior.' In these expressions the adjectives ' piercing,' ' clear,' ' soft,' ' hard,' ' rough,' and ' smooth ' primarily belong to sensible qualities ; and the substantive ' head ' stands for mind, ' heart ' for moral affections. Still, we do not call such expressions *tropes ;* for by constant use these meanings have become the literal meanings of the words. It may be laid down as a *rule* that a given meaning may be considered as literal if it is much used by good writers without any regard to the original meaning of the same word ; for the practice of good writers is the rule of language. Still, the practice is not always easy to ascertain. There is a multitude of words that are in a state of transition between the figure and the letter. " Literal and figurative expressions," says J. Q. Adams in his *Lectures on Rhetoric* (Lect. xxxii.), " are so blended together in the practice of speech that the boundaries between them are imperceptible : like the colors of the rainbow, of which the dullest eye can perceive the varieties, while the keenest cannot catch the precise point at which every separate tint is parted from its neighboring hue." In such cases, and in many analogous difficulties, it is the task of a delicate and correct taste to discriminate.

Though it is impossible to lay down an exact rule by which literal can always be distinguished from figurative language, practically it is not so difficult in most instances to determine whether a given sentence is faulty or not. Take this sentence : " In this error we see a capital violation of the most obvious rules of policy and prudence." - ' Error ' originally means a wandering—it regards the feet ; ' capital ' regards the head ; ' violation ' suggests violence ; ' obvious ' refers to a meeting of two persons ; ' rules ' are lines, etc. Here is a strange medley of images, if these words really suggested the things which they primarily signified ; but they do not, and this sentence of Junius is correct. But it is different with the following sentence of Dr. Johnson : " Barbarous or impure words and expressions may be branded with some note of infamy, as they are carefully to be eradicated, whenever they occur ; and they occur too frequently even in the best writers." To ' eradicate,' not only primarily in Latin, but also as used in its English form, means to pull up by the roots, and we cannot think of any object that can be ' branded with infamy ' and is at the same time capable of being rooted up.

178. **Exercise 2.**—Let the pupil criticise the following figures :

" The colonies were not yet ripe to bid adieu to British connection." " E'en wit's a burden when it talks too long." " There is not a single vein of human nature that is not sufficient to extinguish the seeds of pride." " Up to the stars the sprawling mastiffs fly, and add new monsters to the frighted sky." " No human happiness is so serene as not to contain some alloy." " Hope, the balm of life, darts a ray of light through the thickest gloom." " These are the first-fruits of my unfledged eloquence, of which thou hast often complained that it was buried in the shade." " The wheels of the spiritual ocean have been exerting themselves with perpetual motion." " Her cheeks were blooming with roses and health." " Come, sealing night, and scarf up the tender eye of pitiful day." " He is fairly launched upon the road of preferment."

> " And there, with eyes that goad me yet,
> The ghost of my Ideal stands."

ARTICLE II. ALLEGORY.

179. An **Allegory** (ἀλληγορία) is the treatment or description of one thing under the image of another. It is, therefore, an extended metaphor. When Moore addresses the poetry of Ireland as " Dear Harp of my country!" he uses a metaphor ; when he continues to describe that poetry under the same image of a harp, he writes a beautiful allegory :

> " Dear Harp of my country ! in darkness I found thee,
>   The cold chain of silence had hung o'er thee long,
> When proudly, my own Island Harp, I unbound thee,
>   And gave all thy chords to life, freedom, and song.
> The warm lay of love and the light note of gladness
>   Have wakened thy fondest, thy liveliest thrill ;
> But so oft hast thou echoed the deep sigh of sadness
>   That even in thy mirth it will steal from thee still " ; etc.

See also Moore's " I saw from the Beach."

180. **Literature abounds** in such gems of thought. Parnell's " Hermit " is an allegorical story in verse, elegantly illustrating the secret dispensations of Providence. The ode of Horace, " *O Navis, referent,*" is a touching appeal addressed to Rome, which is represented under the image of a weather-beaten vessel in danger of perishing. The **Parables** of Holy Scripture are so many allegories ; for instance, that of the Prodigal Son, exhibiting the tender mercy of our Heavenly Father, that of the Good Samaritan, the Barren Fig-tree, etc. Pope's " House of Fame " is an elaborate allegory of the descriptive kind. Dryden's " Hind and Panther " is one of the most remarkable allegories in any language. The poet wrote it soon after his conversion to the Catholic Church. The " milk-white Hind " is the Church of Rome ; the " spotted Panther " is the Church of England ; while the Independents, Quakers, Calvinists, and other sects are represented by " bears," " hares," " wolves," and other animals. The opening lines are justly styled by Johnson " lofty, elegant, and musical " :

> " A milk-white Hind, immortal and unchanged,
>   Fed on the lawns, and in the forest ranged ;
>   Without unspotted, innocent within,
>   She feared no danger, for she knew no sin.
>   Yet had she oft been chased with horns and hounds,
>   And Scythian shafts, and many winged wounds,
>   Aimed at her heart ; was often forced to fly,
>   And doomed to death, though fated not to die."

"The wit in the 'Hind and Panther,'" says Hallam, "is sharp, ready, and pleasant; the reasoning is sometimes admirably close and strong ; it is the energy of Bossuet in verse."—*Jenkins' Literature.*

Allegories are subject to the **laws** laid down for metaphors, especially to that of *consistency*, which requires that all the portions of the picture obviously apply to one object in a literal and to the other in a figurative meaning. The French poet Lemierre has elegantly said,

> " *L'Allégorie habite un palais diaphane* " —
> " In crystal palace Allegory dwells,"

to signify that through every part of the literal sense the figurative must be distinctly seen.

ARTICLE III. SYNECDOCHE AND METONYMY.

181. We class **Synecdoche** and **Metonymy** together because they answer the same purpose and are subject to the same rules, differing in both these respects from the metaphor and allegory.

(*a*) **Their purpose**: "Metaphor has been invented," says Quintilian (viii. 6), and the same holds true of allegory, "for the purpose of exciting the mind, giving a character to things and setting them before the eye ; while the synecdoche is adapted to give variety to language." It will, however, readily appear, from the examples to be given, that synecdoche and metonymy do much more than merely give variety to language ; but it is true that they do not paint to the eye.

(*b*) Hence they are **not guided by the same rules** as the metaphor and allegory. The latter two, because they paint to the eye, must present consistent images, such as, if drawn on canvas, would make up one picture ; but this rule is not applicable to synecdoche and metonymy, as they do not paint. Hence it is practically very important to distinguish between these two classes of figures, lest we judge them by laws to which they are not subject.

The **primary laws** for synecdoche and metonymy are, that they must be *clear* and *produce a happy effect*.

§ 1. *Synecdoche.*

182. A **Synecdoche** (σύν, ἐκδοχή, a taking together, a comprising) is a trope founded on the relation of a *whole* to its several *parts*. As the words whole and part have various applications, the figure occurs in various forms.

(*a*) *Physical parts :*

> " Your head must come
> To the cold tomb."
> *—Shirley.*

(*b*) *Singular for plural :*

> " The ploughman homeward plods his weary way."—*Gray.*

(*c*) *Genus for species,* or *species for genus :*

> " Hands that the rod of empire might have swayed,
> Or waked to ecstasy the living lyre."—*Gray.*

Here the genus ' rod ' stands for the species ' sceptre '; the species ' lyre ' for the genus of ' musical instruments,' or it stands for ' poetry,' of which it is the accepted symbol.

(*d*) *The material for the object itself ;* as, ' oaks ' for ships :

> " Let India boast her plants, nor envy we
> The weeping amber and the balmy tree,
> While by our oaks the precious loads are borne,
> And realms commanded which those trees adorn."—*Pope.*

(*e*) *A proper name for a common,* or vice versa. This is called **Antonomasia**; as, ' The Roman Orator,' for Cicero ; ' a Milton,' for a poet ; ' a Cromwell,' for a tyrant ; ' an Aloysius,' for a holy youth ; ' a Hampden,' for a moral hero.

> " Some village Hampden, that with dauntless breast
>   The little tyrant of his field withstood ;
>   Some mute, inglorious Milton here may rest,
>   Some Cromwell, guiltless of his country's blood."—*Gray.*

§ 2. *Metonymy.*

183. While synecdoche exchanges the name of an object for that of its part, **Metonymy** *transfers* ($\mu\epsilon\tau\acute{\alpha}$, $o\nu o\mu\alpha$) the name of an object to another object really distinct from it, but connected with it by an *external relation.* It puts

(*a*) An *effect for a cause;* as, " Death fell in showers," for ' bullets fell.' Pope says :

> " For not to know some trifles is a praise "

—that is, ' a cause of praise.' Moore puts ' death ' for the ' army ' :

> " The minstrel boy to the war is gone ;
>   In the ranks of death you will find him."

(*b*) A *cause for an effect :* " Dust thou art, and unto dust thou shalt return " (Gen. iii. 19)—that is, ' Thou art drawn from dust.'

> " Amid thy bowers the tyrant's hand is seen."—*Goldsmith.*

—*i.e.,* ' destruction ' caused by the tyrant's hand.

(*c*) The *container for the contained :* Thus our Blessed Saviour said :

> " O my Father ! if this chalice cannot pass away, except I drink it, thy will be done."—*Matt.* xxvi. 42.

Johnson says of Charles XII. of Sweden :

> " He left the name at which the world grew pale,
>   To point a moral or adorn a tale."—*Vanity of Human Wishes.*

(*d*) The *sign for the thing signified :*

> " Sceptre and crown
>   May tumble down,
>   And in the dust be equal made
>   With the poor crooked scythe and spade."—*Shirley.*

(*e*) The *protecting deity* for the object protected ; thus the ancients put 'Neptune' for the sea, 'Bacchus' for wine, 'Ceres' for corn, etc.   This use is out of date.

(*f*) *The head of a family for his descendants ;* as :

'May God enlarge Japheth, and may he dwell in the tents of Sem, and Chanaan be his servant."—*Gen.* ix. 27.

(*g*) *The place for what is found in it ;* as, 'Arabia,' for its perfumes :

"And all Arabia breathes from yonder box."—*Pope.*

(*h*) *Abstract for concrete* terms ; as, "Length of days is in her right hand" (Prov. iii. 16), for 'A long life' is the gift of Wisdom.

184. Metonymy is **further diversified** by *attributing to an effect what properly belongs to its cause ;* as :

"Sad, silent, and dark be the tears that we shed."—*Moore.*

—*i e.,* 'Let us weep while we are sad, silent, and unnoticed.'

> "Take back the virgin page
> White and unwritten still ;
> Some hand more calm and sage
> The leaf must fill."—*Moore.*

'Calm' and 'sage' are qualities of the mind that guides the hand.

This use of the metonymy is often harsh or obscure ; as :

> "When sapless age and weak, unable limbs
> Should bring thy father to his *drooping* chair."—*Shakspeare.*

Conversely *we attribute to a cause what properly belongs to its effect :*

> "And the merry bells ring round,
> And the jocund rebecks sound."—*Milton.*

ARTICLE IV. IRONY, HYPERBOLE, AND PERSONIFICATION.

185. 1. **Irony** is a trope founded on the *contrast* between

two objects ; as when Cicero calls the unjust and reckless Verres " that upright and careful man " :

> " But Brutus is an honorable man ;
> So are they all, all honorable men."—*Shakspeare.*

When irony is very bitter it is called **Sarcasm**, a dangerous weapon. *Junius' Letters* contain many ironical passages, in keeping with the envenomed spirit of that writer.

186. **2. Hyperbole** is a trope founded on *exaggeration*. It should be used sparingly ; and it is never proper unless the subject exceed the common measure. It is dictated by violent emotion, and therefore must always be very brief. "*Violenta non durant*"—" Vehemence is short-lived."

187. **Examples**:

> " What a *world of happiness* their melody compels ! "—*Poe.*

> " Strike—till the *last* armed foe expires ! "—*Halleck.*

> " And *each particular hair to stand on end,*
> Like quills upon the fretful porcupine."—*Shakspeare.*

> " He was so gaunt, the *case of a flageolet was a mansion for him.*"
> —*Shakspeare.*

> " That sound might *wake the dead.*"—*De Vere.*

But even in a hyperbole nature assigns a limit to exaggeration. The following is unnatural :

> " Draw them to Tiber's bank, and weep your tears
> Into the channel till the lowest stream
> Do kiss the most exalted shore of all."—*Shakspeare.*

188. The hyperbole says more than it means ; its opposite, the **Litotes** ($\lambda\iota\tau\acute{o}\tau\eta s$, simplicity), *means more than it says ;* thus the expression, " Youth is not over-thoughtful," is a euphemism for ' Youth is giddy.' One of our statesmen finishes an oration, intended to avert an Indian war, with a beautiful instance of this trope :

"The darkness of midnight will glitter with the blaze of your dwellings. You are a father: the blood of your sons shall fatten your corn-field You are a mother: the war-whoop shall *wake the sleep of the cradle.*"

The further horrors of Indian warfare are here veiled with equal judgment and elegance under a double figure.

189. **3. Personification** consists in representing inanimate objects and abstract notions as endowed with *life* and *intelligence.* It may exist in various degrees:

1st Degree.—When merely some *properties* or *qualities* of animals or persons are ascribed to inanimate objects or abstract notions ; as:

> "One faithful harp shall praise thee."—*Moore.*
>
> "O the cold and cruel winter !"—*Longfellow.*

2d Degree.—When inanimate objects or abstract notions are represented as performing the *actions* of intelligent beings ; as:

> "Patriotism, which sinks self and scorns death, is a noble virtue."—*Headley.*
>
> "Hope for a season bade the world farewell,
> And Freedom shrieked as Kosciusko fell."—*Campbell.*
>
> "*Lympha pudica Deum vidit et erubuit,*"

says Crashaw, describing the miracle by which our Blessed Saviour changed water into wine. Dryden thus translates the verse with exquisite taste:

> "The modest water saw its God and blushed."
>
> "Within their buds let roses sleep,
> And virgin lilies on their stems."—*Shirley.*
>
> "Can Honor's voice provoke the silent dust,
> Or Flattery soothe the dull, cold ear of Death?"

3d Degree.—When they are represented as *feeling* like men, or as *speaking* or *listening* to us ; as:

> " Within the hollow crown
>   That rounds the mortal temples of a king,
>   Keeps Death his court ; and there the antic sits,
>   Scoffing his state, and grinning at his pomp."
>
> *—Shakspeare.*

> " Earth felt the wound, and Nature from her seat,
>   Sighing through all her works, gave signs of woe
>   That all was lost."*—Milton.*

> " O gentle Sleep,
> Nature's soft nurse, how have I frightened thee," etc.

> " Sweet Auburn, loveliest village of the plain," etc.
>
> *—Goldsmith*

> " O unexpected stroke ! worse than death !
>   Must I thus leave thee, Paradise ! thus leave
>   Thee, native soil," etc.*—Milton.*

190. Source of the pleasure.—Man naturally loves communion with his fellow-man ; and when his passions are excited or his imagination is aroused, he is prone to invest objects around him with such qualities as raise them to a state of fellowship with himself.

191. Hence it follows: 1. That poetry, which is the language of the passions and of an excited imagination, is full of personifications. Prose admits the lower degrees of personification very readily in all literary productions, and it admits the highest degree when the heart is under the influence of lofty, violent, or tender emotions. 2. No objects should be personified in the highest degree that are not of sufficient dignity or importance to awaken such emotions. The last two lines of the following quotation evidently violate this rule :

> " Dear fatal name ! rest ever unrevealed,
>   Nor pass these lips in holy silence sealed.
>   Oh, write it not, *my hand!* His name appears
>   Already written—blot it out, *my tears !*"

192. When personification is founded upon resemblance, as it usually is, it is subject to the **rules** for metaphor, but not otherwise. For instance, in the words of Moore,

" One *faithful* Harp shall save thee,"

there is no resemblance ; but the fidelity of the harper is attributed to the harp : it is a metonymy. So, too, in Milton's lines,

" Her *rash* hand in evil hour
Forth reaching to the fruit, she plucked, she ate,"

the rashness of Eve is by metonymy transferred to her hand, which is thereby slightly personified, being made to show a property of a person. Thus personification is usually combined with some other figure, and is then subject to the rules for that figure.

193. This *union of two figures in one* must be distinguished from the **metalepsis** ($\mu\varepsilon\tau\acute{a}\lambda\eta\psi\iota\varsigma$, a partaking), which is a noble figure resulting from the meeting of two independent tropes upon one word, as in

" And desolation saddens all thy green."

'Green' here stands by metonymy for the *fields*—the *abstract for the concrete*—and the fields are *personified* by being put in connection with 'saddens.'

194. **Directions to discover the tropes and their species.** —Ask yourself :

1. What idea does the writer wish to convey ?

2. Do the words literally express that idea ? If they do there is no trope. If not,

3. What connection is there between what is literally expressed and what is really meant ?

    A trope founded on *resemblance* is called metaphor ;

    A trope founded on *resemblance prolonged*—allegory.

    A trope founded on a *relation of whole and part*—synecdoche.

A trope founded on an *external relation*—metonymy.

A trope founded on *contrast*—irony.

A trope founded on *exaggeration*—hyperbole.

A trope founded on *diminution*—litotes.

A trope founded on *elevation to intelligence*—personification.

A trope founded on *combination of two tropes*—metalepsis.

An inconsistent or strained trope is a **catachresis** ($\varkappa\alpha\tau\acute{\alpha}\cdot\chi\rho\eta\sigma\iota\varsigma$, misuse). A trope whose real meaning is not clear to an intelligent and attentive reader should be considered as faulty.

195. **Exercise.**—Point out the correct and the incorrect tropes which occur in the following selections :

" I appeal to History ! Tell me, thou reverend chronicler of the grave, can all the illusion of ambition realized, can all the wealth of a universal commerce, can all the achievements of successful heroism or all the establishments of the world's wisdom, secure to empire the permanence of its possession ? "—*Phillips.*

" How many centuries of national existence did Austria go through before this mighty change was effected ! How many national sins did she expiate ! What a spot of glory not merely in imperial but in human annals has she left ! "—*Alison.*

" The accusing spirit that flew up to Heaven's chancery with the oath blushed as he gave it in ; and the recording angel, as he wrote it down, dropped a tear upon the word and blotted it out for ever."
—*Sterne.*

" Our knees shall kneel till to the ground they grow."—*Shakspeare.*

" Our web of life is a mingled yarn, good and ill together : our virtues would be proud, if our faults whipped them not ; and our crimes would despair, if they were not cherished by our virtues."—*Shakspeare.*

> " Music that gentler on the spirit lies
> Than tir'd eyelids upon tir'd eyes."—*Tennyson.*

"But the tender shoot of other times has become a giant in the world's extended forest."—*Dickerson.*

"As War was driving his ebon car upon his remorseless mission."—*Id.*

"One drop of balm alone, one drop of heavenly, life-giving balm, mingles in this bitter cup of misery."—*Everett.*

"Our modern prayers have no wings: they creep with us on our own low sphere."—*Card. Wiseman.*

"Peace, the loathed manna, which hot brains despise."—*Dryden.*

"Forth from the curtain of clouds, from the tent of purple and scarlet,
Issued the Sun, the great high-priest, in his garments resplendent."—*Longfellow.*

"My slenderer and younger taper imbibed its borrowed light from the more matured and redundant fountain of yours."—*Curran.*

"Stalwart and stately in form was the man of seventy winters,
Hearty and hale was he, an oak that is covered with snowflakes."
—*Longfellow.*

"While the bell from its turret sprinkled with holy sounds the air."
—*Id.*

"When the breeze of joyful dawn blew free
In the silken sails of infancy."—*Tennyson.*

"On the ancient stock of Saxon independence the English engrafted the shoots of modern liberty; in its stead the French planted the unknown tree of equality. In the British Isles the plant has become deeply rooted, and expanded widely in its native air; time will show whether the French have not wasted their endeavors in training an exotic unsuited to the climate and unfruitful *in* the soil."—*Alison.*

"Lost! somewhere between sunrise and sunset, two golden hours, each set with sixty diamond minutes. No reward is offered, for they are lost for ever."

CHAPTER II.

FIGURES OF WORDS.

196. Figures of Words, or Diction, are ornaments of style consisting of unusual forms of expression, but without any departure from the literal meaning. As they regard the expression rather than the thought itself, they are the least noble among the figures. Still, that they are no inconsiderable source of strength and beauty will appear from the examples to be adduced.

197. 1. Repetition repeats the same word:

"O Rome! Rome! thou hast been a tender nurse to me."

"In an ugly, dark room an old woman, ugly and dark too, sat listening to the wind and rain. . . . A heap of rags, a heap of bones, a wretched bed, . . . the black walls and blacker ceiling," etc.—*Dickens*.

> "Strike—till the last armed foe expires ;
> Strike—for your altars and your fires ;
> Strike—for the green graves of your sires,
> God, and your native land ! "—*Halleck*.

"First in war, first in peace, first in the hearts of his countrymen."—*Curtis*.

> "Come one, come all ! this rock shall fly
> From its firm base as soon as I."—*Scott*.

198. 2. Polysyndeton multiplies conjunctions for the purpose of making the sentence more impressive ; while **Asyndeton** omits them all to denote greater rapidity:

> "He woke to die 'midst flame and smoke,
> And shout, and groan, and sabre-stroke."—*Halleck*.

Of the asyndeton we can give no more striking instance than the words in which Cæsar expressed the rapidity of his conquest : *Veni, vidi, vici—*" I came, I saw, I conquered."

199. **3. Antithesis** unites contrasted words or phrases in the same sentence :

" Sink or swim, live or die, survive or perish, I give my hand and my heart to this vote."—*Webster.*

> " Ring out the darkness from the land ;
> Ring in the Christ that Is to be."—*Tennyson.*

" The God of hosts in slender Host doth dwell,
Yea, God and Man, with all to either due ;
That God that rules the heavens and rifled hell,
That Man whose death did to us life renew."—*Southwell.*

200. **4. Accumulation** of synonyms dwells on one thought :

" You cannot tell me how, but that some unknown dread, some indescribable apprehension, some indefinable danger, affrighted you," etc.—*Clay.*

" He is no benefactor nor deserving of honor, whatever may be his worldly renown, whose life is passed in acts of force, who renounces the great law of Christian brotherhood, whose vocation is blood, who triumphs in battle over his fellow-man."—*Charles Sumner.*

201. **5. Gradation** or **Climax** makes the sentence rise step by step in strength or dignity :

" So the rule of right, which binds the single individual, binds two or three men when gathered together ; binds conventions and congregations of men ; binds villages, towns, and cities ; binds states, nations, and empires , clasps the whole human family in its sevenfold embrace ; nay, more,

> ' Beyond the flaming bounds of space and time,
> The living throne, the sapphire blaze,'

It binds the Angels of heaven, the Seraphim full of love, the Cherubim full of knowledge ; above all, it binds in self-imposed bonds a just and omnipotent God."—*Charles Sumner.*

202. **6. Correction** consists in retracting an assertion as soon as made, and substituting something more suitable, which is more emphasized by this artifice ; as :

" He has sat quietly in his seat, without moving a finger or raising his voice.   Without raising his voice, did I say ?   His voice was raised, not for us but for our assailants."—*Calhoun.*

CHAPTER III.

FIGURES OF THOUGHT.

203. Figures of Thought are ornaments of composition consisting in an unusual turn given to the thought for the purpose of imparting to it special strength or beauty. As the expression and the thought expressed are intimately connected, it is often hard to tell whether the peculiar happy turn which constitutes the figure should be attributed to the thought or to the expression, and therefore whether it is a figure of thought or a figure of words. But it matters little, as both classes of figures are to be directed by the same rule.

204. Rule for figures of words and of thought.—Look to the end or purpose for which they are used—namely, to add strength or beauty. If a figure does either or both, it is well used; if not, it is faulty. The figures have no charm in themselves, but only in their effects upon the reader or hearer. If this rule is carefully observed all wordiness and declamation will be avoided; for these are the only abuses to which these figures are liable.

205. The chief figures of thought are:

1. **Preterition,** when we pretend to omit an argument, thereby calling attention to it.

"I was going to awake your justice to this unhappy part of our fellow creatures by bringing before you some of the circumstances of this awful plague of hunger. Of all the calamities which beset and waylay the life of man, this comes the nearest to the heart, and is that wherein the proudest of us all feels himself to be nothirg more than he is—but I find myself unable to manage it with decorum. These details are so degrading to the sufferers and to the heare.s, they are so humiliating to human nature itself, that I consider it more advisable to throw a pall over the hideous object and leave it to your general conceptions."—*E. Burke.*

206. **2. Reticence,** which purposely leaves a sentence unfinished ; as :

" By these [mercenary armies] France and Spain, though blessed by nature with all that administers to the convenience of life, have been reduced to that contemptible state in which they now appear ; and by these Britain—but if I was possessed of the gift of prophecy, I dare not, except by divine command, unfold the leaves on which the destiny of that once powerful kingdom is inscribed."—*John Hancock.*

207. **3. Concession,** which yields a point with a view to making a more telling point.

" Yes, I have ambition, but it is the ambition of being the humble instrument in the hands of Providence to reconcile a divided people," etc.—*Clay.*

" I agree with my honorable friends in thinking that we ought not to impose a government on France. I agree with them in deprecating the evil of war ; but I deprecate still more the double evil of a peace without securities and a war without allies."—*Grattan.*

208. **4. Paradox,** which advances what is seemingly absurd to make the assertion more striking : as :

" Do not despond, Athenians, even though your situation is very bad. For what is worst in the past is best for the future," etc.—*Demosthenes.*

" The very excess of his [Burke's] tenderness made him cruel, and the vehemence of his detestation of injustice made him unjust."—*Shaw.*

209. **5. Self-questioning,** in which the orator puts a question and answers it himself ; as :

" And what was it which gave to our Lafayette his spotless fame ?

The love of liberty. What has consecrated his memory in the hearts of men? The love of liberty," etc.—*Everett.*

"What is it you can do? This is the question. I answer: Be true to your religion ; be true to your fatherland ; be true to your families and to yourselves ; be true to the glorious republic that opened her arms to receive you and give you the rights of citizenship."—*Rev. T. Burke, O.P.*

210. **6. Suspense,** which keeps the mind in uncertainty awhile, thus arousing attention to what comes next.

"You will read, sir, that Cæsar triumphed four times: first for his victory over the Gauls, secondly over Egypt, thirdly over Pharnaces, lastly over Juba, the friend of Cato. His first, second, and third triumphs were, we are told, magnificent. Before him marched the princes. . . . His fourth triumph approaches, as magnificent as the former ones. It does not want its royal captive, its soldiers crowned with laurels, nor its multitude of spectators—but they send up no shout of exultation ; they heave loud sighs ; their cheeks are frequently wiped ; their eyes are fixed upon one object that engrosses all their senses, their thoughts, their affections—it is the statue of Cato."—*Knowles.*

211. **7. Forestalling an objection;** as :

"But we are told the sanction of virtue is in the social laws of nations. They are sufficient to make man an honest, upright, moral being, such as your religion requires him to be. This objection is so directly at variance with common sense and daily experience that it scarcely deserves an answer."—*Rev. C. F. Smarius, S.J.*

212. **8. Vision** is a vivid description which presents a fact as passing before our eyes ; as :

"But lo ! the time is come ; the awful words have been spoken ; the mouth of unfailing Truth has declared his own body to be there. All are reverently and silently awaiting their turn to partake of the tremendous gift ; the first have tasted it ; Peter is burning and John is melting into tears. The life-giving portion is proffered to Judas, and he stretches to receive it. Oh ! in pity let us hope that he understands not, notwithstanding the words just spoken, what it is ! O Son of God ! exclaim, if thou canst : Father, forgive, for he knows not what he doth."—*Cardinal Wiseman.*

213. **9. Mimesis** is the vivid description of a person's character ; as :

" It is now sixteen or seventeen years since I saw the Queen of France, the Dauphiness, at Versailles; and surely there never lighted on this orb, which she scarcely seemed to touch, a more delightful vision. I saw her just above the horizon, decorating and cheering the elevated sphere she just began to move in, glittering like the morning star, full of life, splendor, and joy."—*E. Burke.*

214. **10. Apostrophe** addresses absent persons as if present, or personified objects as if listening ; as :

" Hail, sacred tabernacles, where thou, O Lord, dost descend at the voice of a mortal ! Hail, mysterious altar, where Faith comes to receive its immortal food ! " etc.—*Archb.shop P. J. Ryan.*

" Accept, O Prince I these last efforts of a voice once familiar to your ears. With you all my funeral discourses are now to end. Instead of deploring the death of others, it shall be my study to learn from you how my own may be blessed," etc.—*Bossuet.*

215. **11. Comparison** or **Simile** illustrates the subject by comparing it with something else :

" Boundless as ocean is a mother's love."—*S. H. Messenger.*

' Men whose lives glided on like rivers that water the woodlands, Darkened by shadows of earth, but reflecting an image of heaven. '
—*Longfellow.*

" The diamond's sparkle and the ruby's tint are darksome com-pared to friendship's transcendent lustre. But the diamond can be imitated; so, too, alas! may friendship be assumed. As all precious gems are rare, so are friends. A true friend, like the ivy that clings to the walls of the old deserted castle, is ever by one's side to comfort us in sorrow and rejoice with us in prosperity."—*J. J. Hamlyn.*

216. **12. A Wish** or **Prayer** is often used as an elegant and powerful figure ; as :

" Thus lived and thus died our sainted patriots ! May their spirits still continue to hover over their countrymen, inspire all their councils, and guide them in the same virtuous and noble path ! And may that God in whose hands are the issues of all things confirm and perpetuate to us the inestimable boon which through their agency He has bestowed, and make our Columbia the bright exemplar for all the struggling sons of liberty around the globe! "—*Wirt.*

217. **13. Exclamation** and **Interrogation**, when they are used to adorn the style or move the heart ; as :

" Has God rejected the beautiful in this temple of creation ? . . . Who was the first painter that touched with his brush the flowers of the valley and tinged with deep azure the ocean ? . . . Who was the first inspirer of music? Who was the first decorator that studded with gems the Milky Way, and spread his arch of splendor across the concave of this his temple ?"—*Archbishop P. J. Ryan.*

218. **14. Allusions** hint at some fact sufficiently known, in illustration of the present subject. These, as well as **Maxims** and **Quotations,** are figures if they beautify the style ; as :

" And why are these eternal gates thus lifted up? And why is this sublime spectacle revealed, if not that we may be induced to take the dove's wings and fly—fly from this earth, which the waters of bitterness and iniquity still cover, and bear the olive-branch of our reconciliation to this open ark, where alone our feet can rest ?" —*Cardinal Wiseman.*

" Slowly as out of the heavens with apocalyptical splendors
    Sank the city of God, in the vision of John the Apostle,
    So with the cloudy walls of chrysolite, jasper, and sapphire
    Sank the broad, red sun, and over its turrets uplifted
    Glimmered the golden reed of the angel who measured the city."
—Longfellow.

219. **Exercise 1.** Collect elegant figures from the speeches of Webster, Calhoun, Clay, Burke, Pitt, Chatham, Cardinals Wiseman, Newman, Manning, Fathers Burke and Smarius ; or from any selections in prose or verse—*e.g.,* from your reader or hand-book of elocution.

220 **Exercise 2.** Write an address, full of figures, to stir up indolent students or to enkindle in an audience feelings of patriotism, generosity in behalf of a disabled soldier, or any other noble sentiment.

BOOK III.

STYLE IN LITERARY COMPOSITION.

221. We have so far considered the chief elements of literary composition; we now proceed to combine these elements, and to study the more complex subject of *style*.

Style (from *stylus*, the ancient instrument for writing) is the manner in which a person expresses his thoughts and feelings by means of any of the fine arts. We speak of different styles in music, painting, architecture, etc. In literature style is the manner of expressing one's thoughts and feelings by means of language. A man's thoughts and feelings are not, in themselves, perceptible to other men. Style sets them forth in a sensible form; it gives them body and shape, beauty to please, and power to influence others. We study style with a view to increase this beauty and power in our compositions.

222. For this purpose we are to consider in so many chapters: 1. Beauty in itself; 2, Sublimity, Wit, and Humor, which are species of beauty; 3. Taste, which directs the use of these sources of pleasure; 4. Different species of style; 5. Improvement of style.

CHAPTER I.

BEAUTY.

223. Beauty is the power which objects have of pleasing the beholder : beautiful objects please by merely being considered ; *quæ visa placent*, says St. Thomas.

Whence comes this power of an object to please? From the perfection or excellence of the object itself. Is, then, the beauty of an object the same as its excellence? It is that excellence inasmuch as it is perceived, and thus made capable of giving pleasure to the beholder ; if hidden or obscured it could not please him. Beauty is "excellence perceived," or "striking excellence"—*splendor veri*, "the brightness of reality," as Plato puts it. Hence one point is evident, that nothing can be beautiful inasmuch as it is bad or imperfect : falsehood is not beautiful, sin is not beautiful, disorder is not beautiful.

224. How, then, can **works of fiction** please, since they are false? They do not please inasmuch as they are false, but inasmuch as they are true to nature and contain beautiful characters, beautiful scenery, a beautiful plot, beautiful language, etc. But may not a vicious character be beautiful? The description of it, done with skill and fidelity to nature, may be so, but not the character itself.

225. But does not **vice** please the vicious? The mere beholding of vice does not please the mind, but a vice may please by gratifying a passion of the heart ; thus, doing wrong to another may please an angry man. But the beautiful pleases *by the mere fact that it is perceived.* Whatever gratifies one of the passions pleases, and may, therefore, be mistaken for true beauty; but it is false or only apparent beauty. True beauty pleases because its perfection is perceived and approved by the intellect.

226. We must here notice the difference between the beautiful and **the good**: A thing is good when its possession pleases; beautiful, when its very perception gives pleasure. Thus a ragged, soiled one-hundred-dollar note may please the possessor, but not the beholder.

From our definition of the beautiful so far explained another consequence follows—namely, that those things which are most perfect in themselves are also most beautiful to those who clearly perceive them. Thus inanimate things contain, as a class, the lowest degree of perfection and are least beautiful; vegetation rises higher, animals higher still; man surpasses all other material beings in excellence and in beauty, because he is intelligent; angels are higher still; God is **the highest possible beauty** to those blessed beings that behold Him as He is. If He does not always seem so to us, it is because we know Him so little, and also because we let our lower nature obscure the light of our intellect. When, in a better world, God will stand revealed to our sight as He is, our purified souls will see in Him absolute beauty, which will make us supremely happy; therefore that sight is called the **Beatific Vision.**

227. The fact that man is more perfect and beautiful than all lower beings is the reason why literature delights in **personification**—that is, in attributing to lower objects the actions and feelings of living and intelligent beings. Yet even **lower objects** have their beauty: that *color* is more beautiful which is better proportioned or adapted to our organ of sight; *straight lines* and *figures* are beautiful, as suggestive of usefulness; *curves* and *waving lines*, as combining regularity with variety: the waving line is called

the line of beauty, the *spiral* that of grace ; *motion* is beautiful, as exhibiting variety and as being suggestive of life.
This suggestiveness of higher beauty is founded on *associations of ideas*, and is often a source of great pleasure to the
mind, even when things are beheld which are of a very inferior nature ; thus the violet is suggestive of modesty, the
lily of purity, etc.

228. It is certain that unity, variety, proportion, design,
life, etc., are all sources of pleasure to the beholder. Some
critics are of opinion that in all beauty there is **one un-
derlying principle.** One class of writers maintain that this
principle is the blending of *unity with variety*, others that
the one principle is *order with due proportion*, or suitableness to the faculties of the beholder. It is not clear that
all beauty can be traced to one such principle; but it is
certain that *the very perfection of an object*, inasmuch as it
is properly considered, whether in itself or in its associations, is the real source of the pleasure produced.

229. We shall next consider **artistic beauty.** The mere
reproduction by human skill of some natural beauty is
doubly pleasing: first, on account of the natural beauty
reproduced, and, secondly, on account of the intellectual
power displayed by men in its reproduction. Thus a
painted bunch of grapes which almost deceives the eye
is more admired than the bunch which nature produced.
And though photography gives us a more perfect likeness
than drawing can do, still the latter is more admired as
being more the effect of human skill and intellect. But
while all correct imitation is beautiful because skilful and
intellectual, still mere imitation of nature is only the lowest
beauty of art. Artistic skill of a higher kind aims at the
expression of more than natural beauty—namely, *ideal
beauty.*

230. Now, **ideal beauty** is that higher conception of

beautiful things which the artist forms to himself by removing from them all such imperfections as would hinder the full appreciation of them, and by associating with them suggestions of greater perfection than the objects themselves contain.

231. The presentation of ideal beauty is the object of all higher art, of the **fine arts** as such. The ancients aimed at this when their painters and sculptors selected for their subjects the ideal forms of Apollo, Hercules, etc., idealizing human perfections to represent their gods and demigods. Thus, too, Homer is not satisfied with the presentation of human heroes as they really existed, but he portrayed them as the mind loves to contemplate them ; and, rising even higher, he presents to us a panorama of superior ideal beings, exhibiting far more power of intellect and will than it is natural for man to possess. Thus he gives us his gods and goddesses, the most wonderful creations of the pagan mind. In fact, the tendency of all true art has ever been upward into the region of relig us thought. Not until **Christianity** came to reveal to us a far higher perfection did art produce its noblest creations. The spirits, good and bad, described by Milton in his "Paradise Lost" are grander creations than Homer's ; but especially the Saviour of the world, dying upon the cross or reclining upon the straw of the manger, and by His side the purest and fairest of mere created beings, the Blessed Virgin Mother, are subjects for the pencil and the pen which modern artists and poets have fully appreciated. Hence Christian art is far more elevated in its ideals than pagan art could possibly have been.

CHAPTER II.

SUBLIMITY, WIT, AND HUMOR.

232. Sublimity, Wit, and **Humor** give pleasure to the mind by the very fact that they are perceived. They come, therefore, under the definition of beauty, of which they are species. Still, sometimes the term beauty is taken in a narrower meaning, as distinguished from them by certain peculiarities of these three species. We shall next consider those peculiarities.

Article I. Sublimity.

233. Sublimity is that species of the beautiful which imparts pleasure of a peculiarly elevated nature. As beauty is *striking perfection*, so sublimity is *striking greatness*, which is a special kind of perfection. It produces in the beholder a sort of internal elevation and expansion, raises the mind above its ordinary state, and fills it with a degree of astonishment which it cannot well express. The emotion is delightful but serious; when greatest it awes the mind.

The **sources of the sublime** are various—some physical, others moral.

234. 1. The **physical** are chiefly :

    (*a*) *Boundless views*, in the contemplation of which the mind is lost.

    (*b*) The exhibition of *vast power* or strength, not accompanied by any apprehension of danger to ourselves.

The ocean combines to a remarkable extent these two sources of the sublime :

" Roll on, thou deep and dark blue ocean—roll !
  Ten thousand fleets sweep over thee in vain ;
  Man marks the earth with ruin—his control
  Stops with the shore ; upon the watery plain
  The wrecks are all thy deed, nor doth remain
  A shadow of man's ravage, save his own,
  When, for a moment, like a drop of rain,
  He sinks into thy depths with bubbling groan,
Without a grave, unknelled, uncoffined, and unknown."
                                        —*Byron.*

(*c*) *Unusual magnificence,* as in Byron's lines on St. Peter's at Rome :

" But lo ! the dome—the vast and wondrous dome,
  To which Diana's marvel was a cell—
  Christ's mighty shrine above his martyrs' tomb !
  I have beheld the Ephesian miracle—
  Its columns strew the wilderness, and dwell
  The hyena and the jackal in their shade ;
  I have beheld Sophia's bright roofs swell
  Their glittering mass i' the sun, and have survey'd
Its sanctuary the while th' usurping Moslem pray'd ;

" But thou, of temples old, or altars new,
  Standest alone, with nothing like to thee :
  Worthiest of God, the holy and the true,
  Since Sion's desolation, when that He
  Fcrsook his former city, what could be
  Of earthly structures, in His honor piled,
  Of a sublimer aspect ? Majesty,
  Power, Glory, Strength, and Beauty, all are aisled
In this eternal ark of worship undefiled."—*Id.*

(*d*) *Loud and deep sounds,* spreading far and wide, as that of the thunder.

(*e*) *Solemn and awful objects,* bordering on the terrible, and whatever makes us sensible of our littleness compared to the grandeur around us, as solitude, deep silence, obscurity, mystery.

We have said that *order* is an element of beauty in its usual acceptation ; but *disorder* is not unfavorable to the sublime—not disorder in itself, but in connection with grandeur, which it makes incomprehensible to the human mind. The same holds of obscurity, mysteriousness, etc.

235. **2. Moral sublimity** arises from the exhibition of such power of the mind and will as produces astonishment in the beholder. When two of the Horatii were slain, and their father heard that his third son had fled, he was indignant ; and when asked what the youth should have done, " He should have died," he said. The history of the Christian martyrs is full of such examples ; but grander than all is the scene on Calvary, when nature trembled at the crimes of men, and the Victim of all this wickedness, the Son of God Himself, opened His lips, not to complain, but to beg pardon for the perpetrators of the deicide : " Father, forgive them, for they know not what they do."

236. The **style** in which the sublime is to be expressed is either of the greatest simplicity or of the highest magnificence. We have seen specimens of magnificence in Byron ; the style of Holy Writ, which contains the loftiest examples of the sublime, is usually of the simplest kind :

" In the beginning God created heaven and earth. And the earth was void and empty, and darkness was upon the face of the deep : and the spirit of God moved over the waters. And God said : Be light made. And light was made,"—*Gen.* i. 1–4.

" The sublime," says Lacordaire, " is elevation, profundity, and simplicity, blended in a single trait." (See Lacordaire's *Jesus Christ*, p. 29.)

237. **Other examples from Holy Writ:**

" In the horror of A VISION by night, when deep sleep is wont to hold men, fear seized upon me, and trembling, and all my bones were affrighted: and when a spirit passed before me, the hair of my flesh stood up. There stood one whose countenance I knew not, an image before my eyes, and I heard the voice as it were of a gentle wind : Shall man be justified in comparison of God, or shall a man be more pure than his maker? Behold, they that serve Him are not steadfast, and in His angels He found wickedness: how much more shall they that dwell in houses of clay, who have an earthly foundation, be consumed as with the moth ?"—*Job* iv. 13-19.

"Wilt Thou give strength to THE HORSE or clothe his neck with neighing? Wilt Thou lift him up like the locusts : the glory of his nostrils is terror. He breaketh up the earth with his hoof, he pranceth boldly, he goeth forward to meet armed men. He despiseth fear, he turneth not his back to the sword. Above him shall the quiver rattle, the spear and shield shall glitter. Chafing and raging he swalloweth the ground : neither doth he make account when the noise of the trumpet soundeth. When he heareth the trumpet he saith : Ha, ha ! he smelleth the battle afar off, the encouraging of the captains, and the shouting of the army."—*Job* xxxix. 19-25.

"GOD hath measured the waters in the hollow of His hand, and weighed the heavens with His palm ; He hath poised with three fingers the bulk of the earth, and weighed the mountains in scales, and the hills in a balance."—*Isaias* xl. 12.

The following **passages** are full of sublime thoughts and images : the fifteenth chapter of Exodus, which contains the Canticle of Moses, sung by the Jews after their miraculous crossing of the sea ; Psalm ciii.; the forty-third chapter of Ecclesiasticus ; the thirty-eighth of Job.

238. **Exercise.**—Point out the beautiful and the sublime images accumulated in the following poem, "The Fairest Fair":

" Mountains, that upwards to the clouds arise,
    Odorous with thyme, whereon the wild bees linger
Jewelled with flowers of a thousand dyes—
    Their petals tinted by no mortal finger ;

How solemn in their gray-worn age they stand,
Hills piled on hills in silent majesty !
Lofty and strong, and beautiful, and grand :
All this and more is my Beloved to me.

" Come forth into the woods—in yonder valley,
Where rippling waters murmur through the glade ;
There, 'neath the rustling boughs of some green alley,
We'll watch the golden light and quivering shade :
Or couched on mossy banks we'll lie and listen
To song-birds pouring forth their vernal glee.
Wave on, ye woods ; ye fairy fountains glisten :
But more, far more, is my Beloved to me.

" Know ye the land where fragrant winds awaken
In spicy forests hidden from the eye ;
Where richest perfumes from the boughs are shaken,
And flowers unnoticed bloom, and blush, and die ?
Sweet is the eternal spring that there reposes
On wondrous isles that gem the sunny sea,
And sweet the gales that breathe o'er beds of roses :
But sweeter far is my Beloved to me.

" The roaring torrents from the ice-cliffs leaping—
I see them foaming down the mountain-side ;
Through the green dells and valleys onward sweeping,
They fill the hollows with their mighty tide :
Their voice is as the voice of many waters ;
Onward they rush, exulting to be free ;
But ah ! their thunder fails, their music falters :
Far more than this is my Beloved to me.

" A gentler sound wakes in the hush of even,
The whisper of a light and cooling breeze ;
It stirs when twilight shades are in the heaven,
And bows the tufted foliage of the trees ;
It fans my cheek ; its music softly stealing
Speaks to my heart in loving mystery.
Ah ! gentle breeze, full well thou art revealing
The joy that my Belovèd is to me.

" Night comes at last, in mystic shadows folding
    The nodding forest and the verdant lawn,
Till the day breaks, and nature starts, beholding
    The golden chariot of the coming dawn :
Then on each bough the feathered chanters, waking,
    Pour forth their music over bush and tree.
Cease, cease your songs, ye birds ; my heart-strings breaking
    Lack words to say what JESUS is to me.

" Yea, all the fairest forms that Nature scatters,
    And all melodious sounds that greet the ear ;
The murmuring music of the running waters,
    The golden harvest-fields that crown the year,
The crimson morn, the calm and dewy even,
    The tranquil moonlight on the slumbering sea—
All are but shadows, forms of beauty given
    To tell what my Belovèd is to me."

                    —*Augusta Theodosia Drane.*

ARTICLE II. WIT.

239. **Wit** causes pleasure by a peculiar quickness in perceiving, and felicity in expressing, such hidden relations of things as amuse the hearers. Take this example : " You must either be a knave or a fool," said two lawyers to an Irishman sitting between them. "No ; I am between both," was the prompt reply. Here is a relation which would not have struck one person in a thousand. To be true wit, however, it is necessary that, as soon as the relation is pointed out, the hearers or readers understand it. Besides, the unexpected thought must come apparently unsought, else no peculiar quickness of conception is noticed. When a person evidently tries to be witty he disgusts instead of pleasing.

240. A **pun** is a witticism consisting in a play on words. Hancock, encouraging those who had signed the Declara-

tion of Independence to mutual fidelity, remarked : "We must all hang together." "Yes," said Franklin, "or we shall all hang separately." An occasional pun, when truly witty, undoubtedly gives pleasure. But an habitual punster, like every professed wit, is universally pronounced a bore. And with reason : first, such persons evidently try to be witty ; secondly, they often fail ; thirdly, they acquire a habit of trifling, and will often spoil a serious conversation for a wretched pun ; fourthly, they are often sarcastic or otherwise offensive.

241. But wit, when united with common sense, kindness of heart, and beauty of thought, is, in its own place, not only an innocent charm of social intercourse, but also a **powerful weapon** in the arena of oratorical contests.

It appears to be a kind dispensation of Providence that the seasoning of wit and humor is often copiously granted to those whose homely fare stands most in **need** of such condiments to make life **more supportable.**

ARTICLE III. HUMOR.

242. **Humor** is not an elevated species of beauty, but it is more valuable than wit ; it fills many a bright **page,** especially in English literature. One great **advantage** of humor is that it is always good-natured, and thus contributes directly to diffuse happiness all around. Lamb, Hood, Thackeray, and Dickens, in England ; Irving, Lowell, Holmes, and Saxe, in the United States, have deserved much credit for their genial productions.

243. Humor is that species of beauty which delights by a good-natured exhibition of **incongruities**; it addresses itself to our perception of the ludicrous. Some persons appear to be almost destitute of this perception ; others **are** overpowered by it beyond the bounds of reason. **The**

ir.congruity itself is not beautiful, but the good-natured exposition of it by the common sense of the humorist.

244. Humor implies:

1. In the object, *incongruity—i.e.*, want of proportion, as big words and bad grammar. A humorist has a peculiar talent for perceiving and expressing such ludicrous things.

2. In the effect, *surprise* at finding such incongruity where it was not expected : a thing is not ludicrous if it is just what could be expected.

3. In the humorist, strong common sense and *good nature—i.e.*, kindliness, even towards the persons ridiculed.

245. In order to be truly pleasing, humor requires strict regard to the laws of **decorum**: it must never attempt to ridicule the unfortunate, the truly great and wise, nor be employed on subjects held sacred by the hearers.

" It is a beautiful thing to observe the BOUNDARIES which nature has affixed to the ridiculous, and to notice how soon it is swallowed up by the more illustrious feelings of our minds. Where is the heart so hard that could bear to see the awkward resources and contrivances of the poor turned into ridicule ? Who could laugh at the fractured, ruined body of a soldier ? Who is so wicked as to amuse himself with the infirmities of extreme old age ? or to find subject for humor in the weakness of a perishing, dissolving body ? Who is there that does not feel himself disposed to overlook the little peculiarities of the truly great and wise, and to throw a veil over that ridicule which they have redeemed by the magnitude of their talents and the splendor of their virtues ? Who ever thinks of turning into ridicule our great and ardent hopes of a world to come ? Whenever the man of humor meddles with these things, he is astonished to find that in all the great feelings of their nature the mass of mankind always act and think aright, that they are ready enough to laugh, but that they are quite as ready to drive away with indignation and contempt the light fool who comes, with the feather of wit, to crumble the bulwarks of truth and to beat down the Temples of God ! "—*Sydney Smith.*

246. The description of a **humorous character** supposes in its subject a blending of strikingly incongruous traits, as shrewdness with apparent simplicity in Sam Weller. Every act and word must accord with the character, and frequently remind us of its incongruous elements, as in Shakspeare's Falstaff.

CHAPTER III.

TASTE.

247. **Taste** is the power of perceiving and properly appreciating the beauties of nature and of art. Some call it the *Æsthetic faculty ;* but it is no special faculty at all : it is an exercise of the intellect. As such it is common to all men, though in different degrees of perfection. This difference is due partly to variety of natural powers, and partly to difference of education and of early associations.

248. Good taste should be characterized by two qualities, **delicacy** and **correctness.** The former, when highly developed, enables it to distinguish the nicest shades and varieties of beauty, in the same manner as some persons have so delicate a palate as to distinguish readily the flavor of any viand. The latter quality—correctness—enables it to discern accurately what is true from what is false beauty.

249. Of the two characteristics, correctness ought to be chiefly taught, both because it is more capable of being developed and because the want of it is more offensive. If correctness be carefully taught by precepts and examples, delicacy will follow of itself. The direct object of rhetorical rules is to accustom the student to appreciate true and reject false beauty. The difference between these two is that **true beauty** pleases, not only at first sight, but also after the closest scrutiny, and receives the full approbation of man's highest faculty—the intellect ; while **false beauty** cannot bear to be closely examined without displaying a

want of good sense, of naturalness, delicacy, appropriateness, etc.

250. **The precepts of rhetoric** are not arbitrary laws, but the conclusions which the greatest thinkers have drawn from a careful study of literature. Aristotle's mind, the keenest, perhaps, that ever existed, examined the productions of the greatest geniuses that had preceded him, and drew a clear line between true and false beauty. Cicero, Horace, Quintilian, and others continued his labors, and subsequent ages have accepted most of their decisions, because these were found to be conformable to human reason. Still later critics have added their share to this treasury of common sense.

251. **Human reason** itself is the judge of beauty. Now, in matters of taste human reason speaks through the great critics and rhetoricians who have been recognized for ages as the judges of literature. Their unanimous verdict is practically the utterance of mankind itself. This is the **standard of taste**: what it approves is true beauty, what it condemns is false beauty. From time to time some eccentric genius will appear to set at naught all the rules of rhetoricians, imagining that his conceited mind is the great luminary of the world. His brilliant imagination may attract to him a number of admiring followers. Carlyle, in England, was a man of this character, but his departures from the laws of taste were too glaring to mislead many. Other geniuses of less offensive eccentricities have done more real harm to good taste by blending minor faults with superior beauties. It is the part of criticism to point out in the works of even the greatest geniuses any admixture of false beauty. It blames many long speeches and other extravagances in Homer; a want of spirit in some passages of Virgil; excessive self-praise and labored periods in Cicero; a considerable amount of coarse language, wan-

ton irregularities, ill-placed puns, etc., in Shakspeare. In fact, this last author, with all his uncommon beauties, is anything but a safe model on vhich to fashion the taste of young writers.

252. May there be, then, no **varieties in good taste ?** There may be in different men a preference for different kinds of true beauty, and still all these may have good taste. One loves more what is bold or grand, another what is gentle and modest; one admires more the ideal, another the real ; one loves sentiment and imagination, another sober sense. But if one person pronounces an object beautiful and another not beautiful, under the same circumstances, one or the other is clearly mistaken. In this sense it is not true that there is *no disputing about taste.* Varieties of taste are a kind dispensation of Providence that diversifies the aspect of human society as it diversifies the flowers of the field.

253. We add a few **general rules regarding taste** which apply to all kinds of composition.

Rule 1.—Let **good sense** pervade every literary production. This rule applies to poetry as well as to prose, to pleasantry as well as to philosophy and religion. But it is often **violated** by two kinds of writers : first, by those whose imagination and feelings are too lively to be controlled by their judgment, as are many orators, poets, and novelists ; and, secondly, by some conceited philosophers and literati who put their individual views above the wisdom of all the world b sides. Such are, for instance, the **Transcendentalists,** as they are called, Ralph Waldo Emerson, Matthew Arnold, and others, who extol culture and delicacy of taste above common sense.

254. Such, too, are the members of what is called "the **Satanic School.**" Southey, in the preface to his "Vision of Judgment," was the first to use this degrading appella-

tion. Of the writers who have been included under it, Byron, Shelley, Moore, Bulwer, Rousseau, Victor Hugo, Paul de Kock, and George Sand are the most prominent.

"Immoral writers," says Southey, "men of diseased hearts and depraved imaginations, who, forming a system of opinions to suit their own unhappy course of conduct, have rebelled against the holiest ordinances of human society, and, hating that revealed religion which, with all their efforts and bravadoes, they were unable entirely to disbelieve, labor to make others as miserable as themselves by infecting them with a moral virus that eats into the soul. The school which they have set up may properly be called the Satanic School ; for though their productions breathe the spirit of Belial in their lascivious parts, and the spirit of Moloch in their loathsome images of atrocities and horrors, which they delight to represent, they are more especially characterized by a satanic spirit of pride and audacious impiety, which still betrays the wretched feeling of hopelessness wherewith it is allied."—*Southey.*

It is just to add that Moore and Bulwer in their later years wrote in a better spirit.

255. *Rule* 2.—Every composition should have **unity**— unity of subject, unity of plan, unity of general tone, etc. But how this rule applies to various works we shall examine in detail when we come to speak of each species of composition. We shall here confine ourselves to the rule as stated by Horace :

> "*Denique sit quidvis simplex dumtaxat et unum.*"

> "Then learn this wandering humor to control,
> And keep one equal tenor through the whole."—*Francis.*

256. *Rule* 3.—Let perfect **appropriateness** characterize every part of your productions—the selection of your subject, your treatment of it, the thoughts, ornaments, expressions, etc., adapting every detail to the various circumstances of persons, times, places, etc., etc. There is a tendency in certain minds to ignore such proprieties. Some

preachers of great repute have gone so far as to introduce pantomime into the pulpit. Such an example, if not condemned by critics, would tend to debase the taste of the young. The New York *Sun* some time ago contained the following report :

" Pantomimic Efforts that made the Plymouth Congregation Laugh.—Mr. B—— preached last evening upon the difficulty of acquiring correct religious habits, and the comparative ease of maintaining them when once they have become second nature. ' Many look upon religion,' he said, ' as an insurance policy against final loss by fire.' He described that kind of religion so funnily that the congregation laughed outright. ' They go to church every Sunday,' he said, pulling his coat close around him, drawing his face down dolorously, and rolling up his eyes. ' The hymns are doled out to them, a good, sound, dry sermon is preached to them, and the most eloquent passage of all is their going out. They attend prayer-meetings, too—most dismal prayer-meetings !' Here his lower jaw dropped, more of the whites of his eyes showed, and his hands were clasped before him," etc.

CHAPTER IV.

VARIETIES OF STYLE.

257. **Literary style** is the manner in which a person expresses his thoughts and feelings by means of language. It is not a person's language merely. The expression of the thought and feelings is intimately connected with the conception of them. Hence style depends on our conceptions as well as on our language. In fact, a work may be translated from one language into another, and the chief peculiarities of its style remain the same.

ARTICLE I. SOURCES OF VARIETY IN STYLE.

258. To understand the **sources of variety in style**, consider the different ways in which the same thought or feeling may be conceived by the mind. Thus suppose I become convinced that the pleasures of this world cannot satisfy the human heart. I may reach this conviction intellectually, by considering that our hearts long for infinite and lasting happiness, and that this world is necessarily finite and of short duration. I may express this reasoning in abstract language, and my style will be **philosophical.**

259. But in conceiving and expressing the same conviction I may be powerfully assisted by my imagination, and I may thus describe the fleeting show of this world's delights under various images, in a **figurative** and **descriptive** style, as is done in the fifth chapter of the Book of Wisdom :

" All those things are passed away like a shadow, and like a post that runneth on,

" And as a ship that passeth through the waves ; whereof when it is gone by, the trace cannot be found, nor the path of its keel in the waters :

" Or as when a bird flieth through the air, of the passage of which no mark can be found, but only the sound of the wings beating the light air, and parting it by the force of her flight ; she moved her wings, and hath flown through, and there is no mark found afterwards of her way :

" Or as when an arrow is shot at a mark, the divided air presently cometh together again, so that the passage thereof is not known :

" So we also being born, forthwith ceased to be ; and have been able to show no mark of virtue ; but are consumed in our wickedness."

260. While this brief passage is descriptive, the whole fifth chapter develops the same thought in a **narrative** style, bordering on the **dramatic.** It will be readily perceived that the chapter needs only metre to give it the **poetic** style. Thus language and mode of thought combine to shape the style of any composition.

261. " Wolsey's Soliloquy " presents the same thought as the Book of Wisdom, and expresses it in poetic language :

> " This is the state of man : to-day he puts forth
> The tender leaves of hope ; to-morrow blossoms,
> And bears his blushing honors thick upon him :
> The third day comes a frost, a killing frost ;
> And, when he thinks, good easy man, full surely
> His greatness is a-ripening, nips his root,
> And then he falls, as I do.   I have ventured,
> Like little wanton boys that swim on bladders,
> This many summers in a sea of glory ;
> But far beyond my depth : my high-blown pride
> At length broke under me, and now has left me,
> Weary and old with service, to the mercy
> Of a rude stream, that must for ever hide me.
> Vain pomp and glory of this world, I hate ye ;
> I feel my heart new-opened."—*Shakspeare.*

262. Horace deplores the shortness of earthly joys in the **lyric** style. See the fourteenth ode of his second book :

> " Swift fly the rolling years, my friend !
> Nor can your anxious prayers extend
>   The fleeting joys of youth ;
> The trembling hand, the wrinkled cheek,
> Too plainly life's decay bespeak
>   With sad but silent truth.
>
> .   .   .   .
>
> The purple vineyard's luscious stores,
> Secured by trebly-bolted doors,
>   Excite in vain your care :
> Soon shall the rich and sparkling hoard
> Flow largely o'er the festive board
>   Of your unsparing heir."—*Ralph Bernal.*

263. When thoughts are fully developed, as in the fifth chapter of Wisdom, just quoted, we have the **diffuse** style; when briefly expressed, the **concise.** Each of these is beautiful in its proper place (see Nos. 71, 72).

If an author grasps his subject vigorously and expresses it forcibly, his style is said to be **nervous** and strong ; this is always a desirable quality, while its opposite, **feebleness,** is always a defect.

The **vehement** style is characterized by a glowing ardor, pouring out strong feelings with the rapidity and fulness of a torrent, as in most speeches of Demosthenes ; it adds strong feeling to strong thought.

264. A chief source of difference in style, among various persons who write on the same subjects, is the difference of their **characters.** A firm character will produce a manly style, a weak, vacillating character a confused style ; a generous, open character is favorable to clearness, richness, beauty of expression, while narrow-minded and deceitful dispositions will give a very different coloring to the thought. Whatever improves a person's character improves

his style. The social virtues are the sources of charming ornaments to all literature.

ARTICLE II. ORNAMENT OF STYLE.

265. One of the principal sources of variety in style consists in the **ornament** used to adorn the thought and the expression, in tropes, figures of thought, figures of diction, and harmonious constructions. In this respect Blair appropriately distinguishes five kinds of style, according to five degrees of ornament.

266. 1. The **dry style** rejects all ornament; it is proper in text-books on grammar, arithmetic, and any exact science, in legal documents, in business transactions, etc. The language of an educated man should always be correct and perspicuous, exhibiting great purity, propriety, and precision; but what is merely ornamental would, in the writings just mentioned, savor of affectation.

267. 2. The **plain style** uses ornament sparingly. Whatever subject admits of any play of the imagination or the emotions affords room for the ornaments of composition. All such productions are properly styled **literature,** and no others. Now, among these the plain style is appropriate to such as are either too exact to allow the imagination any great indulgence or too familiar or insignificant to justify much painstaking. Plain facts are best expressed in plain language, in proper words, with refined feeling, and with an occasional admixture of modest ornament. Dean Swift, even on important subjects, always wrote in the plain style, which best suited his earnest character. Clearness, strength, and a blunt honesty are his peculiar qualities.

268. 3. The **neat style** uses ornament more freely, but not copiously; and its ornament is ever modest, never strikingly brilliant or bold. It is a style equally capable of manly beauty and the most delicate refinement. To this

middle region belongs the bulk of good literature. Subjects of any elevation should be treated with neatness as a rule; plainness is an exception already explained; while the highest ornaments should be reserved for subjects and occasions of unusual dignity or excellence.

Washington Irving's prose works and Goldsmith's poems exhibit the perfection of the neat style.

269. 4. The **elegant style** possesses all the virtues of ornament without any of its defects. The noblest subjects, especially the loftiest portions of such subjects, call for the highest refinement and magnificence that human thought and human language can bestow. The solemn panegyrical oration, the highest efforts of eloquence at the bar, in the pulpit, and in the popular assembly; the most important events narrated in dignified histories, real or fictitious; the description of the grandest scenes in nature; the most pathetic emotions poured out in lyric verse—present proper occasions for elegance of style.

270. Most great historians, philosophers, orators, novelists, and essayists compose **habitually in the neat style,** being more taken up with the matter treated than with the beauty of the expression: such are Lingard, Blair, Pitt, Chatham, Calhoun, Dickens, Cooper; Archbishop Spalding, Cardinals Newman and Manning, Brownson, and such poets as Pope, Longfellow, and Scott, and many other writers of didactic and ballad poetry. All these, however, rise to the elegant style when the occasion requires. Others aim more habitually at elegant language, such as Prescott, Father Faber, Edmund Burke. Webster, Irving, Cardinal Wiseman, Lowell; and in poetry Shakspeare, Milton, Willis, Moore, Byron, Young, etc.

271. **Compare the following three descriptions** of morning, noticing how they rise in ornament above one another :

" See, the day begins to break
    And the light shoots like a streak
    Of subtile fire ; the wind blows cold,
    While the morning doth unfold ;
    Now the birds begin to rouse,
    And the squirrel from the boughs
    Leaps to get him nuts and fruit ;
    The early lark, that erst was mute,
    Carols to the rising day
    Many a note and many a lay."—*Fletcher.*

" Lo ! here the gentle lark, weary of rest,
    From his moist cabinet mounts up on high,
    And wakes the morning, from whose silver breast
    The sun ariseth in his majesty ;
    Who doth the world so gloriously behold,
    The cedar-tops and hills seem burnish'd gold."
                                    —*Shakspeare.*

Full many a glorious morning have I seen
    Flatter the mountain-tops with sovereign eye,
    Kissing with golden face the meadows green,
    Gilding pale streams with heavenly alchemy."
                                    —*Shakspeare.*

272. 5. The **florid style** is marked by an excess of ornament, so that the reader is distracted from the matter
treated and forced to notice how the writer labors to adorn
his composition. This excess is always objectionable, but
especially in serious works. Still, it may be combined with
considerable excellences, and thus leave the composition
valuable, though not perfect. This is the case with Har-
vey's *Meditations among the Tombs* and Rev. Xavier Mc-
Leod's *Devotion to the Blessed Virgin in North America.*
Both these works are well suited to develop a taste for
ornament in prose composition.

CHAPTER V.

IMPROVEMENT OF STYLE.

Article I. Practical Rules for Style.

273. There are certain rules regarding style that should be observed by all writers on all subjects. The chief are these :

1. The **Rule of Clearness.**—Write so that no one can help seeing your exact meaning at the first glance. This is the most important rule of all. To write with clearness the great means is to have clear ideas yourself ; else how can you convey them to others? Study your subject diligently before you write.

274. 2. The **Rule of Strength.**—Make your thoughts impressive by presenting them strikingly, with proper ornaments and feelings. A languid, feeble style is worthless. Still, distinguish strength from vehemence, as explained above (No. 263).

275. 3. The **Rule of Simplicity.**—The word *simplicity* has many meanings : such as the absence of many parts, as in a simple story ; the absence of much ornament, as in the dry and the plain style ; the absence of refinement, as in the simple manners of rustics ; the absence of shrewdness or intelligence, as in the simplicity of the credulous. Our rule means, write with *naturalness*, so as to avoid all appearance of labor. Labor there must be in writing ; but the labor should not be noticed by the reader. **Virgil** and **Gibbon** labored at their productions with uncommon industry, striving to express every thought to the best advan-

tage. Virgil's lines flow smoothly and as naturally as the warbling of a bird ; Gibbon's sentences are evidently labored, and often harsh and strained.

276. A simple style often appears so **artless** that a beginner imagines nothing is easier than to imitate it ; it is the perfection of art to reach all its purposes without making itself known.   Such is the style in the *Sketch-Book* of Washington Irving, many essays of Addison, the novels of Conscience, Hawthorne's *Tanglewood Tales*, the *Stories for Children* of Canon Schmid, the fables of Æsop, of Phædrus, of La Fontaine, Rosa Mulholland's *Robinson Crusoe.* The ancients had more of this apparent artlessness than the moderns : Herodotus, Theocritus, Anacreon, Homer, Virgil, and Ovid abound in it.   There is, however, in many recent writers, a return to the simplicity of classic taste.

277. When this simplicity assumes the character of child-like innocence it is called by the French term *naïveté*, of which Xenophon furnishes a pleasing example in his narrative of Cyrus' conversation at the court of Astyages.

278. A slight **appearance of carelessness** in the midst of refinement is not unpleasant in proper season, as in familiar letters ; it resembles the manners of a truly refined gentleman among his intimate friends.   But young people cannot let themselves down to it with safety.   An appearance of carelessness is admired in those only who have established a name for superiority of mind.

279. 4. The **Rule of Appropriateness** is the most difficult of all to observe, and is necessary on all occasions.   It requires that we adapt our style to our subject, to our hearers or readers, to our own talent and our age, and to circumstances of place, time, etc.   "He is truly eloquent," says Cicero, "who can express what is simple plainly, what is great nobly, and what is ordinary with decency and mo-

deration "—*Is est eloquens qui et humilia subtiliter, et magna graviter, et mediocria temperate potest dicere* " (*Or.*, 29). Dr. Johnson, though a writer of great eminence, could not adapt his style to his theme, and it was wittily said of him that if he made little fishes talk he would make them speak like whales. **Excess of ornament** is a violation of appropriateness. It is bad taste, in language as in dress, to be ever displaying fineries.

280. Still, this excess is more easily **excused in the young,** whose imaginations are more developed than their judgments. Cicero is not displeased with the youth whose compositions are rather flowery :

" I wish to see exuberance in the youthful mind," he says; " for as it is easier to prune the superfluous branches of a vine than to add to its growth, so I like to see in the youth's production something to lop off" (*De Or* , ii. 21).

Article II. Writing as a Means of Improvement.

281. **Writing** is the most important source of improvement in style and in all the other parts of literary composition. " The pen," says Cicero, " is the best and most efficient teacher of eloquerce "—*Stylus optimus et præstantissimus dicendi effector ac magister*. Without practice no precepts are of any avail. For this reason we have so far proposed a variety of exercises, applying the several precepts in appropriate ways. Through the remainder of this work, however, fewer suggestions of this kind will be needed. The precepts themselves will directly suggest the exercises. All that the teacher need do is to select models for imitation, and themes or subjects for narrations, descriptions, etc., suited to the age and other circumstances of his pupils. But the exercises should by no means be neglected : in them lies the solid fruit of literary studies

282. For the writing of **original composition** these rules should be carefully observed by the pupil :

Rule 1.—He should **think over the whole matter** to be treated, and trace a plan of it in his mind or on paper before he writes the first line of the composition itself.

Rule 2.—He should **compose slowly,** doing the best he can in the first draught ; he will thus improve far more than by putting down every word or idea that presents itself. As in penmanship, so in composition, by writing well we learn to write rapidly, but by writing rapidly we do not learn to write well.

Rule 3.—Still, when the **mind is warmed up** by the subject the writer may allow himself, to some extent, to be carried away by his ardor, provided he does not wander from his theme.

Rule 4.—After writing should come **correction**—a task often neglected because less interesting. But the mind of the master should rule here, not the whim of the scholar. The *limæ labor*—the careful finish—is the straight road to perfection in any art.

Rule 5.—When a composition is written for the eye of the public it should, if possible, be laid by for a while, and then carefully retouched. No one should ever **publish** what an honest and judicious friend condemns, no matter how perfect the composition appears to himself.

ARTICLE III. READING AS A MEANS OF IMPROVEMENT.

283. That **reading** is a copious source of improvement in composition is beyond dispute. Still, on this subject many vague and some erroneous notions are entertained. We shall enter into some details, suggested in part by President Porter's *Books and Reading*.

284. I. **As to the matter** or thought, reflect that when

you read you listen to a **real person**, speaking deliberately and for definite purposes, who undertakes to instruct or to please you. Therefore:

285. 1. **If you read for instruction,** begin by ascertaining whether the author is capable of imparting correct information. (*a*) Is he a *man of authority* on those matters? Or is he simply a fluent writer who can converse plausibly on any subject, though his knowledge of it may be very superficial? Such are many essayists. (*b*) Is he *a man of sound principles?* Can you abandon yourself with perfect confidence to his guidance? If you have reason to distrust him, see whether it would not be more expedient to look for information elsewhere, or at least whether there are not some points on which you ought to mistrust his insinuations.

286. *Remark* that **nearly every book instils certain principles** which may do the more evil as they are less suspected—*e.g.*, Gibbon's *History of the Decline and Fall of the Roman Empire* instils unbelief, seeing in the exchange of a temporal for a spiritual supremacy nothing but decay: it is thus that a pagan would have written. Hume, in his *History of England*, fails to appreciate any virtuous intentions in the nobles and the people; sneering at all things, he chills enthusiasm for every public and private virtue. *Blackwood's Magazine*, a Tory organ, is devoted to strengthen the throne and the Church of England; while the *Westminster Review*, with an opposite aim, tends to undermine the foundations of both.

As the *Fabiola* of Cardinal Wiseman instils purity, generosity, piety, thus many novels instil licentiousness, scepticism, worldliness.

287. 2. **If you read for pleasure,** see (*a*) whether the **writer** is a **moral** and conscientious man. If he is, do not stop to quarrel with every expression to which an improper meaning

might be attached. Like the bee, sip the honey and leave the poison for the spider. If he is not, ascertain first from others whether it is proper to read that work at all, or whether, at least, you are not to be on your guard against some particular danger. If such information cannot be had, see (*b*) whether the **pleasure** afforded is of a **healthy** kind, which not only cheers but also expands and elevates the mind, or at least produces a calm serenity.

288. **Southey's rule** may be of use:

" Would you know whether the tendency of a book is good or evil, examine in what state of mind you lay it down. Has it in- duced you to suspect that that which you have been accustomed to think unlawful may, after all, be innocent, and that that may be harmless which you hitherto have been taught to think dangerous? Has it tended to make you dissatisfied and impatient under the con- trol of others? and disposed you to relax in that self-government without which both the laws of God and man tell us there can be no virtue and consequently no happiness? Has it attempted to abate your reverence for what is great and good? . . . has it de- filed the imagination with what is loathsome? Throw the book into the fire."

289. **II. As to the style:** 1. We improve more by read- ing **a few excellent writers** than by reading a multitude of indifferent ones.

2. Even in reading the best authors we learn more by reading **a few select passages** carefully and frequently than entire books cursorily—*non multa sed multum*.

3. There is an **abundance of good writings** of which the thoughts are proper, so that for style alone we need never read anything really dangerous.

4. The **best** should be read **from earliest childhood**.

5. **Faulty writers** do positive harm to the style of the young; now, many modern writers, highly admired by some, are full of faults.

6. Not mere reading, but a careful study by **analyzing**, is necessary for the acquisition of a good style.

7. Even in select models **distinguish the perfect** from the faulty ; but be slow to condemn before understanding well.

290. **III. To read critically** is to judge for yourself of the real value of a book. This supposes the reader to be well versed in the matter treated, and to have read seve-ral other works on the same or on a similar subject, so as to be able to compare. Young people are rarely qualified to do so; it will be safer for them to seek information in particular cases from those of greater experience. Still, **some few hints** may be suggested :

1. See what the book professes to treat, what end to ob-tain. Is that end in itself desirable? Is it of present utility ?

2. Can it be reasonably expected that the author, as far as he is known, is qualified to attain it ?

3. Does he actually attain it ?

4. Does he do so better than is done by any book yet published on that subject in the same language ? else what is the use of a new book?

291. **IV. Read attentively.**—1. Do not, as a rule, read a book that cannot keep you awake and interested.

2. Read for a definite purpose—*e.g.*, to know such an author's views on such a question.

3. Know, however, that not every book requires the same closeness of attention.

4. Distracted reading does no good ; pause when there occurs a thought worth entertaining.

5. In serious reading pause from time to time—*e.g.*, at a new chapter—to review in mind the matter read.

6. Some readings are so suggestive that but little should be read at a time ; the more we reflect, the more we im-prove.

292. **V. What shall I read ?** *Answer :* 1. **On what matter do you need most information** to do well what is expected of you ? After settling this you may next inquire what book will best supply this particular want—*e.g.*, one engaged in studying the ancient languages will do well to read Ancient History, that he may understand the facts and circumstances to which classical literature constantly refers.

 2. Generally **prefer what is of present use** to the information which may perhaps be useful some future day. Still, do not so confine yourself to your present narrow sphere as to neglect acquiring a certain amount of general information to fit you for a wider field of action in after-life.

 3. **Do not read what you cannot at present understand,** and be honest enough to acknowledge your ignorance ; but adapt your reading to your age and circumstances. Children should generally read narrations, descriptions, etc., in prose and verse, but these should always be such as inculcate sound principles ; later on they will read essays, treatises, etc.

 4. Generally **avoid wordy writers,** who say little in many words.

 293. **VI. Poetry.**—1. As all will not enjoy the same authors and the same pieces, read only such as you can appreciate. You cannot readily enjoy poetry when you cannot **sympathize with the writer** ; and as we should never sympathize with what is vicious, we must be most careful to select pure-minded authors.

 2. The moral influence of a piece is good, no matter what the subject, if it **throws our affections aright** and leaves on the mind fit images and contemplations. Milton makes Satan odious, Byron and Goethe make the reader sympathize with the evil spirit against God.

BOOK IV.

VARIOUS SPECIES OF PROSE COMPOSITIONS.

CHAPTER I.

IMITATION.

294. The young are gifted with a remarkable power of **imitation**; it is the most important instinct which the all-wise Creator has provided for their early development, and it suggests the method to be followed by the educator. No kind of exercise is better adapted to their age than the imitation of whatever is excellent in thought and style. It must be noticed, however, that they can be made to imitate advantageously those literary beauties only which they can to some extent understand and appreciate. Hence some exercises in imitation are suitable to children, others to those whose judgment is more mature and whose education is more advanced.

295. The **importance** of imitation is even greater than that of precepts: precepts without models to imitate would not carry a learner far on the road to literary excellence; while many have become skilful writers without the guidance of precepts, by the sole means of imitation, supposing, of course, a fair amount of natural talent.

Longum iter per præcepta, says Seneca, *brevis et efficax per exempla*—"The way that leads through precepts is long, that through examples is short and direct."

296. Still, **imitation is not all-sufficient,** for its productions are usually inferior to the originals, not having their naturalness and their power. Besides, what is most valuable in a writer, his genius, ease, tact, etc., cannot be imitated. Exercises of imitation may be almost infinitely varied, but all may be reduced to **two kinds.** We may imitate a model either by writing on the *same subject* or on *another subject.*

ARTICLE I. IMITATIONS ON THE SAME SUBJECT.

297. The ways in which learners may imitate a model by **writing on the same subject** are chiefly five :

I. They may read a composition, or hear it read, and then try to **reproduce the same thoughts** in their own words; and they may even attempt to improve on the original.

These models should be suited to the age, degree of progress, and other circumstances of the pupils ; a judicious choice of the proper models must be made by the teacher. He will find a supply of such pieces in readers, selections for elocution, etc.

This exercise may be improved by dictating a brief **analysis** of the model, so that the pupil may develop it more regularly.

298. II. Pupils may write a **prose** composition, reproducing in their own style the thoughts contained in a piece of **poetry.** For instance, let them write a description of a happy village, or of the village inn, the village schoolmaster, etc., in imitation of Goldsmith's " Deserted Village." Or let them read the poem " Evangeline " of Longfellow, and then narrate the same story in prose.

299. III. They may **translate** a masterpiece of composi-

tion from an ancient or a modern language into their mother-tongue. Such exercises are of constant use in a classical course of education. They are highly recommended by Cicero (*De Or.*, i. 34) and by Quintilian (x. 5). Pliny points out the following **advantages of such translation:**

" It gives the learner propriety and beauty of expression, a copious supply of figures, facility in explaining every thought ; and, by the power of imitation, it stimulates him to invent for himself beauties similar to those of his models. Shades of thought which a reader might not notice cannot escape the attention of the translator, and thus his understanding and his judgment are improved by constant practice."—*Letters*, vii. 9, § 2.

300. That these and other advantages may be secured, the translation must be carefully and **judiciously done,** so that the full and exact meaning of the original be expressed with great propriety in the vernacular. It is not at all necessary that there be a word in English to correspond to every word of the original, nor that the sentences in both be of the same length and construction. But two extremes must be avoided : on the one hand, we should not give a mere paraphrase instead of a translation, and, on the other, we should not follow the original so closely as to do violence to our own idiom.

301. **Two further directions** for translation may usefully be added :

1. The manner of translation should be **regulated by the object** to be attained : thus for a legal or theological document fidelity and closeness are more important than beauty of style ; while the latter should receive more care in works of less exact thought which are translated for the general reader.

2. In works of literary merit the translation should **retain the characteristic beauties** of the original style ; for instance, Cicero's fulness, fluency, and harmony ; Demos-

thenes' closeness and energy ; Livy's ease ; Cæsar's exactness ; Ovid's sweetness ; Homer's rapidity and fire ; Virgil's delicacy, etc.   (See Newman's *Historical Sketches*, vol.
ii., advertisement.)

302. IV. A fourth kind of imitation consists in a **double
translation.** If the object is, for instance, to perfect one's
self in Latin composition, a passage of Cicero or Livy may
be translated into English ; then, after some interval of
time, it is to be translated back into Latin, and the result
to be compared with the original. This exercise is well
suited for self-improvement, especially with persons of more
mature minds.

303. V. A very useful kind of imitation consists in first
analyzing a model—for instance, an oration—and then **developing this analysis,** so as to produce a composition resembling the original.   (See for the preparation of such
analysis our *Art of Oratorical Composition*, b. iii. c. iv.)

ARTICLE II. IMITATION ON A DIFFERENT SUBJECT.

304. We may strive to reproduce the beauties of a model by applying them to a **different subject** in three principal ways, of which the first two are suited to younger persons, the third to more advanced students.

305. I. The first manner consists in taking the **elegant
words and phrases,** constructions and figures of our model,
and applying them, with some judicious changes, to a similar subject.   Take as an example the following extract
from a speech by Patrick Henry (March, 1775) :

" They tell us, sir, that we are weak, unable to cope with so for-
midable an adversary. But when shall we be stronger? Will it be
the next week? or the next year? Will it be when we are totally
disarmed, and when a British guard shall be stationed in every
house? Shall we gather strength by irresolution and inaction?

Shall we acquire the means of effectual resistance by lying supinely on our backs and hugging the delusive phantom of hope, until our enemies shall have bound us hand and foot? Sir, we are not weak, if we make a proper use of those means which the God of nature hath placed in our power. Three millions of people, armed in the holy cause of liberty, and in such a country as that which we possess, are invincible by any force which our enemy can send against us. Besides, sir, we shall not fight our battles alone. There is a just God who presides over the destinies of nations, and who will raise up friends to fight our battles for us."

In close imitation of this write a strong appeal to sinful men who put off their conversion :

" You may tell me that you are weak, unable at present to subdue your unruly passions. But when will you be stronger? Will it be the next week? or the next year? Will it be when these passions shall have grown still stronger by more protracted indulgence? when your wills shall have been further weakened by habitual excesses? Will you gather strength by irresolution and inaction? Will you acquire the means of effectual resistance to your depraved inclinations by lying supinely on your backs and hugging the delusive phantom of hope that you shall be able to shake off the yoke at some future day, when your passions shall have bound you hand and foot? No; you are not too weak now, if you make proper use of those means which a merciful God has placed at your disposal. Men so intelligent and noble in many other respects, men accustomed to make sacrifices for other purposes, which they fully appreciate, are capable of accomplishing any object to which they generously devote their attention. Besides, you are not to fight your battles alone. There is a good God who earnestly wishes every sinner to be converted, who speaks to your hearts this very day, and who is ready now to second your earnest efforts "; etc.

306. II. The second is a much **looser method of imitation**: it consists in reading carefully a story, a description, a letter, or any elegant passage of a good author, and then endeavoring to compose on a similar subject, profiting by any hint which the model may suggest with regard to style, or plan, or anything else that may improve the composi-

tion. This method of imitation is not subject to definite rules, but it relies on that instinctive power of imitation which is productive of the happiest results, provided the models be judiciously chosen ; that is, provided they be excellent in themselves and well suited to the stage of the learner's progress. An **example** would be The Combat of Goliath and David written in imitation of The Combat of the Horatii and Curiatii, as related by Livy (ii. 10).

307. III. The **more advanced exercise** consists in first studying a model thoroughly, examining its excellences of various kinds—the beauty and appropriateness of the thoughts, the order in which they are developed, the harmony of the periods, the elegance and power of the figures, the closeness of the reasoning, the clearness of the arguments, the delicate politeness of the refutation, etc.—and then writing a similar composition on another theme which is capable of analogous treatment.

308. For instance, in imitation of the **first oration of Cicero against Catiline** a speech may be written denouncing some evil practices or some wicked men that are ruining the youth of the country, such as the reading of obscene literature or the wretches who spread it broadcast over the land. It is not necessary that the imitation follow the entire model step by step. Sometimes we may imitate the main division only and the general spirit of a model.

309. Thus we find, for instance, that Demosthenes, in his **Third Olynthiac** Oration, 1. Shows the necessity of seizing the proffered opportunity ; 2. Explains how it is to be improved ; 3. Enforces these measures by proving that success is certain, if that plan be adopted, and that action is imperative (*Art of Orat. Comp.*, p. 120). Now, on this plan an address to the members of a debating society may readily be composed : 1. Showing the necessity of profiting by

the opportunities for self-improvement which the society affords; 2. Explaining what must be done to derive fruit from the exercises; 3. Enforcing these suggestions by proving that the task is easy, but that earnest application is absolutely necessary to insure success.

The greatest writers of all ages have made use of such imitations while striving to improve on their models. Cicero imitated Plato in his dialogues; Virgil imitated Homer and Theocritus; Horace, Pindar; Pope imitates Virgil's Eclogues, *etc.*

ARTICLE III. SELECTION OF MODELS.

310. Much depends on the **judicious choice of models** to be proposed for imitation. Even for the youngest children none but excellent examples should be selected, suited to their tender age, of course, but exquisite in their kind. In fact, perfection in the model is more necessary in proportion as the pupils' judgment is less developed; for such learners have no other guide than the instinct of imitation, and cannot discern what should be imitated in the model from what is unworthy of their imitation.

311. Besides, what is thus learned in early years can scarcely be unlearned later on. Very many children have their taste depraved for life by their first picture-books or sensational stories. Quintilian, in his excellent work on the *Education of an Orator*, insists earnestly on the necessity of putting nothing before children that they may not imitate to advantage. *Optima quidem et statim et semper—* "Choose the best models at once and ever after." He would have the very talk of the child's nurse to be grammatical :

"First of all, let the talk of the child's nurses not be ungrammatical. Chrysippus wished them, if possible, to be women of some knowledge ; at any rate he would have the best chosen that circumstances may allow. To their morals, doubtless, attention is first to be paid ; but let them also speak with propriety. It is they that the child will hear first ; it is their words that he will try to imitate. We are naturally most tenacious of what we have imbibed in our infant years, as the flavor with which you scent new vessels remains in them ; nor can the colors with which wool is stained be effaced hereafter. Those very habits which are of a more objectionable nature adhere with the greater tenacity ; for good ones are easily changed for the worse, but when will you change bad ones into good ? Do not, then, accustom the child, even when yet an infant, to phraseology which must be unlearned " (b. i. c. i. 4, 5).

312. Those writers, as a rule, are the **best models for imitation** who combine regularity of plan with ease and naturalness of development. Such are chiefly Cicero and Demosthenes, Livy and Herodotus, Cæsar and Xenophon, among the ancients ; and among the moderns, Edmund Burke and Erskine, Pitt and Chatham, Webster and Calhoun, Clay and Everett ; Lingard and Alison, Prescott and Irving ; Addison and Walter Scott, Dickens and Cooper; Cardinals Wiseman, Manning, and Newman.

313. Some writers are useful models for the acquisition of **special excellences**; thus we may learn vigor and condensation of thought from Thucydides and Tacitus, vivid description from Sallust, a forcible and direct style from Macaulay, Brownson, and Father Burke. While perhaps no author is commendable in every respect, beginners especially should confine themselves to those who approach nearest to perfection; or, better still, such passages from any good author should be selected for them by a prudent teacher as are every way fit models for imitation.

314. **The teacher will, besides,** 1. Vary his selections to suit the capacities and circumstances of his pupils ; 2.

Point out in what the beauty of those pieces consists, and in what particular respects they are chiefly to be imitated; 3. Vary his selections so as to improve, now some, then other talents of his pupils. A learner trained on one model or to one kind of style only, would not bring all his powers into play ; he would not acquire a well-developed mind nor all the beauty of language which is within his reach.

CHAPTER II.

LETTERS.

315. A **letter** is a written communication on any subject from one person to another. Letters deserve most careful study; for, 1. No species of composition is more generally used by all classes of persons. 2. A negligently written letter may entail very injurious consequences. 3. Many will judge of a person's character and attainments from his epistolary correspondence.

It makes a considerable difference in our style whether we write as officials or business men, or as individual members of society. We may, therefore, usefully distinguish letters into **two kinds**—*official* or *business* letters and *unofficial* letters. We class official and business letters together, because they are mainly subject to the same rules.

ARTICLE I. OFFICIAL OR BUSINESS LETTERS.

316. We call **official** or **business letters** all those written by a person in the capacity of an officer, a professional man, a merchant, or a tradesman. In all such correspondence the following are the leading rules:

Rule 1.—Be very **clear**, so that your exact meaning cannot fail to be understood at first sight. Read your letter over with close attention to see that all your thoughts are correctly, fully, and clearly expressed.

Rule 2.—Take care that the **handwriting** be legible, else you may get *boots* for *books*, *matches* for *hatchets* or *latches*, *two ponies* instead of 100 *pansies*.

Rule 3.—Be **brief** and to the point; business men have no time to waste.

Rule 4.—Confine yourself to **strict business.** If you wish to add matters of friendship, it is well to write them on a separate leaf, that the business portion may be separately filed.

Rule 5.—Write **grammatical and idiomatic** English, but without any attempt at figures—in the plain style.

Rule 6.—Observe the received **formalities,** which are now to be explained.

The **formalities of epistolary correspondence** are not uniform in all countries. The general tendency of Americans is towards simplicity in forms: they consult the convenience of all persons concerned, showing proper respect for every one, but using few idle compliments. We shall notice the points most generally agreed upon, without condemning such departures from these directions as are authorized by common sense and respectable practice.

317. Here is an **example** of official correspondence. It is taken from General Sherman's *Memoirs;* most of the letters in that work are on the same simple plan:

HEADQUARTERS ARMIES OF THE UNITED STATES, }
CITY POINT, VIRGINIA, December 26, 1864. }

Major-General W. T. Sherman, Savannah, Georgia :

GENERAL : Your very interesting letter of the 22d inst , brought by Major Gray, of General Foster's staff, is just at hand. As the major starts back at once, I can do no more at present than simply acknowledge its receipt. The capture of Savannah, with all its immense stores, must tell upon the people of the South. All well here.   Yours truly,

U. S. GRANT, *Lieutenant-General.*

318. We call attention to some **special formalities** in general use.

1. Write on white paper with black ink, leaving a half-inch margin at the left side. Use letter or note size, but never tear nor cut off a part. Decided colors, odd patterns, gaudy pictures are in bad taste.

2. Leave at least one inch vacant on the top of the first page.

3. Put on the first line, and to the right, your own post-office **address**; and, either on the same line or on the next, the **date**—that is, the month, day, and year ; also the hour, if necessary.

319. 4. On the next line, and beginning near the margin, put the **name, title,** and **address** of the person or firm you write to. This inside address, as it has been called, may occupy one or two, or even three, lines. It should be complete enough to distinguish the party addressed from all others (as the letter will be filed without the envelope); but it need not be so detailed as the outside address on the envelope.

It is more formal, when addressing dignitaries, to omit or abridge the directions at the head of the letter, and to write the whole address below the signature to the left.

320. Care should be taken to give every one his **proper title.** The following titles are in common use:

In writing to the Pope, " His Holiness, Leo XIII."

To a cardinal, " His Eminence."

To an archbishop, " The Most Rev. P. R. Kenrick (with or without D.D.) "

To a bishop, " The Rt. Rev. —— (D.D.) "

To a priest, " Rev. ——."

To the President and Vice-President of the United States, " The President," " The Vice-President."

To a governor or foreign minister, " His Excellency."

To members of Congress and other high officers of the State, to judges, aldermen, etc., " The Hon."

After the name of a lawyer or a justice of peace, " Esq." (nothing before it).

To a military officer, " General," " Colonel," " Captain," " Lieutenant."

To private persons, " Mr.," " Master " (for a young boy), " Messrs." or Misses (for a firm), " Mrs. John Brown " (for the wife of John Brown), " Mrs. Mary Brown " (for his widow), " Miss Brown " (for his eldest daughter), " Miss Julia Brown " (for a younger daughter), etc.

321. 5. Next comes the **salutation**:

" Holy Father " or " Your Holiness," " Your Grace," " Your Lordship," " Rev. Father," or " Your Reverence."

" Mr. President," " Mr. Vice-President."

" Your Excellency," " Your Honor."

" General," " Colonel," etc.

" Sir," " Gentlemen " or " Ladies," " Madam," " Miss."

The word " Dear " denotes acquaintance and respect, but not familiarity : the terms "Sir," " Madam," " Miss " look rather formal without " Dear."   " My Dear " is considered by some as more familiar, by others as less so.

322. 6. Begin the first **paragraph** at the point where the salutation ends, or on the next line just below it.   The other paragraphs will commence about half an inch from the margin.

323. 7. The letter should end with the **subscription,** which consists of two parts—viz., an expression of respect and the signature.   The expression of respect often forms part of the last paragraph ; at other times it stands separately, and then it usually begins about the middle of the line.   The following forms are common in official correspondence:

" I am, with respect, your obedient servant " ; " I have the honor to be your obedient servant " ; " Very respect-fully yours " ; " Yours truly " ; " Sincerely yours " ; " Yours thankfully," etc.

324. 8. Make as few **folds** in the letter as possible. With a full-sized sheet turn the lower on the upper edge and make a fold in the middle; fold the double into three parts. See that the letter does not adhere to the inside of the envelope. The envelope should be suitable to the paper, and both should be of an approved pattern.

325. 9. **On the envelope** put the stamp near the right upper corner. About the middle of the envelope write the name and title of the party addressed; on the next line, a little more to the right, the number of the house and the name of the street (or, for small places, of the town and county); below, the name of the city; and, lastly, that of the State. Take great care that the directions be so explicit as to prevent all possibility of mistake.

10. In **answering** business letters (or any letters that require a direct answer) begin by mentioning the items to which you are replying; thus:

"Yours of the 25th inst. came to hand. You desire to know . . ."

"Your order for . . . is received."

"Your favor of the 30th ult. enclosing check for seventy-five dollars (\$75) on Farmers' Bank, St. Louis, is received and credited to your account, in full payment for . . . "

326. 11. A **note** may be written in the third person throughout; *e.g.:*

"Mr. Jno. Green will call on Mr. W. Smith on next Thursday at three P.M."

This is often a convenient form for postal cards.

327. 12. When sending a **telegram** the great rule is to convey all the necessary information briefly and in such language as is most apt to be correctly transmitted. Proper names are often mistaken and punctuation marks utterly neglected in the transmission. The formalities of titles, etc., may be dispensed with in telegrams.

328. 13. When it is necessary to add an item after the letter is finished, we begin by making **P. S.** (postscript) near the margin below the last line of the letter, and then state briefly what we have to say; if there is no evident reason for our former omission, we premise a word of excuse.

329. Exercise 1.—Write a letter purporting to order from the publisher a dozen copies of this text-book, or of another book designated by the teacher; and submit the letter to him for criticism on all particulars.

330. Exercise 2.—Write a letter purporting to send payment for the books received.

331 Exercise 3.—Write in the name of the book-firm to acknowledge receipt of payment.

332. Examples :

A Note.

> *Mr. & Mrs.* ———
>
> *request the pleasure of*
>
> . . . . *Company*
>
> *at dinner on Friday,*
>
> *Jan.* 19*th, at* 7½ *o'clock.*

A Card.

> *Mr. & Mrs.* ———
> *At Home,*
> *Wednesday, April the eleventh,*
> *from four until six o'clock,*
> *and from eight until eleven o'clock.*
> *No.* ——— *Second Avenue.*

No. — H Street,
Washington.

Dear Julia,

    Will you not come to dine with us to-morrow, Saturday, at 7 o'clock ? We shall be so glad to see you. I hope that you have no other engagement.

    Affectionately yours,

        Agnes Smith.

Jan. 2d, Friday.

An Envelope.

[Stamp]

Mrs. Lily Tulip,
   Elm Grove Mansion,
     Acacia,
       Linwood Co.,
         Florida.

      Rosebud Village, Merrydale Co., Ind.,
          April 1, 1886.

Mrs. Lily Tulip,
  Acacia, Florida.

   My Dear Mother:

      I have just received your kind favor of the 25th ult. in which you inform me that you desire me to return as soon as convenient. Much as I enjoy the scenery here, and especially the affection of my excellent uncle and aunt, I shall be happy to comply with your wishes. You may look for me on next Saturday morning. I have so many good things to say to you, but the postboy is waiting for this letter. Do take good care of your health: here all are well and send love.

     Your loving daughter,

        Flora.

ARTICLE II. UNOFFICIAL LETTERS.

333. **Unofficial letters** are such as are written by any person in his private capacity, as an individual member of society. They may be dictated by friendship, by charity or kindness, by politeness, by respect, by gratitude, by self-interest, or by any other reasonable motive.

There is one important **difference** between official and unofficial letters—namely, that the former exclude sentiment, and the latter admit it freely; the former proceed solely from the head, the latter often from the heart, though, of course, under the guidance of the head. Now, when the heart is interested the imagination is stirred, and literature, in the strict meaning of the word, is the result; then there is room for tropes and figures and other ornaments of style, and, in particular, for the display of the most delicate taste. Epistolary correspondence does not admit the bolder figures of oratory: any attempt at splendor is objectionable in letters. We must charm by gentler beauties, by appropriateness, by modest plays of the imagination, by genial warmth of sentiment.

334. The **style** of these letters should generally be:

(*a*) *Correct*, as is the language of educated men in conversation; still, somewhat more chastened—*i.e.*, free from all that is rather tolerated than approved. Apparent negligence may be sometimes agreeable; real negligence never.

(*b*) *Appropriate* to the subject, the persons, the occasion, etc.; on important matters grave, on common ones neat, elegant and playful on trifling ones, etc.

(*c*) *Concise*, pruning away long introductions, unnecessary developments, diffuse reasoning, especially to men of little leisure. Familiar letters may be more diffuse.

(*d*) *Modest*, avoiding long periods, bold figures, etc.

(*e*) *Graceful*, selecting neat constructions and all kinds of modest ornaments, such as obvious comparisons, natural metaphors, brief narrations and descriptions, pithy sayings, witty and humorous reflections, etc.

335. We shall treat with some detail of the principal species of such letters :

I. **Letters of friendship** are such as are dictated by mutual affection between relatives and friends. They should be natural, easy, frank, without the least affectation. "I wish you to open to me your soul, not your library," said Mme. de Sévigné, who wrote exquisitely herself. Such letters may treat of any subject of common interest to the parties concerned. Their language is that of the heart. Kindness, affection, charity, good-nature should dictate, prudence and common sense supervise them.

336. **Their charm will depend** chiefly on the intelligence and the amiable character of the writer. Whatever, therefore, will quicken or develop our intelligence, but especially whatever will improve our character, making us more sociable, unselfish, considerate, etc., will improve our familiar correspondence. Persons too dull to have any original thoughts, those incapable of warm feelings, pretentious persons who cannot write without affectation, vainglorious ones who can think of nothing but self, deceitful characters incapable of candor, are not likely to succeed in this species of composition. On the other hand, intelligent persons with warm-hearted, modest, and open characters are sure to succeed, provided they do not take a wrong view of their task. What is that task? It is to make others happy for time and eternity. See what your friend would like to hear ; anticipate his queries ; speak of yourself for the sake of your friend. Avoid overwrought sentimentality : it is distasteful, because unreal. Genuine goodness and gentle piety are attractive.

337. "A light, easy, playful **style** is most appropriate in

friendship " (*American Gentleman*). Still, the modest ornaments of style are here in place. Happy turns of expression, delicate allusions, innocent hints, ingenious faultfinding, pleasing anecdotes, and pen-pictures have a pleasant effect, but all must be natural. "If you run after wit," says Montesquieu, "you will catch folly." "Most persons write ill," says Chesterfield, "because they aim at writing better than they can, by which means they acquire a formal and unnatural style ; whereas to write well you must write easily and naturally."

338. **In telling news** be not a gossip, do not make known the secrets of others ; handle the names of others with respect, so that, if they should happen to see the letter (as they may sooner or later), they could not be offended with you ; be charitable and prudent. Relate facts with order and clearness, in a pleasant style.

339. II. **Letters of Congratulation**—such as are written on occasion of the New Year, a birthday, a patronal feast, or when a friend has met with some uncommon good-fortune—should be dictated by genuine friendship and sincere esteem, and expressed modestly without any exaggerated praise. Never flatter—*i.e.*, never praise what you feel does not deserve it—but let your friend see that you love him and that you rejoice with him for his sake, not for the advantage his success may bring you.

340. In **New Year's letters**, etc., express gratitude for all that parents and others have done for you, sorrow for the grief you may have caused them, a promise of more thoughtful conduct in the future, with a hope that God will grant you time to fulfil your promise. Add good wishes, and a prayer for the blessings of Heaven on the new year. The writing should be most careful, to show respect and to prove you have profited by your opportunities to learn. In all such letters one good thought, one happy

hit, is more pleasing than four rambling pages : it is more creditable to the writer and more acceptable to the reader.

341. III. **Letters of Condolence.** These require great skill and care. Act like the humane surgeon who touches the wound gently, and only to heal it. If your correspondent knows the sad news already, sympathize sincerely with him : " What a loss sustained ! what hopes disappointed ! " Hit as it were accidentally on a motive of · consolation drawn from reason, or, better, from religion, and develop it skilfully. If you are to announce the bad news yourself prepare the way slowly ; suggest motives of resignation to God's will beforehand ; state the news at last as delicately as you can Express your grief again before you conclude.

342. IV. **Letters of Introduction or Recommendation** require special prudence. Think first whether it is proper to write such a letter at all for such a person.

> " Consider well for whom you pledge your name,
> Lest without guilt you bear another's shame."—*Horace.*

Avoid two dangers : do not offend the applicant for a recommendation; do not deceive your correspondent by exaggerated praise of the one recommended.

If the applicant is *worthy* state his merits, express reasonable confidence in him, ask your friend's interest in his behalf as a personal favor to yourself. If he is *unworthy* or doubtfully worthy, give him a letter which he will prefer not to present ; for every such letter is an open letter, which the bearer is expected to read before delivering. It may be necessary to write by mail to the third party, informing him, before the letter is presented to him, of certain facts which could not be mentioned in the recommendation. Write on the envelope, below the address, towards the left : " To introduce Mr. ——."

343. V. **Letters of Petition** should be modest and every way moderate. Ingratiate yourself in a manly way ; state your reasons briefly but forcibly ; show your appreciation of the trouble your correspondent may be put to in consequence of the favor ; promise gratitude.

In answering such letters favorably be brief and show your pleasure at rendering the little service asked. Say as little as possible of the trouble it costs, or of limitation or conditions. In refusing show how reluctantly you do so ; give good reasons for it. Express your hope of finding, some other time, a better opportunity of showing your affection or esteem.

344. VI. **Letters of Thanks** should never be neglected when a favor has been received. Express your appreciation both of the favor and of the kindness with which it was bestowed. Hope for an opportunity, not of repaying the person, but of showing your gratitude.

345. We add some further directions for epistolary **correspondence in general :**

1. Give *advice* sparingly : do not volunteer it except for very special reasons ; if asked give it cautiously, modestly, appearing to mistrust your views unless there is a principle at stake. If there is, state it modestly but firmly : in this, as in all things else, honesty is the best policy.

2. If you must *find fault*, do so reluctantly and as gently as circumstances will allow ; but if it is your clear duty to do it at all, do it with manly firmness.

3. To *excuse* yourself rather exaggerate than hide your fault ; express sorrow ; then touch upon palliating circumstances, or explain how the mistake arose ; promise care for the future.

346. Eminent letter-writers are few. Cicero's is the best collection : he corresponded in a charming style with the greatest men of his age on all manners of subjects ;

but he wrote simply what the circumstances actually suggested, without any intention of publishing his letters.

Pliny's are highly, even excessively, polished.

Dean Swift's are unaffected, but they want discretion and betray many of his defects of character.

Pope's are entertaining, witty, and refined, but too evidently labored.

Chesterfield's are natural, but often indelicate, and in other ways wanting in a Christian spirit.

Lady Mary Montagu has much ease and vivacity, and a very agreeable epistolary style.

In French, Madame de Sévigné is considered a charming model of familiar correspondence; still, she is too talkative for English taste.

The letters of Eugénie de Guérin are among the most perfect models in this species of literature.

347. **Exercises.**—Write one letter of each species, the particular circumstances being suggested by your teacher.

CHAPTER III.

NARRATION.

348. Narration is defined a species of composition which relates the particulars of a real or fictitious event. In a wider meaning, narration is the statement of successive facts; it enters into histories, biographies, travels, novels, etc. We shall consider: 1. The *general rules* for all good narration; 2. The rules for *Simple Narration*; 3. Those for *Complex Narration*; 4. The *style* of narration.

ARTICLE I. RULES FOR NARRATION IN GENERAL.

349. The first rule regards the **choice of a subject.**
Rule 1.—The writer should select a subject with which he is **sufficiently acquainted,** else he cannot expect to write a sensible composition.

350. *Rule* 2.—He should choose a subject **not too lofty** for his talents, nor too intricate for his ability to handle successfully.

These two rules apply to all compositions; but they are often violated in the choice of subjects for narration. The reason is that many of the most perfect specimens of narration, in ancient and modern writers, are of wars and battles, and other stirring subjects, which are too intricate and too little understood by the young to be good subjects for imitation. Such subjects accustom beginners to unreality and conceit, and do more harm than good.

351. *Rule* 3.—The subject should **suit the end** intended by the writer. If he desires to *please* let him choose facts

which are beautiful or interesting in themselves, or which may readily be beautified ; if he aims at *moving* his readers he must select a story that speaks to their hearts ; if he wishes to *instruct* he must relate an event that is itself instructive, or from which he can draw a useful lesson. If all these ends be intended together he should choose very carefully some matter which is suited for all these purposes.

352. If the subject deals with real facts the rule of **fidelity** to the truth is essential. It requires that not only the main facts shall be true as they are narrated, but also that all the striking and important details be faithfully stated as they are known to have happened. Little details which are only the filling-up of the picture may be supplied by the writer's knowledge of human nature. But care must be taken that the author does not give a false coloring to his picture by offering his own speculations as real facts. It would be a great fault to introduce any important but fictitious circumstance into the narrative of a real event.

353. *Rule* 4.—The rule of **probability** applies to both real and fictitious narratives. It requires that everything narrated must appear natural, plausible, or true to nature. To make a narration look probable or plausible the writer must show how far the effects mentioned proceeded from known causes, and how far they were merely accidental. He must exhibit the words and actions as in keeping with the characters of the persons, with the times, places, etc. He must do all this without appearing to reason much, simply by presenting the facts and circumstances in a natural manner.

354. *Rule* 5.—To make a narration truly artistic—*i.e.*, a beautiful piece of literary composition—the rule of **unity** is important. All the details of the narrative must be so selected and disposed as to appear parts of one whole story, so that all the attention of the reader is concen-

trated upon a single fact. When the story is brief and simple the rule of unity is easily observed ; but not so when the details are many and the narrative is prolonged.

355. **The art of telling a good story well** lies chiefly in this process : that, after a proper introduction, you excite and partly satisfy the curiosity of the reader without hurrying the events too much, suspending the action occasionally without allowing it to languish. Such suspense often adds intense interest to the narrative, which must afterwards be brought to a natural and full close, satisfying all reasonable curiosity and expectation.

Article II. Simple Narration.

356. **A narrative is simple** if it is free from intricacy and multiplicity of details, and so brief that, when it has been read, the whole story is easily remembered—taken in, as it were, at one glance; else it is *complex*. Addison illustrates the truth, " The humble are exalted," by this simple story, " The Drop of Water " :

" A drop of water fell out of a cloud into the sea, and, finding itself lost in such an immensity of fluid matter, broke out into the following reflection : ' Alas ! what an insignificant creature am I in this prodigious ocean of waters ; my existence is of no concern to the universe ; I am reduced to a kind of nothing, and am less than the least of the works of God.' It so happened that an oyster, which lay in the neighborhood of this drop, chanced to gape and swallow it up in the midst of this its humble soliloquy. The drop lay a great while hardening in the shell, till by degrees it was ripened into a pearl, which, falling into the hands of a diver, after a long series of adventures, is at present that famous pearl which is fixed on the top of the Persian diadem."

357. Dodsley inculcates moderation in pleasure by the " Fable of the Two Bees " :

" On a fine morning in May two bees set forward in quest of honey;

the one wise and temperate, the other careless and extravagant.
They soon arrived at a garden enriched with aromatic herbs, the most
fragrant and the most delicious fruits. They regaled themselves
for a time on the various dainties that were spread before them ; the
one loading himself at intervals with provisions for the hive against
the distant winter, the other revelling in sweets without regard to
anything but his present gratification. At length they found a wide-
mouthed vial, that hung beneath the bough of a peach-tree, filled
with honey ready tempered and exposed to their taste in the most
alluring manner. The thoughtless epicure, in spite of all his friend's
remonstrances, plunged headlong into the vessel, resolving to in-
dulge himself in all the pleasures of sensuality. The philosopher,
on the other hand, sipped a little with caution ; but, being suspi-
cious of danger, flew off to fruits and flowers, where, by the moderation of his meals, he improved his relish for the true enjoyment
of them. In the evening, however, he called upon his friend to
inquire whether he would return to the hive ; but he found him sur-
feited in sweets, which he was as unable to leave as to enjoy. Clog-
ged in his wings, enfeebled in his feet, and his whole frame totally
enervated, he was but just able to bid his friend adieu, and to lament
with his latest breath that, though a taste of pleasure might quicken
the relish of life, an unrestrained indulgence is inevitable destruction."

358. One of the most perfect models that can be proposed of a simple narration is from the masterly pen of
Cicero, " Dionysius and Damocles " :

" Dionysius, the tyrant of Sicily, showed how far he was from being happy, even whilst abounding in riches and all the pleasures
which riches can procure. Damocles, one of his flatterers, was com-
plimenting him one day upon his power, his treasures, and the magnificence of his royal state, and affirming that no monarch ever was
greater or happier than he. 'Have you a mind, Damocles,' said the
king, 'to taste this happiness, and know by experience what my
enjoyments are, of which you entertain so high an appreciation ?'
Damocles gladly accepted the offer. Then the king ordered that a
royal banquet should be prepared, and a gilded couch placed for
him, covered with rich embroidery, and sideboards loaded with gold
and silver plate of immense value. Pages of extraordinary beauty

were ordered to wait on him at table, and to obey his commands with the greatest readiness and the most profound submission. Neither ointments, chaplets of flowers, nor rich perfumes were wanting. The table was loaded with the most exquisite delicacies of every kind. Damocles fancied himself amongst the gods. In the midst of all his happiness he sees, let down from the roof, exactly over his head as he lay indulging himself in state, a glittering sword hung by a single hair. The sight of destruction, thus threatening him from on high, soon put a stop to his joy and revelling. The pomp of his attendants and the glitter of the carved plate gave him no longer any pleasure. He dreads to stretch forth his hand to the table. He throws off the chaplet of roses. He hastens to escape from his dangerous situation, and at last begs the king to restore him to his former humble condition, having no desire to enjoy any longer so dreadful a kind of happiness."

359. If we study this piece with care we shall **notice the following points** in particular: 1. There is a brief introduction to the story. 2. The facts are related in the natural order. 3. The quotation of the tyrant's words enlivens the narrative. 4. The description of the feast adds elegance. 5. Every detail either throws light upon the facts, or makes them more interesting or impressive. No item could be omitted without detracting from the happy effect of the whole. 6. We see the reason of everything that is said or done. All these are points worthy of imitation.

360. Care ought always to be taken to **select those circumstances** of an event which mark it strikingly. A few well-chosen details may convey a more vivid impression of a fact than a multitude of less telling incidents. Thus Walter Scott, in narrating the "Taking of Roxburgh Castle," selects only a few items; but they stamp the impression of the sudden surprise indelibly on the mind:

"You must know Roxburgh was then a very large castle situated near where two fine rivers, the Tweed and the Teviot, join each other. Being within five or six miles of England, the English were extremely desirous of retaining it, and the Scots equally eager to obtain possession of it. I will tell you how it was taken.

"It was upon the night of what is called Shrovetide, a holiday which people paid great respect to and solemnized with much gayety and feasting. Most of the garrison of Roxburgh castle were drinking and carousing, but still they had set watches on the battlements of the castle, in case of any sudden attack ; for as the Scots had succeeded in so many enterprises of the kind, and as Douglas was known to be in the neighborhood, they conceived themselves obliged to keep a very strict guard.

"An Englishwoman, the wife of one of the officers, was sitting on the battlements with her child in her arms, and looking out on the fields below. She saw some black objects, like a herd of cattle, straggling near the foot of the wall and approaching the ditch or moat of the castle. She pointed them out to the sentinel, and asked him what they were. ' Pooh, pooh !' said the soldier, ' it is Farmer Such-a-one's cattle' (naming a man whose farm lay near the castle). ' The good man is keeping a jolly Shrovetide, and has forgot to shut up his bullocks in their yard ; but if the Douglas come across them before morning he is likely to rue his negligence.' Now, those creeping objects which they saw from the castle-wall were no real cattle, but Douglas himself and his soldiers, who had put black cloaks above their armor, and were creeping about on hands and feet, in order, without being observed, to get so near to the foot of the castle-wall as to be able to set ladders to it. The poor woman, who knew nothing of this, sat quietly on the wall, and began to sing to her child. You must know that the name of Douglas had become so terrible to the English that the women used to frighten their children with it, and say to them when they behaved ill that they ' would make the Black Douglas take them.' And the soldier's wife was singing to her child :

> 'Hush ye, hush ye, little pet ye ;
> Hush ye, hush ye, do not fret ye :
> The Black Douglas shall not get ye.'

"'You are not so sure of that,' said a voice close beside her. She felt at the same time a heavy hand, with an iron glove, laid on her shoulder, and when she looked round she saw the very ' Black Douglas ' she had been singing about standing close beside her, a tall, swarthy, strong man. At the same time another Scotsman was seen ascending the walls, near to the sentinel. The soldier gave the alarm and rushed at the Scotsman, whose name was Simon Ledehouse, with his lance; but Simon parried the stroke, and, closing with the sentinel, struck him a deadly blow with his dagger. The rest of the Scots followed up to assist Douglas and Ledehouse, and the castle was taken. Many of the soldiers were put to death, but Douglas protected the woman and the child. I dare say she made no more song about the Black Douglas."

361. Washington Irving, in narrating the first landing of Columbus, was naturally led by the importance of the event to give a full and detailed account of what took place on that solemn occasion. But he has carefully avoided overloading his picture with useless circumstances; his narration is in exquisite taste. (See *Life of Columbus*, vol. i. b. iv. c. i.)

ARTICLE III. COMPLEX NARRATION.

362. It is not easy to draw the line between simple and complex narration; nor does it matter much by what name we call a narrative, provided it be clear and interesting. But the reason we speak of **Complex Narrations** is, to show how certain difficulties are to be overcome which do not occur in the pieces so far explained. These **difficulties** are: (*a*) multiplicity of detail; (*b*) a want of obvious connection between various events; and (*c*) intricacy, when various series of facts run into one another.

363. These difficulties are to be overcome by the study of **order**—*i.e.*, a skilful disposition of the parts with a view to obtaining certain results; here the results aimed at are clearness and interest.

364. There are **various kinds of order**. 1. The most common is the **order of time**, called also the historical order. An example of this order is found in the history of

Joseph and his brothers (Genesis xxxvii. to xlvi.). Another example is "The Sorrowful Night" (Prescott's *Conquest of Mexico*, ii. p. 361). All that is necessary in the historical order is that the events unfold themselves naturally before the eyes of the reader, without confusion.

365. 2. The **order of importance** relates first the principal events, omitting such details as might cause confusion, and returning afterwards to supply them. This order is partly historical, and is often the clearest in relating complicated facts. It is used by Livy in his account of the passage of the Rhine by Hannibal. He narrates first how the soldiers effected the crossing of that rapid stream in the face of a numerous army of hostile Gauls, and then returns to relate other matters omitted in the first account (Livy, xxi. 26–29).

366. 3. The **distributive order** consists in relating separately two or more series of facts which happen about the same time in different places, and which conspire to produce one main result. Thus Livy, in narrating the battle of Cannæ, tells first what was done on one wing, then in the centre, and then on the other wing; thus enabling the reader to follow the account with ease and pleasure. He does not give us three separate narrations ; but, by presenting both the armies together to our view before the battle, and as soon again as the rout of the Romans began, he exhibits all the events as the parts of one harmonious whole.

367. 4. The **romantic order** arranges events not so much with a view to clearness as to interest, beginning with a striking fact or scene which is not the first in the order of time, but which is suitable to arouse attention : the writer later on supplies such other facts as had first been omitted. This order is often pursued where the purpose is pleasure and the story is long. In the body of the narration in-

terest may similarly be promoted by delaying the explanation of some facts till a proper degree of suspense has been attained. But inversions are by no means necessary, and the most regular order is usually the most tasteful and pleasing. First-class writers create sufficient interest by the naturalness of their story, their felicity in the choice of items, and the propriety and elegance of their expressions; but inferior writers make constant use of tricks and artificial contrivances, as bad cooks do of strong condiments to atone for the absence of the genuine flavors which please a healthy taste.

368. **Classical taste** favors neatness and regularity, in arrangement as in everything else; but romantic taste loves wildness and striking peculiarities as productive of more excitement. This is at present the prevailing taste of the general reader, but by no means of our best writers nor of the refined portion of society. Goldsmith, Irving, Prescott, Lingard, Wiseman, Newman, and many others are classical in their taste and resemble Livy, Ovid, Virgil, Homer, Plato, Cicero, and Demosthenes. Whatever order is adopted, a long story should be divided into chapters, each of which should exhibit some particular group of facts, so that a brief heading may comprise the whole matter of that division.

369. To insure **unity in a complex narration** one fact must be made more prominent than all the rest, the centre of attention and interest, or the issue to which everything tends. For this purpose the narrator may give prominence to one leading character in whom the interest of the narrative is centred; such would be either Napoleon or Wellington in the battle of Waterloo. When the story is long or very intricate there may be secondary centres of interest, and distinct groups of events, provided the groups and the persons be themselves clustered around one

striking or commanding figure, and directed to one important result.

370. It is a useful exercise to **compare in detail two distinct accounts** of the same event as given by two different writers ; for instance, the **defeat of Braddock,** in Bancroft's *History of the United States* (vol. iv., pp. 186–192, Ed. 1852), and in Irving's *Life of George Washington* (vol. i. pp. 173–182, Ed. 1860). It will be observed that Irving premises a clear description of the battle-ground, concentrates attention on one army, keeps Braddock and Washington ever in sight, making the general the central figure, which we can easily follow ; while in Bancroft, who is less attentive to these points, there appears to be confusion. This will be seen more clearly if we read the latter account first ; else, without noticing it, we are apt to allow the distinct views of Irving to guide us through the less distinct account of Bancroft. With Irving's clear narration of the battle we may compare the no less distinct description of the battle of Poictiers in Lingard's *History of England* (vol. ii. pp. 314 to 316, Ed. of 1840). Lingard appears to gain by the comparison. He concentrates attention more effectually upon the leading points. If we compare with his narrative the taking of Badajos as related by Alison (vol. iii. pp. 467–469, Ed. 1848), we shall notice that Alison describes very graphically, and distributes the events judiciously and most carefully. But he seems to overload his account with minor details, which make it difficult to follow.

371. This last remark is further illustrated by a comparison of Alison's narrative of the **Battle of Waterloo** (*History of Europe*, vol. iv. c. lxxvii. pp. 532–539, Ed. of 1848) with Abbott's in his life of Napoleon (Griswold's *Prose Writers of America*, pp. 609 to 612). Both are very able narrations of one of the most important events in the history of the world ; and they are worthy specimens of

the style of both distinguished authors. The two passages should be carefully read, and compared together in detail. They offer some striking **points of difference:**

Abbott's sympathies are entirely with Napoleon, Alison's are decidedly with Wellington. Both make their favorite hero the centre of the action. Hence results at once a striking difference in the style. The dashing spirit of Napoleon and of his enthusiastic followers pervades the account of the former; the cool, calculating skill of the Iron Duke and of his unyielding legions characterizes the elaborate narration of the latter. Abbott writes as the biographer of one man in whom all interest is naturally centred; Alison, as the painstaking historian of modern Europe, strives to do justice to many individual heroes. Abbott writes for the general reader; Alison for the careful student of history and military tactics. Hence the former's account is more pleasing, more. artistic ; the latter's more useful and more scientific. As a specimen of literature Abbott's is singularly beautiful ; the charge of the Imperial Guard in particular is sublime.

ARTICLE IV. STYLE OF NARRATIONS.

372. The **style** ought to be regulated by the end or purpose of the writer: 1. When *instruction* is aimed at clearness ought to be the chief quality. It should, however, be accompanied by neatness, and even elegance, as the occasion may require, and as the writer's talents can afford: no one should aim higher than he can reasonably expect to reach.

2. If emotion or *persuasion* is aimed at vividness is the chief quality, exhibiting, as if present to the view, whatever can move the heart.

3. If *pleasure* is the chief object the language ought to

be polished accordingly, not by loading it with gaudy ornaments, but by setting forth the subject with becoming
dignity and elegance.

Familiar facts can be most gracefully related in what the
ancients called the *stylus tenuis*—a style of simplicity and
neatness combined, which is unpretending but may be very
charming in its apparent artlessness.

> " *Ut sibi quivis*
> *Speret idem, sudet multum, frustraque laboret*
> *Ausus idem."—Ars Poet.*, 240.

> "From well-known tales such fictions would I raise
> As all might hope to imitate with ease;
> Yet while they strive the same success to gain,
> Should find their labor and their hopes are vain."
>
> *—Francis.*

As a specimen of this style in narration we may refer to
Irving's well-known story of Rip Van Winkle in his *Sketch-
Book.*

373. Persons who have not acquired a cultivated style
should aim at narrating briefly and clearly, in correct language, without attempting any great elegance of style.

374. Narration is said to be **graphic** when the various
scenes are so painted that the imagination is arrested by
them. This quality of style is obtained by mingling descriptions with the narrative. Long descriptions are rarely appropriate; but brief descriptions and characteristic
epithets may occur at every step. Of this style of narration we find a beautiful example in the account of the
Romans surrounded in the defile of Caudium (Livy, ix.
2–6).

375. The story should, as a rule, be **told feelingly;**
that is, the writer should enter into the sentiments, the
spirit of the narration: now exulting, now sympathizing,
now indignant, now grateful, etc. The expression itself

ought to be tinctured by the thoughts and feelings : now rapid, now slow ; now solemn, now familiar, etc. One of the clearest signs of a depraved taste is the absence of such harmony between the scene presented and the style in which it is narrated. This want of taste is very noticeable in Froude's narration of the execution of Mary, Queen of Scots. On the other hand, no one can help feeling how much the narration of the same sad event is set off to advantage by Robertson, Miss Agnes Strickland, and Dr. Lingard.

To accustom students to narrate in an orderly manner the following exercises may be of use :

376. **1st Exercise,** by *analysis :* After reading the history of Joseph and his brothers, mention briefly in the order of their occurrence the facts connected, 1. With the sale of Joseph to the Egyptian merchants ; 2. With his elevation to power ; 3. With the recognition of him by his brothers. This kind of analysis can be applied to any narration

377. **2d Exercise,** by *observation :*
Mention briefly the various stages, 1. In the growth of corn, from the seed to the ripe ear ; 2. In the growth of a peach-tree, from the planting of a peach-stone to the decay of the tree ; 3. In the rising and development of a summer storm ; 4. In the transition from autumn to winter, and from winter to spring.

378. **3d Exercise.**—Point out *defects* in the following order of facts. Landing of Columbus : (*a*) signs of land appeared at last ; (*b*) there had been a mutiny on board the vessel ; (*c*) great joy of the sailors ; (*d*) Indians stood wondering on the shore ; (*e*) it was Easter day ; (*f*) Columbus planted the standard of Spain ; (*g*) he landed with several companions ; (*h*) the Indians took them for visitors from heaven.

379. 4th Exercise, *criticism :*

Read a narration and point out in it how the rules are observed or are violated. Consider chiefly these points : 1. Is there unity? 2. Is anything superfluous? 3. Is everything in its proper place? 4. Is it easy to follow the narrative? 5. Does everything appear natural? 6. Are the reasons of every act apparent? 7. Are the essential scenes clearly described? 8. Is any important item omitted?

Note 1.—It must be remembered that unity is not secured by the fact that the narration is limited to the events of a day, a year, etc.; there must be a leading event developed throughout.

Note 2.—Complex narration will occur in tracing one effect to various causes—*e.g.*, the American Revolution—or the various effects of one common cause.

380. 5th Exercise.—*Narrate* the change that has come over the world through the inventions of printing, of steam-power, or of the telegraph.

Unity in these complex narrations is secured by keeping the one cause or the one effect continually before the reader's mind.

CHAPTER IV.

DESCRIPTION.

381. We mean by a **description** the delineation of some object or scene. Narration deals with successive facts ; description with objects that exist at the same time. We rarely find any literary production of great length which is entirely descriptive ; but descriptions are often introduced into narratives with happy effect. Sometimes they serve the purpose of making the narration impressive, by moving the passions of the reader. At other times they are intended to make the events more intelligible. Thus we have seen that some narratives of battles are hard to follow because the writer has neglected to give us a clear description of the battle-field. Descriptions frequently serve as ornaments, affording an agreeable variety to the narration, and presenting scenes of striking interest to the imagination.

We shall divide this chapter so as to treat, first, of the description of things ; secondly, of the description of persons or characters.

Article I. Description of Things.

382. *Rule* 1.—In all cases the description should be of a piece with the rest of the composition, and not look like a purple patch sewed on a common garment.

383. *Rule* 2.—Descriptive passages must have a natural connection with the main subject, or be properly introduced.

384. To acquire skill in description it is necessary to form a **habit of close observation,** to study natural objects and the various characters of men. The exercises laid down in a preceding chapter on Object-Lessons are a useful preparation for descriptive compositions.

385. We have already remarked, when treating of narrations, that **brief descriptions** are constantly blended with them to great advantage, making them vivid and impressive. But **long descriptions** are not of very frequent occurrence, because they labor under serious difficulties ; the study of these difficulties and of the ways to overcome them will suggest the chief precepts for the management of descriptions.

386. I. **The first difficulty** is that it is impossible to express in words all that the eye would take in if the scene were actually witnessed.

This difficulty is obviated by making a judicious **choice of the salient features** of the scene. For, in reality, when we behold a landscape, for example, the mind does not pay attention to all the particulars presented to the eye ; it notices distinctly a few striking points, and sees the rest vaguely or not at all. Hence we learn that the great art of description, as of painting and drawing, consists chiefly in the skilful selection of those very items which the eye would rest on if the whole scene were present. We may apply to description what Macaulay remarks of history:

"No history and no picture can present us with the whole truth; but those are the best pictures and the best histories which exhibit such parts of the truth as most nearly produce the effect of the whole. . . . An outline scrawled with a pen which seizes the marked features of a countenance will give a much stronger idea of it than a bad painting in oils. Yet the worst painting in oils that ever hung in Somerset House resembles the original in many more particulars."—*Essays, History.*

Though Macaulay's practical use of this principle is not always defensible, the principle itself is universally acknowledged.

387. Another point of comparison between history and painting is likewise applicable to description:

"History has its foreground and its background, and it is principally in the management of its perspective that one artist differs from another. Some events must be represented on a large scale, others diminished; the great majority will be lost in the dimness of the horizon, and a general idea of their joint effect will be given by a few slight touches."—*Id.*

So in description a few objects will be **fully dwelt upon**, others **briefly pointed out,** and the rest will be suggested by some general terms.

388. We quote as an **example** of this process a passage of Washington Irving's *Sketch-Book* in which he describes his first landing in England:

"It was a fine sunny morning when the thrilling cry of ' Land !' was given from the masthead. None but those who have experienced it can form an idea of the delicious throng of sensations which rush into an American's bosom when he first comes in sight of Europe. There is a volume of associations with the very name. It is the land of promise, teeming with everything of which his childhood has heard or on which his studious years have pondered.

"From that time until the moment of arrival it was all feverish excitement. The ships-of-war that prowled like guardian giants along the coast, the headlands of Ireland stretching out into the Channel, the Welsh mountains towering into the clouds—all were objects of intense interest. As we sailed up the Mersey I reconnoitred the shores with a telescope. My eye dwelt with delight on neat cottages with their trim shrubberies and green grass plots. I saw the mouldering ruin of an abbey overrun with ivy, and the taper spire of a village church rising from the brow of a neighboring hill. All were characteristic of England.

"The tide and wind were so favorable that the ship was enabled to come at once to the pier. It was thronged with people, some idle lookers-on, others eager expectants of friends or relatives. I could distinguish the merchant to whom the ship was consigned ; I knew him by his calculating brow and restless air. His hands were thrust into his pockets ; he was whistling thoughtfully, and walking to and fro, a small space having been accorded him by the crowd in deference to his temporary importance. There were repeated cheerings and salutations interchanged between the shore and the ship as friends happened to recognize each other.

" All was now hurry and bustle—the meetings of acquaintances, the greetings of friends, the consultations of men of business I alone was solitary and idle. I had no friend to meet, no cheering to receive. I stepped upon the land of my forefathers, but felt that I was a stranger in the land "

389. The same happy selection of circumstances may be noticed in his description of a poor man's funeral in the sketch entitled " The Widow and her Son," and in the following pen-picture by Longfellow :

" The first snow came. How beautiful it was, falling so silently all day long, all night long, on the mountains, on the meadows, on the roofs of the living, on the graves of the dead ! All white save the river, that marked its course by a winding black line across the landscape ; and the leafless trees, that against the leaden sky now revealed more fully the wonderful beauty and intricacies of their branches. What silence, too, came with the snow, and what seclusion ! Every sound was muffled, every noise changed to something soft and musical. No more tramping hoofs, no more rattling wheels ! Only the chiming sleigh-bells, beating as swift and merrily as the hearts of children."

390. II. The second difficulty arises from the fact that a description, unlike a painting, can present only one feature at a time. To realize the whole scene the reader must exert himself and group the various features in his imagination. Now, ordinary readers are not apt to take so much trouble, unless they feel an unusual interest in the

scene presented ; they soon fail to follow the guidance of the writer, the scene becomes confused, and all effort to follow the description is abandoned.

391. **One means of removing** this inconvenience is never to attempt a long description, except when sufficient attention has been aroused, either by the importance of the matter itself or by some special sympathy or curiosity awakened in the reader. The main points, then, to be studied in this connection are:

1. To see by what process we can arouse the reader's attention ; and especially,

2. To study how we can lessen the strain on his imagination.

392. 1. **To arouse attention** we may show the importance of conceiving the scene distinctly ; we may also enlist the feelings of the reader in our subject. Nothing is more conducive to attention than a deep interest felt in the objects described. Whatever will inspire sympathy, love, affection, or any of the gentler emotions or stronger passions, will quicken the imagination to realize the scene described. We may instance the lengthy description of Westminster Abbey in Irving's *Sketch-Book*. The reflections introduced at every step sustain the attention amid scenes which it is difficult to delineate in a striking manner. Instead of such reflections as Irving introduces in that description, we may keep the reader's sympathies enlisted in a subject by viewing it in connection with one of the persons or characters in whom special interest is felt. Thus Irving describes the scene at the landing of Columbus as seen by that hero ; and Abbott, the various phases of the battle of Waterloo as observed by Napoleon. Thus, too, Homer describes the chief Grecian heroes through the lips of Helen, who points them out to Priam from the top of the Trojan walls.

393. 2. To lessen the exertion required of the reader's imagination several means may be suggested :

(*a*) Place the reader in a **favorable position** to observe the whole scene.

394. (*b*) Begin with a striking feature, or with a view of the general outline, and proceed next to fill up the scene in an orderly manner. Both these rules are well exemplified in this extract from Prescott's *Conquest of Mexico* (vol. ii. b. iii. c. 6) :

" Nothing could be more grand than tne view which met the eye from the area on the truncated summit of the pyramid. Toward the west stretched that bold barrier of porphyritic rock which nature has reared around the Valley of Mexico, with the huge Popocatepetl and Iztaccihuatl standing like two colossal ·sentinels to guard the entrance to the enchanted region. Far away to the east was seen the conical head of Orizaba soaring high into the clouds, and nearer the barren though beautifully-shaped Sierra de Malinche throwing its broad shadows over the plains of Tlascala. Three of these are volcanoes higher than the highest mountain peak in Europe, and shrouded in snows which never melt under the fierce sun of the tropics. At the foot of the spectator lay the sacred city of Cholula, with its bright towers and pinnacles sparkling in the sun, reposing amidst gardens and verdant groves, which then thickly studded the cultivated environs of the capital. Such was the magnificent prospect which met the gaze of the conquerors, and may still, with slight change, meet that of the modern traveller, as from the platform of the great pyramid his eye wanders over the fairest portion of the beautiful plateau of Puebla."

395. (*c*) Use all the ornaments of style that may please the imagination ; as Irving does in this description of a farm-yard :

" A great elm-tree spread its broad branches over it, at the foot of which bubbled up a spring of the softest and sweetest water, in a little well formed of a barrel, and then stole sparkling away through the grass to a neighboring brook that babbled along among the alders and dwarf willows. Hard by the farm house was a vast barn that might have served for a church, every window and crevice of which seemed bursting forth with the treasures of the farm; the flail was busily resounding within it from morning to night; swallows and martins skimmed twittering about the eaves; and rows of pigeons, some with one eye turned up, as if watching the weather, some with their heads under their wings or buried in their bosoms, and others swelling and cooing and bowing about their dames, were enjoying the sunshine on the roof. Sleek, unwieldy porkers were grunting in the repose and abundance of their pens, whence sallied forth, now and then, troops of sucking pigs, as if to snuff the air. A stately squadron of snowy geese were riding in an adjoining pond, convoying whole fleets of ducks; regiments of turkeys were gobbling through the farm-yard, and guinea-fowls fretting about it, like ill-tempered house-wives, with their peevish, discontented cry. Before the barn-door strutted the gallant cock, that pattern of a husband, a warrior, and a fine gentleman, clapping his burnished wings and crowing in the pride and gladness of his heart—sometimes tearing up the earth with his feet, and then generously calling his ever-hungry family of wives and children to enjoy the rich morsel which he had discovered."

396. (*d*) Let the **rule of unity**, necessary in all compositions, be strictly observed in every description—that is, let only one object be described, or let a variety of objects be united by one leading idea into a moral whole, the embodiment of one sentiment. Thus Bancroft, in his *History of the United States* (vol. ii. p. 266, old edition), describes the site where New York was afterwards built, and gives unity to all the leading parts by means of the one dominant idea of wildness; next (p. 268) he presents the site as it is now, as an embodiment of civilization.

397. (*e*) It is a great help, where it can be done, to introduce into a long description **a connected narrative** that will unite the various parts of the scene, as when a person is made to visit successively various portions of a landscape.

398. (*f*) Sometimes we may introduce brief narratives

of **incidents** or of historical reminiscences ; at other times reflections of an agreeable or elevated kind. These precepts are exemplified in numerous passages of Prescott's *Conquest of Mexico*, in particular in his description of the Valley of Mexico (vol. ii. p. 68).

399. The **style** in description should be concise : every word should add light to the picture, and no useless feature should be presented to the imagination. Still, description need not be bare of ornament ; on the contrary, it may be richly adorned, as we have èxplained (No. 395). We add one instance in point from the pen of Fenimore Cooper, " Venice at Night " :

" The moon was at the height. Its rays fell in a flood on the swelling domes and massive roofs of Venice, while the margin of the town was brilliantly defined by the glittering bay. The natural and gorgeous setting was more than worthy of that picture of human magnificence ; for at that moment, rich as was the Queen of the Adriatic in her works of art, the grandeur of her public monuments, the number and splendor of her palaces, and most else that the ingenuity and ambition of man could attempt, she was but secondary in the glories of the hour.

" Above was the firmament gemmed with worlds and sublime in immensity. Beneath lay the broad expanse of the Adriatic, endless to the eye, tranquil as the vault it reflected, and luminous with its borrowed light. Here and there a low island, reclaimed from the sea by the patient toil of a thousand years, dotted the lagunes, burdened by the group of some conventual dwellings, or picturesque with the modest roofs of a hamlet of the fishermen. Neither oar, nor song, nor laugh, nor flap of sail, nor jest of mariner disturbed the stillness. All in the near view was clothed in midnight loveliness, and all in the distance bespoke the solemnity of nature at peace. The city and the lagunes, the gulf and the dreamy Alps, the interminable plain of Lombardy and the blue void of heaven, lay alike in a common and grand repose."

400. **1st Exercise.**—Analyze various model passages of the best authors, noticing :

1. What object or aim the author wishes to attain;
2. What features he has selected for distinct treatment, what others for a brief sketch;
3. How he starts out;
4. What order he follows in the development;
5. What sentiments he has introduced;
6. What special artifices he has used to excite interest, or to enable the reader to follow him with ease.
7. How naturally the description is introduced, and how naturally it is laid aside to return to the narration.

401. **2d Exercise.**—Compare the descriptions of the same or of analogous subjects as drawn by various great writers, noticing how the style will differ with the general aspect of their works. For instance, compare the Pestilence in Athens, by Thucydides (book ii.), with the London Pestilence of A.D. 1665 as described by Lingard (vol. vii. pp. 278–282), by De Foe (Chambers' *Cyclopædia of Literature*, vol. i. p. 621), by Armstrong (*id.* ii. p. 69).

402. **The study of description** is one of the best means of improving the style of narrations, and, in fact, of all literary compositions. It is to his remarkable descriptive power that Prescott, for instance, owes that special charm which makes him so popular among all classes of readers, so that children, who find unadorned history too dry for their taste, will pore over his pictured page as they would over a touching story. As one more specimen of the descriptive style of this author we will refer to the crossing of the Sierra (vol. ii. pp. 461–465).

403. **3d Exercise.**—Mention briefly the items you would select to describe a city, a village, river, picnic-ground, country—putting all the items in good order.

404. **4th Exercise.**—Point out the faults against order in this sketch, a description of a room :

1. The room is nearly square.
2. It is dark and unattractive, having but two small windows on the east side.
3. It is twenty-four feet long and twenty-two feet wide.
4. It is in the southeast corner of the building.
5. It is a low room, the ceiling being only nine feet from the floor.
6. It has a recess on the west side.
7. The walls are plastered.

405. **5th Exercise.**—Describe a pleasant scene in spring, a busy scene in a city, a pompous funeral, a scene of devotion in a church, a scene of distress, one of lively enjoyment, one of solemn grandeur.

ARTICLE II. DESCRIPTIONS OF CHARACTERS.

406.. We mean by **descriptions of characters** the pointing-out of those peculiarities by which certain persons are distinguished from the generality of men. Such compositions are far less in use than descriptions of things ; but they are occasionally very appropriate in historical or fictitious works, and as beautiful, when skilfully drawn, as they are difficult to compose.

407. " The drawing of characters," says Blair, " is one of the most splendid and, at the same time, **one of the most difficult ornaments of historical composition.** For characters are generally considered as professed exhibitions of fine writing; and an historian who seeks to shine in them is frequently in danger of carrying refinement to excess from a desire of appearing very profound and penetrating. He brings together so many contrasts and subtile oppositions of qualities that we are rather dazzled with sparkling expressions than entertained with any clear conception of a human charac-

ter. A writer who would characterize in an instructive and masterly manner should be simple in his style and should avoid all quaintness and affectation; at the same time not contenting himself with giving us general outlines only, but descending into those peculiarities which mark a character in its most strong and distinctive features."—*Blair*, Lect. xxxvi.

408. There are **two kinds** of these descriptions : one depicts *general* and one *individual* characters. The latter describes a real or imaginary person by a multiplicity of traits; the former presents one trait only, common to a whole class of men. The former usually occurs in the course of histories, biographies, or novels; of the latter kind Theophrastus among the ancients has left us some good specimens. Marshall, in his *Comedy of Convocation*, gives us some general characters as elegant as they are unpretending. See also " The Bashful Man " (*Models of English Lit.*, p. 59).

409. One of the most admired descriptions of **individual character** is that of the great Carthaginian general Hannibal, which occurs in the twenty-first book of Livy's history of Rome ; another, that of Catiline in Sallust's history of that depraved Roman (n. 5). The following by Walter Scott is distinct and truthful :

" **Robespierre** possessed this advantage over Danton, that he did not seem to seek for wealth, either for hoarding or expending, but lived in strict and economical retirement, to justify the name of the 'Incorruptible' with which he was honored by his partisans. He appears to have possessed little talent, saving a deep fund of hypocrisy, considerable powers of sophistry, and a cold, exaggerated strain of oratory as foreign to a good taste as the measures he recommended were to ordinary humanity. It seemed wonderful that even the seething and boiling of the revolutionary caldron should have sent up from the bottom, and long supported on the surface, a thing so miserably void of claims to public distinction; but Robespierre had to impose upon the minds of the vulgar, and he knew how to beguile them by accommodating his flattery to their passions and scale of understanding, and by acts of cunning and hypocrisy, which weigh more with the multitude than the words of eloquence or the arguments of wisdom. The people listened as to their Cicero when he twanged out his apostrophes of ' Pauvre Peuple, Peuple vertueux !' and hastened to execute whatever came recommended by such honeyed phrases, though devised by the worst of men for the worst and most inhuman of purposes," etc.

410. The **general character is exemplified** in this selection from Marshall's *Comedy of Convocation:*

" **The Good and Easy Clergyman** was a more agreeable type, and one which he had frequent opportunities of studying. One of this school was incumbent of a large and fashionable chapel not half a mile from his own parish church. His voice and manner were so tender that he seemed to be always on the point of making everybody an offer of marriage. His life appeared to glide away in a mild and amiable conflict between the claims of piety and good breeding. Sometimes his eye would kindle, and you would have said he was going to launch a rebuke against some popular sin ; but good taste came promptly to the rescue, and the sinner's sensibility was greatly spared. His sermons were generally a tender panegyric of the natural virtues. He considered them in every aspect, and drew such ravishing pictures of the ' devoted mother,' or ' the Christian at home,' or ' the good parent's reward,' that people said his sermons were as good as a novel ; and so they were. He was quite sure he never once alluded to hell during his whole career," etc.

411. **Rules for the Description of Characters.**
1st Rule.—They should present the individual, or the class of persons described, by **striking traits** which will enable the reader to form a lively and distinct conception of the subject.

2d Rule.—These traits of character must be **consistent with one another,** and the whole picture must be true to nature, so that the highest probability be attained.

3d Rule.—Above all, the characters of real persons must be presented with strict **regard to truth.** For truth is the chief quality of all historical compositions; and no good can come to mankind from falsehood and misrepresentation. And still it is certain that many descriptions of character, occurring in works of great reputation, are very untruthful, often very unjust to the persons described.

412. There are **two chief causes** of this defect. The first is the difficulty of finding out the truth. It is hard enough for us to understand fully those with whom we daily converse, and to picture them to others in their true light without exaggerating or lessening their merit; it is far more difficult to do so with persons who lived in distant ages and in foreign lands. The second source of difficulty lies in the fact that a character drawn with strict regard for the truth is apt to be too tame for the taste of ordinary readers. Most persons, especially the uneducated, want what is striking and sensational in literature. It is easy enough to pander to such taste and to draw flashy portraits in the brightest colors, or, like Carlyle, " to give sketches alternately in chalk or charcoal, that exhibit his saints and his demons, now in ghastliest white and then in the most appalling blackness " (President Porter, *Books and Reading*, p. 162). But to qualify discreetly our praise and blame, to trace those delicate lineaments of the mind and heart which make up a man's individual character, is a task which few can successfully accomplish.

413. How far a straining after effect has injured the truthfulness of historical writings is well explained by President Porter :

" The fact deserves notice in this connection that, of late, professed historians have indulged somewhat freely in romancing, and so in a sense turned their histories into quasi-historical novels ; especially when they attempt to give elaborate and eloquent portraitures of their leading personages, in which the most lavish use is made of effective epithets and pointed antitheses," etc.—*Id.*

414. As much light may be thrown upon one character by comparing or contrasting it with another, we sometimes meet with **Parallel Characters,** as such descriptions are called. In these, two characters are explained at the same time, every trait in the one being compared with an analogous trait in the other.

415. The following is a specimen of this kind, as elegant in style as it is judicious in thought.

"Homer and Virgil compared":

" Homer was the greater genius, Virgil the better artist. In one we most admire the man, in the other the work. Homer hurries and transports us with a commanding impetuosity, Virgil leads us with attractive majesty. Homer scatters with a generous profusion, Virgil bestows with a careful magnificence. Homer, like the Nile, pours out his riches with a boundless overflow ; Virgil, like a river in its banks, with a gentle and constant stream. When we behold their battles, methinks the two poets resemble the heroes they celebrate : Homer, boundless and irresistible as Achilles, bears all before him, and shines more and more as the tumult increases ; Virgil, calmly daring like Æneas, appears undisturbed in the midst of the action, disposes all about him, and conquers with tranquillity. And when we look upon their machines, Homer seems like his own Jupiter in his terrors shaking Olympus, scattering the lightnings and firing the heavens ; Virgil, like the same power in his benevolence, counselling with the gods, laying plans for empires, and regularly ordering his whole creation."—*Pope.*

See a similar passage with which Blair concludes Lecture xliii. The ancients have left us admirable models of parallel characters ; for instance, the comparison between Cæsar and Cato in Sallust's history of Catiline's Conspiracy (liv.)

416. To facilitate the writing of exercises in this species of composition attention is called to the following **items:**

    1. A general appreciation of the person's worth.

    2. His race, family, age, fortune, station, resources.

3. Bodily aspect, general bearing, complexion, looks, voice, gesture, manners.

4. Qualities of mind and heart, virtues, vices, inclinations.

5. Intercourse with superiors, equals, inferiors, relations, friends, enemies, strangers.

6. Influences acting on him, and exerted by him on others. Etc.

For an analysis of Parallel Characters see " Socrates and Seneca," in *Zanders' Outlines of Composition* (p. 167).

417. **Exercises**:

1 Write a general character of a fop, a troublesome friend, a politician, a spendthrift, a miser. (Compare Saxe's " My Familiar.")

2. Write an individual character of Washington, Napoleon I., St. Francis Xavier, Mary Queen of Scots.

3. Write a contrast between a rich man and a poor man from the cradle to the grave.

CHAPTER V.

ESSAYS.

418. **Essays** are attempts to state one's own reflections upon a given subject. They are of different lengths and kinds, ranging from learned treatises to the first attempts of a school-boy at putting his own thoughts on paper. **As school exercises,** to be beneficial they require careful management. Nothing is easier than for a teacher to tell a pupil to write an essay "On the beautiful" or "On the sublime," etc. ; but nothing is more difficult for a pupil than, unassisted, to carry out such an order. Or, if he finds no difficulty in the task, it is perhaps owing to the fact that sense and nonsense are equally welcome to his youthful mind, provided he can cover a few pages of foolscap with well-sounding sentences.

419. **The main difficulty** in this matter is that the boy is thus called upon to express his thoughts on a subject on which he has no clear thoughts to express, and he has not been instructed how to gather thoughts for himself. The first step, therefore, in treating of essay-writing is to teach pupils how to collect appropriate thoughts by a thorough study of the subject assigned.

420. We have said **appropriate thoughts,** for we wish to warn both teachers and learners against an error which has gained ground in our day, and which directs pupils to write down any thought that comes to their minds, no matter how little it be to the point. "At first," says a modern rhetorician, "aim only at copiousness, correcting no faults

except those of grammar and punctuation, and encouraging the pupil to write freely whatever thoughts come up about the subject, and in whatever order they happen to come up." This will teach fluency, no doubt, but not excellence of composition. Let all remember that good sense is ever the foundation of literary success; that, as Quintilian remarks, nothing but what is excellent should be proposed for the imitation of the young, and children should learn nothing which they are afterwards to unlearn (b. i. c. i. 4, 5). A boy who can write ten lines of good sense on a given subject is really further advanced in composition than one who can dash off a hundred lines of mixed sense and nonsense. The first task, then, is to collect appropriate thoughts.

ARTICLE I. COLLECTING APPROPRIATE THOUGHTS.

421. **To study a subject** is to consider carefully all that belongs to that subject, its nature and its name, its causes and its effects, its circumstances and its antecedents, its resemblance to other subjects or its contrast with them ; recalling also to mind, or reading, what others have done or said concerning the matter in question, etc., etc.

These are called by rhetoricians the **topics of thoughts**; they are fully explained in the study of oratory (see *Art of Oratorical Composition*, b. ii. "On the Invention of Thought"). We shall confine ourselves here to a brief explanation of them.

§ 1. *The Nature and Name of the Subject.*

422. When we begin to study a subject **four considerations** are apt at once to present themselves : 1. What is really meant by the subject—*its definition ;* 2. What class of things it belongs to—its *genus or kind;* 3. Of what

portions it is made up—the *enumeration* of its parts ;
4. The *name* by which it is called.

423. 1. A definition is a brief explanation stating what is
meant by the subject, and how it is distinguished from all
others. This is often the most important of all the topics.
It makes the writer conceive a clear idea of his subject, and
enables him to write a sensible explanation of the same.
Thus the essay "On Honor," in the *Guardian*, is mostly
taken up with the discussion of the true idea or definition of 'Honor'; that "On Modesty," in the *Spectator*,
discusses the definitions of 'Modesty,' of 'Assurance,' and
of 'Impudence'; while Addison begins his essay "On
Cheerfulness," in the same paper, by a brief explanation of
what 'Cheerfulness' is, showing how it differs from 'Mirth,'
with which unreflecting minds often confound it.

> "I have always preferred cheerfulness to mirth. The latter I
> consider as an act, the former as a habit of the mind. Mirth is
> short and transient, cheerfulness fixed and permanent. Those are
> often raised into the greatest transports of mirth who are subject to
> the greatest depressions of melancholy. On the contrary, cheerful-
> ness, though it does not give the mind such exquisite gladness, pre-
> vents us from falling into any depths of sorrow. Mirth is like a
> flash of lightning, that breaks through a gloom of clouds and glit-
> ters for a moment ; cheerfulness keeps up a kind of daylight in the
> mind, and fills it with a steady and perpetual serenity."

These last lines show how figures may be used to set off
a definition to advantage.

424. 2. Genus or Kind.—It is often useful to examine to
what kind or class of things the subject belongs. Thus
Cardinal Wiseman, in his essay "On the Miracles of the
New Testament," shows how these may be viewed either
as exhibitions of Christ's power, proving that he was God ;
or as works of mercy, wrought to relieve the sufferings of
men ; or as teachings of certain truths, as when He healed

the paralytic to prove that a man may receive from God the power to forgive sin.

425. 3. **Enumeration of Parts.**—This topic opens a wide field for the development of thought. In our chapter on " Object-Lessons " we have suggested a useful exercise, which consists in pointing out the parts of an object presented to the senses (b. i. c. i. a. 2). A similar process may often be applied to moral subjects. Thus Henry Giles begins his essay "On the Worth of Liberty " with this paragraph :

"What is the worth of liberty? Within the limits of this inquiry all that I propose to say on the present occasion will be confined. Of course I refer mainly to civil liberty, although I do not exclude all reference to liberty in its more spiritual relations. I do not attempt to define liberty either civil or moral. What civil liberty is we all practically comprehend ; and if we do not, defining it would not enable us. I will simply mention the following as a few of the attributes that belong to it : supremacy of the law ; equality of all before the law ; the representation of all in the enactment or changes of the law. To these we may add the provisions which wisdom and experience suggest by which such conditions can be most thoroughly attained and most inviolately preserved."

In the last lines he enumerates the attributes or moral parts which make up liberty. He would have done well to begin with a good definition of liberty ; for it is not true that "we all practically comprehend what civil liberty " or any other kind of liberty is. Many think it is the absence of all restraint, whereas it is only the absence of all undue restraint.

426. 4. **Name.**—Sometimes the very name of the subject will suggest some appropriate thoughts. For instance, if the subject were "The United States, a Land of True Liberty," the name ' United States ' may remind us that the wisdom of our forefathers knew how to combine in the

Union all the advantages of a strong government, respected by all the world, with most of the advantages of independent legislation for the different States of the Union, so that every part of the land may enjoy as large a share of independence as is compatible with the common good.

§ 2. *Causes and Effects.*

427. 1. **Causes.**—The author of the essay "On Cheerfulness," in the *Spectator*, raises the question, what causes produce this happy disposition in the mind, and devotes to these causes a considerable portion of his paper. The consideration of the causes throws much light on every kind of subjects. The essay "On Gratitude," in the *Tatler*, examines in particular the reasons why we should be grateful to the Creator :

"If gratitude is due from man to man, how much more from man to his Maker? The Supreme Being does not only confer on us those bounties which proceed more immediately from His hand, but even those benefits which are conveyed to us by others. Every blessing we enjoy, by what means soever it may be derived upon us, is the gift of Him who is the great Author of good and Father of mercies."

The essay of Addison "On Laughter," in the *Spectator* (No. 52), is almost entirely drawn from the topic of causes.

428. 2. **Effects.**—Effects suggest still more abundant thoughts, and such as are more easy of development. Often a whole essay is nothing more than a description of effects. Such is an essay in the *Spectator* "On the Advantages of a Good Education," and one in the *Rambler* "On the Disadvantages of a Bad Education."

Exercise.—Write an essay on bad company, on intemperance, on war, on music, on steam, on electricity, drawing all the thoughts from this one topic of effects.

§ 3. *Circumstances and Antecedents.*

429. 1. **Circumstances.**—Every subject may be viewed as connected with various circumstances, under which it exists or may be supposed to exist. For instance, if I am to write an essay on " Our National Banner," I may speak of it as displayed in war and in peace, on land and on sea, at home and abroad, and in various events of our national history. If I write on " Water," I may view it in the rain, in the ocean, in the destructive torrent, in the quiet stream, in the bubbling brook, in the refreshing spring, in the clouds of heaven, in the form of falling snow or of the floating iceberg, etc.

" How common, and yet how beautiful and how pure, is a drop of water ! See it as it issues from the rock to supply the spring and the stream below. See how its meanderings through the plains and its torrents over the cliffs add to the richness and the beauty of the landscape. Look into a factory standing by a waterfall, in which every drop is faithful to perform its part, and hear the groaning and rustling of the wheels, the clattering of shuttles, and the buzz of spindles, which, under the direction of their fair attendants, are supplying myriads of purchasers with fabrics from the cotton-plant, the sheep, and the silkworm."

430. **Exercise.**—Describe a good-natured man, a peevish man ; the display of heroism, of cowardice ; the power of music, of eloquence viewed in various circumstances or situations.

431. 2. **Antecedents.**—It may often be useful in an essay to describe what a man or a thing was at a former time, in order to conjecture thence what may be expected from the same on future occasions. Thus in an essay " On the Early Propagation of Christianity," I may invite the reader to go back in spirit and consider that those wonderful men, the Apostles, who established so sublime a religion in so many lands, had been ignorant and timid fishermen, and

that they could never have accomplished their great mission without the assistance of a higher power, that of God
Himself.

From this same topic an essay on Hume, in the *Dublin
Review* for May, 1842, shows that this writer was utterly
unqualified by his antecedents to become the historian of
England, and therefore that truth cannot be expected from
such a source.

§ 4. *Resemblance and Contrast.*

432. One of the readiest means to understand a subject
clearly and to explain it to others is to compare it with
other matters and trace out certain points of resemblance
or opposition.

1. **Resemblance.**—We may take as an example the labors
of an educator, and compare them with those of the gardener, who raises young plants. The consideration of what
the latter does to foster, to protect from harm, to quicken,
to prune, etc., the objects of his assiduous care, may suggest many analogous duties incumbent on the educator of
human hearts and minds. Again, the enriching of the soul
for heaven may be compared to advantage with the in-
defatigable industry of merchants, who gather wealth for
earth, etc.

Our American essayist, E. P. Whipple, in his essay " On
Words," illustrates the various styles of English writers by
playfully comparing them to various kinds of soldiers.

"Words are more effective when arranged in that order called
style. The great secret of a good style, we are told, is to have proper words in proper places. To marshal one's verbal battalions in
such order that they may bear at once upon all quarters of a subject
is certainly a great art. This is done in different ways. . . . The
tread of Johnson's style is heavy and sonorous, resembling that of an
elephant or a mail-clad warrior. He is fond of levelling an object

.by a polysyllabic battering-ram. Burke's words are continually practising the broad-sword exercise and sweeping down adversaries at every stroke. Arbuthnot 'plays his weapon like a tongue of flame.' Addison draws up his light infantry in orderly array, and marches through sentence after sentence without having his ranks disordered or his line broken," etc.

Addison, in the 153d number of the *Tatler*, compared different characters in conversation to different instruments of music.

433. 2. **Contrast.**—Many subjects may be appropriately illustrated by contrasting them with their opposites, as when modesty is inculcated by making boastfulness odious, when the useful citizen is praised by contrasting him with a man who is a burden to the state. Thus Addison, in the *Guardian* (No. 111), makes the indolence of the British youth of his day odious by contrasting it with the love of knowledge displayed by Julius Cæsar, by Alexander the Great, and by King Solomon.

§ 5. *Authorities and Examples.*

434. Lastly, it may be very useful to consider what others have said and done in connection with the subject on which we are to write. For this purpose we must study authorities and examples.

1. **Authorities** are the sayings of men whose word inspires confidence. Now, though an essay-writer is supposed to give his own views on the subject before him, he is not expected to form those views without considering what thoughtful and well-informed men have said on the same matter. He will exhibit a pleasing modesty by leaning on the judgment of others ; and the authorities quoted, besides showing him to be possessed of learning, will often inspire much more confidence than his own speculations could command. An appropriate quotation of some excel-

lent authority is like a gem in a composition, adding considerably to its brilliancy and its real value. Notice the happy effect of this topic in the following passage of Washington Irving :

" How vain, how fleeting, how uncertain are all those gaudy bubbles after which we are panting and toiling in this world of fair delusion ! The wealth which the miser has amassed with so many weary days, so many sleepless nights, a spendthrift heir may squander away in joyless prodigality. The noblest monuments which pride has ever reared to perpetuate a name the hand of time will shortly tumble into ruins, and even the brightest laurels gained by feats of arms may wither and be for ever blighted by the chilling neglect of mankind. 'How many illustrious heroes,' says the good Boethius, 'who were once the pride and glory of the age, has the silence of historians buried in oblivion !' And this it was that induced the Spartans, when they went to battle, to sacrifice to the Muses, supplicating that their achievements should be worthily recorded. 'Had not Homer tuned his lofty lyre,' observes the elegant Cicero, 'the valor of Achilles had remained unsung.'"

435. 2. **Examples** are remarkable actions of great men proposed for imitation, or referred to as confirming our opinion. Addison, in the *Tatler* (No. 133), begins his essay "On Silence" thus : "Silence is something more magnificent and sublime than the most noble and expressive eloquence, and is, on many occasions, an indication of a great mind." He then refers to several facts of illustrious personages to confirm his proposition, in particular to the silence of the Son of God under calumny and defamation.

ARTICLE II. VARIOUS KINDS OF ESSAYS.

436. The topics just explained will furnish appropriate thoughts for every kind of essays. But the use of these topics, and the treatment and development of them, will differ considerably for the various kinds.

§ 1. *School Essays.*

437. Essays have been written as **school exercises** from time immemorial. The ancient rhetorician Aphthonius explains them with some detail, and in a manner well suited to develop in the student habits of orderly and sensible composition. He proposes to the pupils what he calls a *chria* ($X\rho\varepsilon i\alpha$)—that is, a pregnant or suggestive sentence, borrowed from some author and developed by certain rules. There are three species of this chria:

438. (*a*) The **verbal chria** proposes a wise maxim, as would be the advice Shakspeare puts on the lips of Wolsey:

"Cromwell, I charge thee, fling away ambition."

439. (*b*) The **historical chria** proposes a fact which implies, though it does not express, an important lesson; as:

"Pythagoras required of his disciples that, to learn how to speak, they should be silent for five years."

440. (*c*) The **mixed chria** proposes a fact containing the statement of a maxim; as:

"The mother of the Gracchi exhibited no gold nor pearls; but pointing to her young boys she said, 'These are my jewels.'"

441. To develop any of these species of chria Aphthonius proposes **eight heads** or considerations:

1. A *Commendation* of the sentence proposed, or of its author, by way of introduction. Let it be brief and modest.
2. A *Paraphrase*, expressing the meaning of the sentence in other words, with some further development or explanation.
3. The *Cause* or reason why the maxim is true, or why the fact is such as stated.

4. *Resemblance*, illustrating by comparison with similar things.

5. *Contrast*, illustrating by comparison with contrary things.

6. *Examples.*

7. *Testimonies* or authorities.

8. *Conclusion* addressed to the mind or the heart of the reader. Care should be taken that the transition from one point to another appear natural.

442. One **advantage** derived from so regular an exercise is that the young learn to think and write in an orderly manner, which result is, or should be, one of the great aims of all literary education; for it is one of the chief elements of literary excellence. Still, it is not necessary that the same amount of regularity be observed in all essays, whether written as school exercises or not.

443. There is, besides the regular chria, the free or **loose chria,** as some rhetoricians call it, which allows much more variety of arrangement. Sometimes one or two topics will supply a sufficient amount of appropriate thought, and there is a special advantage in fully developing a few points. In fact, it may be laid down as a rule that one consideration well developed will produce a more effective composition than a great number of separate reflections, each briefly expressed. If we analyze the essays of great writers we shall find that they usually confine their treatment of a subject to few topics.

444. **Example 1.**—Let us consider how Blair does this in his third lecture on Rhetoric. In it he treats of four subjects, giving us, as it were, four different essays, on "Criticism," on "Genius," on the "Pleasures of Taste," and on "Sublimity in Objects."

On *Criticism,* he examines its definition and its nature.

On *Genius*, its nature and a comparison between Genius and Taste.

On the *Pleasures of Taste*, he considers the sources of those pleasures and the authority of Addison.

On *Sublimity in Objects*, the nature and the sources of sublimity.

445. **Example 2.**—His fourteenth lecture is "On Figurative Language." After some introductory remarks he treats :

1. Of the *cause* or origin and of the *nature* of figures.

2. Of the *circumstances* of time, showing that language is most figurative in early ages.

3. Of the *effects* or advantages of figures.

4. He *enumerates* and explains various kinds of figures.

(On Blair's treatment of the topics, see *Art of Oratorical Composition*, 127.)

446. Let the student, then, apply to the study of his subject such topics as he thinks may give him suitable thoughts. He will do well to examine all the topics, and then **select for treatment** those thoughts which appear most appropriate and most within his power of treatment. Let him note in the margin the topic he is developing and the various thoughts suggested by it. For instance, if, with Blair, he considers the nature and the sources of sublimity, let him write in the margin 'Nature,' and then explain what he has to say on that topic ; further on he will write 'Sources,' and then mark, in the order in which he treats them, the different sources, 'Obscurity,' 'Disorder,' 'Moral Sublimity,' and, lastly, the general source, the 'Foundation of the Sublime.'

447. With pupils not sufficiently advanced the teacher may usefully point out the sources which are most likely to furnish appropriate thoughts, and even make out a

sketch to be developed by them, adding special hints for the development of every part.

If he assigns an **essay upon a sensible object,** he will do well to remind the pupils of what has been explained in the chapter on " Object-Lessons," and lay down as a plan the division suggested in Exercise I. of Lesson VI.

It will be proper to begin with such sensible objects as are well known to the students, or on which they can gather information from books put at their disposal.

448. Next will come insensible or **abstract subjects,** such as virtues and vices—for instance, diligence or sloth, courage or cowardice, generosity or selfishness. For the treatment of these the following **plan** may be suggested :

1. Definition or description of the virtue or vice ;
2. Causes in which it originates ;
3. Circumstances in which it is apt to be exhibited ;
4. Effects which it produces ;
5. Comparisons and contrasts ;
6. Authorities and examples.

For the thorough treatment of Order or Arrangement we must refer the student to our *Art of Oratorical Composition* (book iii.)

§ 2. *Magazine Articles.*

449. Modern literature abounds in essays. They fill the pages of our Quarterly Reviews, Monthly Magazines, Weekly and Daily Papers in endless variety and profusion. Many **essays in periodicals** are written with great ability, being the productions of cultivated minds, who strive to condense and to set forth with clearness, for the benefit of the general reader, what has cost them years, perhaps, of study and meditation. But the vast majority of periodical articles are compositions of a very different kind. Even when written by authors of considerable reputation they

are dashed off in haste with a view to excite the interest and to please the craving for novelty of the thoughtless public.

450. As a natural consequence most periodical essays are both **unreliable in matter and defective in form**: far from being good models for the imitation of the young, they falsify taste by preferring apparent to real excellences.

"A magazine," says Macaulay, "is certainly a delightful invention for a very idle or a very busy man. He is not compelled to complete his plan or adhere to his subject. He may ramble as far as he is inclined, and stop as soon as he is tired. No one takes the trouble to recollect his contradictory opinions or his unredeemed pledges. He may be as superficial, as inconsistent, and as careless as he chooses" (*Essays*, "Athenian Orators").

451. **Macaulay's Essays** are striking proofs of these assertions. They contain, indeed, an abundance of original thoughts, suggestive and bold speculations, of real facts and plausible theories; but in many of them truth is blended with fiction, facts are distorted and exaggerated, as if the author were sometimes trying to see to what extent an able pen can trifle with the convictions of ages and still remain within the sphere of plausible argumentation.

452. One of the worst features of periodical essays is that **order,** so essential to real beauty of composition, is much neglected in them, and the minds both of readers and writers lose all power of regular development of thought. Even Orestes A. Brownson, probably the greatest of American essayists, acknowledged in his *Republic* that constant essay-writing had disqualified him for the composition of a regular treatise.

In order that essay-writing may be truly beneficial, systematic arrangement and development must ever be made a prominent point in it, as in all other species of composition. With these cautions great benefit may be derived from the study of our leading essayists, whose productions constitute a rich and important portion of English literature.

453. But while order is necessary in essays, we can lay down **no definite plan** upon which such composition should be written. Maturer minds, at least, must be allowed considerable liberty. Let them study the matter thoroughly and then draw up such a plan in each case as will display their matter to the best advantage. For the study of such power of combination and division we must refer them to the *Art of Oratorical Composition* (book iii.) An essay is in many respects similar to an oration, and we can conceive no better precepts for it than those which ancient and modern rhetoricians have laid down for oratorical composition. Periodical essays may be critical, philosophical, historical, or political.

§ 3. *Critical Essays.*

454. Two things require special explanation in connection with **critical essays**: 1. The general laws of criticism; and 2. The special points to which the critic should attend in composing his essay.

455. **I. General Laws of Criticism.**
The critic is not to be guided by his individual preferences, his likes and dislikes; but he is to judge of literature by the **universally received laws of composition.** These precepts are not the arbitrary dictates of any man or any body of men, but the systematized expression of the judgments pronounced by the most judicious minds in the civilized world, and confirmed by the approbation of many generations. Every new work on Rhetoric or Belles-Lettres is but another attempt to restate those laws or precepts with new illustrations and with particular applica-

tion to special circumstances. In our language Alexander Pope has written a beautiful poetical essay, showing, both by his own example and by his judicious precepts, how the laws of composition ɛre to be applied by the critic. His little work deserves careful study ; but we must here confine ourselves to those directions which are most necessary for the composition of critical essays.

456. **The chief laws of criticism are these:**

1. Let the critic consider with care what is the **real value of the work** he undertakes to criticise. For this purpose it will be useful to compare it with other works written on the same subject, and see in what respects it is superior. Publications which are not, in some important particulars, superior to all other works already existing in the same language are not deserving of recommendation.

457. 2. In judging of the value of a recent work let the critic not be misled by the manner in which it has been received by the press or the general public. The **first welcome given to a book** is not always the result of genuine admiration. " Puffers," says Macaulay, " are a class of people who have more than once talked the people into the most absurd errors, but who surely never played a more curious or more difficult trick than when they passed Mr. Robert Montgomery off upon the world as a great poet." But one of his poems had already gone through eleven editions before Macaulay, by his critique in the *Edinburgh Review* (April, 1830), stemmed the tide of general admiration.

458. 3. Nor should the critic allow himself to be captivated by the **fashions of the day**, or by the mannerism of a prevalent school of art. Acknowledging what is really good in such fashions, which are often reactions against other species of depraved taste, he should judge of per-

fection by the old universal standard and the undoubted maxims of genuine taste.

459. 4. Still, he should not be so **pedantic** as to refuse to see real beauties because marred by some flagrant violations of admitted rules. Shakspeare and others have uncommon beauties mixed with great defects. To reject both were not reasonable; to praise both is not judicious. It is the part of the critic carefully to draw the line between what is good and what is bad.

460. 5. In writing the critique of a commendable composition, more trouble should generally be taken to bring to view its **excellences** than its **shortcomings.** Students in their essays should occupy themselves almost exclusively in showing forth what is really worthy of approbation. To do so will practise their skill and improve their appreciation of the beautiful.

461. 6. Let praise or blame be given with **due moderation.**

> " Avoid extremes; and shun the fault of such
> Who still are pleased too little or too much.
> At every trifle scorn to take offence,
> That always shows great pride or little sense :
> Those heads or stomachs are not sure the best
> Which nauseate all and nothing can digest.
> Yet let not each gay turn thy rapture move :
> For fools admire, but men of sense approve ;
> As things seem large which we through mists descry,
> Dulness is ever apt to magnify."
> *—Pope's Essay on Criticism.*

462. 7. When defects are to be pointed out let it be done with **politeness** and delicacy of speech, so as not to wound susceptibilities more than is necessary. Still, there are occasions when more emphasis is required to counteract the evil which violations of good taste would otherwise produce. Whatever would do injury to religion or moral-

ity should be openly condemned ; and it will generally be found that what is hurtful to these is at the same time a departure from true artistic beauty.

463. 8. Lastly, we must guard the critic against an odious but not uncommon mistake—that of **condemning what he does not thoroughly understand.**

> " But you who seek to give and merit fame,
> And justly bear a critic's noble name,
> Be sure yourself and your own reach to know,
> How far your genius, taste, and learning go ;
> Launch not beyond your depth, but be discreet,
> And mark that point where sense and dulness meet."
>
> —*Id.*

464. **II. The composition of a critical essay.**

It is useful to begin by analyzing the work which is to be criticised, and writing a clear **synopsis** of the same. (See the precepts for Analysis and Synopsis in the *Art of Oratorical Composition*, book iii. c. iv.) This synopsis need not form a part of the critical essay ; but it will aid the writer to understand thoroughly the subject of his criticism. In preparing it he will notice in particular the following points :

1. What the author criticised pretends to prove or to explain, or what appears to be the purpose of his work.

2. What are the difficulties which he has had to overcome.

3. How he enters upon his subject ; what proposition he lays down, if any ; what process he chiefly adopts —whether narrating, discussing, theorizing, etc.

4. What line of thought he follows from the beginning to the end of his composition.

5. What original thoughts occur in the course of the work.

6. To what species of composition the work belongs.

7. What appears to be its chief merit in thoughts, style, etc.

8. How far it accomplishes the purpose for which it was written.

465. The writer should carefully **examine the rules** which rhetoricians have laid down for the species of composition to which the work criticised belongs, and see how they are followed by the author.

After these preparations he will proceed to write the **plan** of his own criticism; in doing which he may profit by the following suggestions:

1. It is often appropriate to begin with a general appreciation of the work criticised; this appreciation should be expressed with accuracy, in a spirit of moderation, and usually of kindness.

2. After this, and sometimes before it, the principles should be explained upon which the criticism is based. If these principles are not generally recognized they should be supported by proofs drawn from reason or from authority.

3. In proceeding to details a lucid order should be followed. It is usually proper to treat first of those items for which the work criticised deserves praise; then to proceed, with expressions of regret, to those items which call for censure.

466. The **style** most appropriate for critical essays is that which is called the *neat* (*supra*, book iii. c. iv. art. 2). As proper models of style we may propose Prescott's, Bancroft's, and Spalding's Miscellanies, Cardinals Wiseman's and Newman's Essays, and Lingard's Tracts.

467. The **tone** of the criticism should usually be kind and respectful, observant of the oratorical precautions and all the laws of literary politeness, even when dealing with

authors who ignore such precepts. (On Politeness and Oratorical Precautions see *Art of Oratorical Composition*, book iv. c. iv. art. 2.)

468. As an **example** we insert a synopsis of Archbishop Spalding's criticism on Prescott's *Conquest of Mexico:*

1. General appreciation of the work, remarks on the style.
2. Brief criticism on the introduction—*i.e.*, the Aztec Civilization.
3. General principles of historical writing—stated, proved, and applied:
    (*a*) Research : diligent and thorough.
    (*b*) Accuracy : general, not universal.
    (*c*) Impartiality : much wanting, proved by quotations.
4. A synopsis of the history, with quotations.
5. Special moral questions debated.
    (*a*) Was the Conquest justifiable? Yes, as shown not *à priori*, but from the facts and from the principles of natural and international law.—The Pope's interference.
    (*b*) Was it stained with wanton cruelty? No. Discussion of details.

§ 4. *Scientific, Historical, and Political Essays.*

469. All the remaining species of essays belong to one of three kinds: **Scientific or Philosophical, Historical,** and **Political** Essays. The first deal with abstract principles, the second with past facts, and the third with future measures. This distinction bears a close resemblance to the division of oratory into Demonstrative, Judicial or Forensic, and Deliberative discourses. (See *Art of Oratorical Composition*, book vi. No. 334.) In fact, essays have almost

everything in common with orations: the invention, the arrangement, the development of thought.

470. Therefore the **precepts** for essay-writing are nearly identical with those treated fully in the *Art of Oratorical Composition.* The chief difference is that essays are read, not spoken. This will affect the **style** and the use of pathos. But even the difference of style is confined to very few points. The essay is not composed in the direct style, which is suitable to speeches (*Ib.* No. 308), nor does it require the same copiousness of treatment (No. 313). Still, this last difference does not affect essays intended for the general reader, especially in an age when readers do so little thinking for themselves.

The earnest pupil who wishes to perfect himself in essay-writing should study thoroughly the work referred to. We shall here add such points as belong more directly to the composition of various essays.

471. **L Scientific or Philosophical Essays.**

Science traces the connection between particular conclusions and general principles. It may treat of religion, of philosophy proper, or of the physical sciences. A Scientific Essay usually takes the form of a **Thesis**—*i.e.*, it lays down a proposition which it undertakes to prove, as 'Man is a free agent'; 'The soul of man is immortal'; 'The theory of spontaneous generation is untenable.'

472. The **plan of a Thesis** usually comprises:

1. An *introduction* to awaken interest. (See *Art of Or. Comp.*, b. iv. c. i.)

2. A *statement* and an *explanation* of the proposition which we undertake to prove.

This should be clear, pointed, and concisely expressed. Any vagueness on this point would be a great defect. (*Ib.* c. ii.)

3. The *proof* or argumentation, containing two parts:

    (*a*) Lay down carefully and establish firmly the first principles from which you intend to draw your conclusion. Do not hurry your readers on to your deductions till they have fully agreed to your principles. Finish this part by reminding them of the truths so far established.

    (*b*) Show by logical and lucid reasoning that your Thesis or proposition follows from those truths. Propose your reasoning in various forms, if necessary; make it striking to every class of your readers. (*Ib.* c. iv. art. i. § 2.)

4. A *refutation* of objections. (*Ib.* § 3.)

5. A *conclusion*, drawing inferences or making practical applications.

473. Scientific essays are at present extensively printed and read in magazines and other periodicals. When intended for the general public they should be written in a popular **style**, elegant and racy, substituting for abstract thoughts al! kinds of clear and apt illustrations. How to adapt such a composition to different classes of readers is explained in connection with Academic Lectures in the *Art of Oratorical Composition* (b. vi. c. iii. art. 3). A noble model for such essays is found in the lectures of Cardinal Manning "On the Four Great Evils of the Day."

474. II. An **Historical Essay** treats of an historical event or an historical character. It may assume various forms; the following are the principal :

475. 1. A connected **Narrative** of an historical event ; such an essay is nothing else than a narration, and the precepts for it have already been given (book iv. c. iii.)

476. 2. A **Biographical Sketch** of an historical personage ; this will be treated under Biography (c. vii.)

477. 3. A **Thesis** to be proved by historical facts ; this

will follow a plan similar to the scientific thesis just explained. Archbishop M. J. Spalding, in the eleventh article of his *Miscellanea* ("On the Spanish Inquisition"), lays down and proves these three theses :

    (*a*) The Spanish Inquisition was mainly a political institution, and the result of extraordinary political circumstances ;

    (*b*) Its cruelties have been greatly exaggerated ;

    (*c*) The Catholic Church is not responsible for the institution itself, much less for its abuses, real or alleged (p. 222).

His whole "Chapter on Mobs" (p. 619) is an historical thesis proving that "mobs cannot put down truth and virtue."

478. 4. A **Dissertation,** presenting different views entertained by different historians on some event or character. This kind of essay is not bound down to any definite plan ; still, it should observe the rules of all good compositions respecting unity of subject, an orderly process, and clear development.

Of this species is the essay of J. C. Calhoun which he entitles " A Discourse on the Constitution and Government of the United States " (*Works,* vol. i.)

Other examples are found in various chapters of Balmes' *European Civilization ; or, Protestantism and Catholicity compared in their Effects on the Civilization of Europe,* a work of extraordinary ability. Chapter ii. contains a brief dissertation "On the Causes of Protestantism."

479. 5. A **disquisition** or systematic inquiry into a special historical question. The essay must confine itself to that one question, and explain lucidly :

    (*a*) What is the exact point at issue ;

    (*b*) What views are entertained by different parties regarding it ;

(*c*). What reasons are urged by them in support of their several views ;

(*d*) What the author considers to be the true solution, and how far it appears to be certain ;

(*e*) What reasons support his conclusion.

See J. C. Calhoun's "Disquisition on Government" (*Works*, vol. i.)

Another example is found in Archbishop M. J. Spalding's criticism of Prescott's *Conquest of Mexico* (analyzed in No. 468) ; he discusses in particular :

(*a*) Was Cortez justifiable in attempting the subjugation of Mexico ?

(*b*) Were the conquerors wantonly cruel ?

480. **III. Political Essays**, like political speeches, are of a practical nature, regarding measures advocated or opposed. They occur most commonly as editorials in newspapers. **Editorials** are such leading articles as formally express the editor's opinions on the current topics of the day ; they must be distinguished from mere news reports, communications, clippings, etc.

481. News articles simply record the facts of the day, while editorials discuss the leading events, commending or condemning, explaining or defending, convincing and exhorting, assigning causes and suggesting remedies, also pointing out tendencies and probable consequences—in a word, giving the philosophy of present history. Hence the style is very different : news must be stated clearly, accurately, briefly ; editorials must be written eloquently.

482. The **importance of Editorials** at present is uncommonly great. They are the teachers of the age, exerting the widest and most telling influence for good or evil, truth or falsehood, sound or corrupt morality. They replace songs in O'Connell's saying : "Give me the making of a nation's songs, and I care not who makes its laws."

483. **Their aim** should be to inculcate and defend sound principles of private morality and public virtue, expose present events in their true light, trace their true causes, tendencies, and probable consequences ; expose public vice and falsehood, unmask false pretenders and public quacks, uphold the noble traditions and aspirations of the country. Editors should be the advocates of right and truth at the bar of public opinion.

484. The **style of editorials** is of a high order, combining popularity with judicial dignity, vigor with moderation, simplicity with the various charms of eloquence.

Editorials, and all essays written for practical purposes, bear a very close resemblance to speeches addressed to popular assemblies. No better precepts can be laid down for the thorough study of them than the rules given for Deliberative Oratory ; these should be as carefully studied by editors as by popular orators. (See *Art cf Oratorical Composition*, book vi. c. i.)

CHAPTER VI.

DIALOGUES.

485. A **Dialogue** is a conversation between two or more persons. Among the ancients this species of composition was carried to great perfection. Their dialogues were of two kinds, the *descriptive* and the *didactic* or philosophical.

486. The **descriptive** kind was used by Lucian for the portrayal of characters. We have elsewhere spoken of the description of characters. **Lucian,** instead of describing them in his own words, introduces his personages as speaking. He makes the pagan gods and the souls of the dead converse among themselves in such a way as to exhibit marked traits of character, and he does this in a lively, interesting manner. His object is to show forth the absurdities of pagan superstitions.

487. **Didactic** or philosophical dialogues were written with great elegance by Plato, and, after his example, by Cicero. These authors introduced learned men discussing some important subject, in an easy and natural manner, with great refinement of thought and language. Their purpose was the same as that of philosophical essays; but the conversational form added special charm to the composition. The personages introduced were such as would command attention; they were placed in situations interesting to the reader, and made to converse in language consistent with their respective characters.

488. As an **example** we may take the dialogue of Plato styled *Phædon.* A discourse on the immortality of the

soul is put on the lips of the philosopher Socrates, and addressed by him to his disciples, under circumstances which make it remarkably impressive. It was the day at the close of which the philosopher was to drink hemlock in punishment of his teachings. His disciples had gathered round him in his prison to show their esteem and affection for their master. Every one must feel that such circumstances add far more weight to the philosopher's words than an abstract essay could possess.

489. **Plato** in his dialogues never speaks in his own person ; but **Cicero** proceeds differently. He dedicates his compositions to some friend, and explains to him who his characters are, why he has chosen them, and under what circumstances they are supposed to discourse. His conversations "On Old Age," "On Friendship," and "On the Orator" are special favorites with classical scholars.

490. **English literature** has not produced any acknowledged masterpieces in this species of composition. But we have many scenes in dramas and in novels exhibiting characters as strikingly as do the dialogues of Lucian—*e.g.*, the quarrel between Brutus and Cassius in Shakspeare's "Julius Cæsar" ; the examination of Sam Weller by Sergeant Buzfuz in Dickens' *Pickwick Papers ;* the character of the Martyr's Boy in Cardinal Wiseman's *Fabiola* (c. ii.).

491. Of the **philosophical dialogue** we have a good specimen in *Brownson's Review* for 1854, styled "Uncle Jack and his Nephew," and another in the *Month* for November, 1869, styled "The Dialogues of Sydney." A late work by St. George Mivart, entitled *Nature and Thought*, is an imitation of Cicero's dialogues. In modern times didactic treatises usually assume the form of essays ; when conversation is introduced at all it is wont to be combined with so much incident as to be classed among Novels. Samuel Johnson's *Rasselas* is of this nature.

492. Dialogues are subject to the following **rules**:

1. They must create interest by presenting lifelike characters, placed in interesting situations, and conversing in a natural and unaffected manner.

2. If didactic they must treat of some theme, and develop it with sufficient regularity, so as to give a clear insight into the views of the author on that subject.

3. They must be replete with wisdom, or at least with good sense.

4. They must be couched in refined language, with tasteful and modest ornament.

493. **Exercise I.** Write a descriptive dialogue exhibiting the character of a miser, a spendthrift, a fop, a flatterer, a young hero. (For a model see *Fabiola*, c. ii.)

494. **Exercise II.** Write a didactic conversation on the advantages of a thorough education, of music, of good company; on the Crusades, the Inquisition, on Galileo. (For a model see a dialogue between Fabiola and her slave Syra in the sixteenth chapter of *Fabiola*.)

CHAPTER VII.

NOVELS.

495. A **Novel** is a fictitious narrative in prose, embracing a complete series of events, and exhibiting some phase of human life.

Such phases of human life are, for instance:

(*a*) *Peculiar conditions of society*, as in Dickens' *Oliver Twist*, Cooper's *The Last of the Mohicans*, his *Leather-stocking Tales*, etc.

(*b*) The *manners of certain periods* of history, as in historical novels generally. Such are Cardinal Wiseman's *Fabiola*, Cardinal Newman's *Callista*, B. O'Reilly's *Victims of the Mamertine*, McKeon's *Dion and the Sibyls*, Bailey's *Pearl of Antioch*, Conscience's *Lion of Flanders*, Lady Fullerton's *Constance Sherwood* and *Too Strange not to be True*.

(*c*) The *workings of the passions*, as in Goldsmith's *Vicar of Wakefield*, Thackeray's *Vanity Fair*, etc.

(*d*) The *tendencies of institutions* and popular movements, as in Bresciani's *Jew of Verona* and *Lionello*, and in Brownson's *Spirit-Rapper*.

(*e*) *Peculiar views of the world*, as in Dickens' *Christmas Carols*.

496. Some novels may be called **philosophical,** being intended to set forth special views and systems of doctrine. To this class belong religious novels. In all such it is important that not only the doctrines inculcated be sound, but also that the composition possess literary beauty and

proper interest, and that the moral tone of the characters be favorable to virtue. We can mention no more excellent model than the *Fabiola* referred to above. Gen. Lew Wallace's *Ben-Hur* deserves praise.

497. Others are called **Society Novels**: these are usually written to ridicule the extravagances of prevalent tastes and practices, thus answering the same purpose as comedy. Such is Bulwer's *My Novel*. Many of these give little attention to plot, being chiefly taken up with the exhibition of character. All such compositions may be useful in their way; but unfortunately not many can be recommended for the perusal of those who care to keep their hearts undefiled by the contamination of vice.

498. **Sensational Novels** are still more objectionable. These stir up the passions by frequent vivid sketches of exaggerated and unreal scenes. They create a morbid craving for exciting stories, and impair that calm of mind which is an essential element of a prudent and considerate character.

499. Well-written novels possess certain **advantages** over other species of literature:

    1. They reach those who will not read more serious books;

    2. They may fill up profitably an occasional hour of needed relaxation, even with earnest men;

    3. They may widen the reader's knowledge of the world;

    4. If well chosen they may improve his heart;

    5. They may enlarge his stock of words and phrases.

500. The **objections** universally urged against promiscuous novel-reading are numerous; the principal are:

    1. They cause great waste of time;

    2. They produce desultory habits of mind, which disqualify a person for earnest attention to duty;

3. They give false views of life;

4. They make the reader familiar with vice and vicious characters, thus lowering his standard of virtue by showing that many others are worse than himself;

5. They often make vices look like virtues, or at least like excusable foibles;

6. They develop in the reader that spirit of the world which is diametrically opposed to the spirit of Christ.

(See further objections to novel-reading in Jenkins' *British and American Literature*, pp. 322, etc.)

501. There are **two schools** of novelists, the *realistic* and the *ideal*. The **ideal** is the older school; it has more of the spirit of poetry. It presents men not as they usually are, but as they may exceptionally be, and as we love to imagine them—more noble, more disinterested, more heroic. Such novels are called Romances; most French novels belong to this class. Their effect on the reader is often elevating, analogous to that produced by epic and tragic poetry; but they are apt to become unreal and extravagant, as were the tales of knight-errantry in the Middle Ages. They are also liable to another objection, for they often exalt passions that should rather be checked, in particular the passion of love, which up to the time of Walter Scott made up the plot of nearly all novels.

502. The **realistic** school is more prosaic; it is also more favorable to common sense. It is well exemplified in the novels of Charles Dickens. It describes men and things just as they are, and makes persons act in a probable, natural manner. This process also has its inconveniences. Brownson is severe on Dickens for making his readers so familiar with vulgar and vicious characters.

503. Most of the precepts that should direct this species

of composition have been treated in this work under the heads of Narration (book iv. c. iii.) and Description (c. iv.) We shall here add a few **special rules.**

Rule 1.—Let the novel be **interesting** to the class of read-ers for whom it is intended ; some novels written for very laudable purposes are undeniably dull.

Rule 2.—It should **aim at a higher purpose** than mere amusement—namely, to deck valuable knowledge and true wisdom in the pleasing garb of fiction, so as to captivate the imagination, and thus more readily gain mind and heart to what is worthy of man.

Rule 3.—It should give a right direction and a **healthy tone** to the passions. No amount of interest can atone for the slightest injury to mind and heart.

Rule 4.--It should, in order to be a true work of art, either portray **characters** in a very natural and pleasing manner, or excite great interest by a well-developed **plot,** combining variety of incident with unity of the general plan.

504. **Novelists.**—De Foe was the father of the Eng-lish novel as distinguished from the more romantic tales of knight-errantry ; Fielding and Richardson soon followed him ; but those novelists are now almost forgotten by the general public. Every year brings new authors into gene-ral notice. But none, perhaps, have gained so continued and general favor as Walter Scott.

Novelists are by this time so numerous that it were vain to attempt a criticism upon their respective merits. Ger-ald Griffin, the Banim Brothers, Marion Crawford, Miss Rosa Mulholland, Christian Reid, Kathleen O'Meara—also known as Grace Ramsay—and especially Bolanden, may be mentioned, in addition to those referred to with praise in the above precepts, as novelists that have written in a moral spirit ; while George Eliot, Victor Hugo, Charles

Reade, Wilkie Collins, George Sand, Balzac, and many others are immoral and often blasphemous. Bulwer's early novels are objectionable, but his later ones are better.

505. **Exercise.**—Analyze a novel according to the following plan :

1. What is known of the author ?
2. To what school or class of novels does the work belong ?
3. Is a definite purpose, philosophical, political, moral, or religious, discernible in the novel ?
4. What is the plot ? Analyze it briefly.
5. In what lies the principal excellence of the work ?
6. What are its leading characters and how naturally are they presented throughout ?
7. Is the style beautiful and properly varied to suit the different characters ?
8. What of the descriptions ? the narration ? the dialogues ?

CHAPTER VIII.

HISTORY.

506. History is **one of the noblest studies** to which man can devote himself. Cicero styles it :

" The witness of ages, the light of truth, the life of our memory, the teacher of our lives, a messenger from the distant past " (*De Or.*, ii. 9).

Frederick Schlegel remarks :

" History constitutes the apparently easy and first elements of all instruction ; and yet the more cultivated the mind of a man becomes, the more multiplied opportunities will he find of applying it and turning it to use, the more will he discern its richness and divine its deeper sense. Indeed, no thinker is so profound as to be able to anticipate with accuracy the course of history, no scholar so learned as to think he has exhausted it, and no sovereign so powerful that he may with impunity disregard its silent teachings " (*Lectures on Modern History, I.*)

507. The **kind of instruction** that history affords is most precious, for it enables us to gather with comparatively little trouble that knowledge which others have acquired by long, and often bitter, experience ; it enables one man to profit by the lives of millions. As he travels in mind through various lands and successive ages, he observes the customs of diverse nations, their manners of worship, of government, of warfare, of commerce, and of agriculture ; their cultivation or their neglect of the liberal and the useful arts ; and he becomes acquainted with the characters of men and the workings of the human pas-

sions. Thus his mind is enlarged, his views are extended, and he gathers wisdom for his own conduct, learning what course of life leads to success, and what other course leads to destruction.

ARTICLE I. NATURE AND GENERAL LAWS OF HISTORY.

508. **History is defined** as the narrative of past events for the instruction of mankind Instruction, then, is its end or purpose. Should this instruction embrace all the information that can be drawn from the study of past ages? Macaulay would require this (Essay on Mitford's *Greece*) ; but in doing so he departs from the approved way and he aims at what is visionary and unattainable. He acknowledges that such an historian as he desires has never existed ; and Prescott remarks : " Such a monster never did and never can exist" (Essay on Irving's *Conquest of Granada*).

The historian who strives to compass more than he can will necessarily neglect some part of his task ; and the danger is that he will neglect what is less attractive but more truly important.

509. There are two classes of details which **the historian will properly omit** and leave to other writers :

1. Whatever affords **mere gratification of curiosity** rather than valuable information. Such matters, as Macaulay acknowledges, are usually left to the historical novelist :

" Mr. Sismondi publishes a grave and stately history, very valuable and a little tedious. He then sends forth as a companion to it a novel, in which he attempts to give a lively representation of characters and manners. . . . We manage these things better in England. Sir Walter Scott gives us a novel ; Mr. Hallam a critical and argumentative history. Both are occupied with the same matter" (*Essays,* " Hallam").

Macaulay has striven to unite both elements, but with little success. His *History of England* has all the charms of a novel ; but " it is not a student's book, and could no more be quoted as an authority than Shakspeare " (*Dublin Review*, June, 1856, " Hallam"). " Everybody reads, everybody admires, but nobody believes in Macaulay " (*Blackwood's Magazine*, August, 1856).

510. 2. What is of no importance for the general student, but **interesting to specialists only,** should not overload the pages of a general history. There are special histories of painting, music, commerce, etc. ; but history proper deals with such matters in so far only as they are intimately connected with great events and lessons of wisdom, which are the specialty of history as such. For history is not a collection of universal knowledge, but a special department of study.

511. What knowledge, then, or **what special instruction is the historian to impart ?** We answer, the knowledge of the great events and important changes which have affected mankind, in as far as the knowledge of these increases the wisdom of succeeding generations. This is what the greatest historians have endeavored to record, and for the proper recording of which they have been considered as great historians. Tacitus troubled himself very little about " rummaging the old-fashioned wardrobe " of Tiberius—a task which Macaulay would impose upon the historian—but he unmasked the hypocrisy of that prince and showed the world how he destroyed the liberty of Rome.

512. Among the great events and important changes that the historian is to record, **the principal are** those which affect religion and systems of government, military achievements, the progress or decay of liberty, of general enlightenment, or of the arts and sciences, and whatever is prominent in the civilization of a people.

513. There is one line of thought in which modern historians are expected to improve on the ancients. We attach more importance now to **the welfare of the people** than to the splendor of public exploits, and justly so, because we understand better than the ancients did that the true end of government is the happiness of the governed. The modern historian must therefore take more pains to point out what measures led to the happiness and what to the sufferings of the common people. This task is more important than the descriptions of battles and sieges, which make up so extensive a portion of ancient histories. On this point Macaulay is correct :

"The circumstances which have most influenced the happiness of mankind, the changes of manners and morals, the transition of communities from poverty to wealth, from knowledge to ignorance, from ferocity to humanity—these are for the most part noiseless revolutions. Their progress is rarely indicated by what historians are pleased to call important events. . . . The upper-current of society presents no certain criterion by which we can judge of the direction in which the under-current flows. We read of defeats and victories, but we know that nations may be miserable amidst victories and prosperous amidst defeats. . . . We have read books called histories of England, under the reign of George II., in which the rise of Methodism is not even mentioned" (*Essays,* " History ").

514. Since the purpose of history is instruction, **the great law for history** is that it shall impart sound knowledge, giving us true facts, faithfully presented and correctly interpreted. Truth is to the mind what food is to the body—an essential requisite for its proper development and healthy condition. For the absence of truth from histories nothing can atone—no style, however beautiful ; no name, however popular.

515. Still, **all errors are not equally important.** If an historian is somewhat mistaken about the number of men who perished in a given battle, about the armor of certain

troops or the name of their commander, such errors do not seriously interfere with the lessons of wisdom which the reader is expected to learn. But those errors are most pernicious which affect practical conclusions; above all, when those conclusions regard the highest interests of mankind. Thus Hume, who so misrepresents many facts as to instil infidelity; Gibbon, who labors to undermine Christianity; Macaulay, who incessantly carps at Catholicity; and Bancroft, who, while patronizing all religions, inculcates indifferentism to all positive teaching—far from instructing, lead men astray on subjects which it is their highest interest to understand aright.

516. It is not here supposed that all these historians have set themselves deliberately to work to misrepresent what they knew to be the truth. **The critic** deals with the literary productions themselves, and with the motives of the writers in so far only as they throw light upon the value of the works. As for the **student of history,** he ought to inquire before reading whether the author is a reliable guide, whether he is sound on the first principles of reason and revelation. If he is not sound on these he will be sure to mislead. "Can the blind lead the blind? do they not both fall into the ditch?" (Luke vi. 39).

ARTICLE II. SOURCES OF HISTORICAL KNOWLEDGE.

517. *Rule* 1.—In gathering materials for a history the writer should, as far as possible, **consult the original documents,** and not be satisfied with taking statements at secondhand. Lingard's conduct in this respect is worthy of imitation:

"To render these volumes more deserving of public approbation," he writes in his preface to the *History of England,* "I did not hesitate, at the commencement of my labors, to impose on myself a severe obligation from which I am not conscious of having on any occasion materially swerved : to take nothing upon trust ; to confine my researches, in the first instance, to original documents and the more ancient writers, and only to consult the modern historians when I had satisfied my own judgment and composed my own narrative. My object was to preserve myself from copying the mistakes of others, to keep my mind unbiassed by their opinions and prejudices, and to present to the reader from authentic sources a full and correct relation of events."

518. It is owing in great part to the **neglect of this rule** that misconceptions and misstatements are handed down from one historian to another. For instance, how often do we not hear of the cruel dungeon in which Galileo is supposed to have been incarcerated, when in reality he was simply forbidden to leave for some time the halls and gardens of a magnificent palace? (See the collection of original documents regarding Galileo in the *Dublin Review*, vol. xvii., New Series. On the transmission of false statements from one historian to another, see an interesting chapter in Cardinal Newman's *Present Position of Catholics in England*, pp. 226, etc.)

519. The original **documents to be consulted** are not only books, deeds, journals, chronicles, memoirs, official records, private letters, etc., but even such relics of the past as buildings, tombs, coins, paintings, tools, and so forth. Lately much light has been thrown on some portions of history by the study of such relics. Still, we must distinguish between the real facts which these studies have discovered and the mere theories which historians and scientists are ever inventing to fill up the void left by the facts.

520. **The Holy Scriptures** are, of course, the most venerable and the most reliable source of historic knowledge : besides being inspired by the Holy Spirit, they are, even from a human point of view, the most ancient and the most

authentic documents. (See Southwall's *Recent Origin of Man*, Preface.) Vain men are ever building up theories, and exploring every remnant of former ages, with the view to find contradictions between God's word and the records of time. But the highest authorities in antiquarian researches, such as the two brothers Rawlinson, Lenormant, Chevallier, and others, have sufficiently shown that there is no real conflict between science and revelation.

521. *Rule* 2.—Distinguish carefully between **reliable and unreliable documents.** Not every document, however ancient, is truthful ; nor is it enough that a writer is a contemporary of an event to be a reliable witness of it. The historian must know how to sift his evidence with acute discrimination, as a judge must do with conflicting testimony. Within this century there has been considerable earnestness displayed by leading historians in discovering the truth on many points which had been misunderstood for ages. Niebuhr has made important discoveries bearing on the history of ancient Rome. Voigt and Roscoe, though not Catholics, have restored the honor of Gregory VII. and of Leo X. ; Hallam and Ranke have labored zealously in the cause of truth, though both are prejudiced witnesses ; Maitland has, to a considerable extent, changed the views of the learned in favor of the middle ages ; and the Cathotholic historian Digby has set forth the true grandeur of those Ages of Faith. (On Hallam see *Dublin Review*, vols. xix., xx., New Series. See also Maitland's *Reformation*, Essay I. "On Puritan Veracity.")

522. As examples of unreliable documents from which writers have often drawn gross falsehoods, we may mention the two historians of the Spanish Inquisition, **Limborch** and **Llorente,** who have supplied Prescott with most of his misrepresentations on that subject. Both are utterly unreliable writers, as is proved to evidence in Archbishop M. J.

Spalding's *Miscellanea* (pp. 216, etc. ; see also Balmes' *European Civilization*, appendix). Prescott admits the extravagant exaggerations of Llorente ; but unfortunately he has thought it proper to consign this important admission to a foot-note which he puts near the end of his work (*History of Ferdinand and Isabella*, vol. iii. p. 492), while he takes special trouble to exalt the authority of Llorente in the chapter on the Inquisition (vol. i. p. 265), to which he purposely appends a sketch of Llorente's life.

523. Late historians owe much of their reliability to the fact that they have gained more free access to authentic documents than was granted to their predecessors. For instance, Agnes Strickland in her *Lives of the Queens of England and Scotland*, and Lingard in his *History of England*, have been allowed to consult the English State papers ; and now the Vatican archives have been thrown open to all comers.

ARTICLE III. QUALITIES REQUIRED IN AN HISTORIAN.

524. The *first quality* which an historian will need in collecting his materials is **industry**—hard, long, and persevering labor. Lucian, in his *Treatise on the Manner of Writing History*, correctly remarks :

" This is not a task for fluent writers or careless compilers ; but more than any other species of literature it requires much thought, if the historian wishes to produce what Thucydides calls a treasure that will endure for ever " (ch. v.)

525. Of industry **the ancients** have given us bright examples. Herodotus travelled over the greater part of the then known world. Thucydides began to collect his documents at the beginning of the war of which he intended to become the historian. Polybius travelled much

to visit those places with which remarkable events were connected. From him we have this celebrated maxim: "Truth is to history what eyes are to animals. As animals are of no use without sight, so history without truth is only amusing and unprofitable narration."

526. Most eminent **historians of modern times** have displayed no less industry. Prescott's laborious research is unquestionable.

"He has thoroughly examined," says Archbishop M. J. Spalding, "and seems to have carefully sifted all the original documents relating to the Conquest [of Mexico]. . . . He obtained no less than 8,000 pages of unpublished documents. He was also greatly aided in this task by men of distinguished talent in Mexico" (*Miscellanea*, p. 252).

527. David Hume, on the contrary, is notoriously deficient in research. He wrote before the critical school of history began ; he consulted no original documents ; he did not weigh his second-hand authorities ; he simply wished to write a pleasant narrative in a faultless style. Hence the *North American Review* says of nim : "That any instructor in our day should place Hume's work in the hands of a youth, leaving him to suppose that it contained the truth, is to us a matter of no little surprise." (See a thorough criticism of Hume in the *Dublin Review* for May, 1842.)

528. The *second quality* needed by an historian is **impartiality**. This does not consist in being indifferent to justice and injustice, good and evil, as the infidel critic Taine pretends to be.

"What matters it," he writes, "if Peter or Paul is a rascal ? That is the business of his contemporaries ; they suffered from his vices, and ought to think only of despising or contemning him. Now we are beyond his reach, and hatred has disappeared with the danger. At this distance, and in the historic perspective, I see in him but a mental machine, provided with certain springs, animated by a primary impulse, affected by various circumstances," etc. (*English Literature*, vol. ii. p. 407).

This is an absurd indifference, which can only be justified on Taine's own theory : " Vice and virtue are products, like vitriol and sugar " (vol. i. Introduction). Still, such indifference is not seldom exhibited by writers of unsound principles.

529. The impartiality required of' the historian is the absence of such **prejudice** as would prevent him from discovering or from acknowledging the truth. For instance, a person raised in a mercantile community and destitute of a liberal education is apt to appreciate no enterprise which does not add to the wealth of the nation. He may readily be blinded by prejudice to such a point that he will judge a grand enterprise like the Crusades by no other rule than that of cold utilitarianism.

How far prejudice has affected historians in regard to religious questions is ably explained by Cardinal Newman in his *Lectures on the Present Position of Catholics in England* (L. i., etc.)

530. The *third quality* needed by the historian is **discrimination**, which will enable him to determine :

    (*a*) What documents are reliable ;

    (*b*) What is the real meaning of obscure passages in reliable documents ; and

    (*c*) Which is the true or the most probable among conflicting testimonies.

The ancients did not generally manifest this critical spirit. Still, even Herodotus takes care to distinguish between what he witnessed and what he heard, between what he considered as probable and what as fabulous. In the present century history is become much more critical than ever before ; but it is far from perfection as yet. For instance, Fra Paolo, alias Pietro Sarpi, continues to be quoted as an authority about the Council of Trent, though it is clearly proved that he wrote under the dictation of passion and bitter hatred.

Judicious discrimination supposes in the historian a keen insight into the characters and the passions of men, so as to discern the selfish motives which may impair the value of his authorities.

ARTICLE IV. HISTORY GENERALLY RELIABLE.

531. Mankind has exhibited in all ages a high appreciation of fidelity in historical records; and historians have, as a rule, striven earnestly to discover and transmit the truth. It may, therefore, be safely asserted that **history is generally reliable.** Several **reasons** contribute to make it so:

1. Man is naturally desirous of discovering the truth on important matters;

2. It is a principle of Ethics that men do not deceive wantonly when important interests are at stake; and, therefore, even questions of life and death are unhesitatingly decided by the testimony of proper witnesses;

3. When historians have gone to great trouble to discover the truth with regard to events, they are not apt to trifle with knowledge so laboriously acquired;

4. If one is tempted by special considerations to misrepresent some weighty events, others will unite their testimony to contradict him, and thus no gross errors are apt to be universally received.

532. What, then, must we think of the well-known saying of Sir Robert Walpole to his son Horace, "Quote me not history; for that I know to be false"? This means that not every assertion found in a history is to be at once received as decisive. Thus understood, the caution is a wise one. We should **read history with a critical spirit,** with careful discrimination between reliable and unreliable au-

thors. When history is thus read it will be found that the vast majority of past events are agreed on by historians, and therefore it would be folly to refuse credence to them. It will appear, besides, that falsifications concurred in by many historians are confined to special classes of events. If copious streams of error have been poured out upon the earth, those streams can be shown to flow from certain sources and along determined channels which it is quite possible to distinguish from the general currents of reliable information.

533. Against our thesis, "history is generally reliable," **it may be objected** that so great an authority as Count de Maistre has said : "The history of the last three centuries is a general conspiracy against the truth." And our Supreme Pontiff, Leo XIII., in a late encyclical letter on historical studies, writes : "Now, if ever, it may justly be said that the art of writing history would seem to be a conspiracy against the truth." But it must be noticed that both these authorities speak of special departments of history, of such as bear upon the Catholic Church.

534. That the **history of the Church** should have been greatly misrepresented by her opponents need not surprise us. Christ had foretold that His Church should be persecuted. "If you had been of the world, the world would love its own," etc. (John xv. 18–22). The persecution of the sword has ceased, but other methods of attack are continuing in all ages.

"It was natural," says the Pontiff, "that those who were attacking the Papacy by every means in their power should not spare history, the witness of such great facts. They have tampered with her integrity, and that with such persistent art as to turn into weapons of offence the very arms that were most suited to the purpose of warding off aggression. The Centuriators of Magdeburgh made themselves conspicuous by their adoption of this system," etc.

He proceeds to show that their example was followed by the opponents of the Church generally. Unfortunately most English writers have ranked themselves with her enemies. How this hostility has led to various systems of falsification we shall have occasion to explain in the next article.

ARTICLE V. SPECIAL SOURCES OF ERROR.

535. **The law of truthfulness** in historical writings is thus expressed by Cicero:

"Who does not know that the first law of history is that it shall dare say nothing false, next that it shall not fear to tell the whole truth, again that the narration suggest no suspicion of favor or enmity?" (*De Or.*, ii. 15).

This wise rule may be **violated in four ways,** which constitute so many sources of error—namely, by *false assertions*, by the *suppression of facts*, by *partiality*, by prejudice or *hostility*. There is a fifth source of error, less familiar to the ancients—*i.e.*, the misrepresentation of facts by *false theories*.

§ 1. *False Statements.*

536. No truly great historian would deliberately stain his pages with **false statements.** When these occur they are usually the result of misinformation, of prejudice, or of such party spirit as blinds the mind to the light of truth. As examples of false statements, the **results of misinformation,** we may refer to the works of Herodotus and Diodorus Siculus, and to the portions of Rollin which are drawn from those unreliable authorities. Lenormant and Chevalier speak with great respect of those authors; but they judiciously add:

"To reproduce as a whole the facts which they relate, and to give them as an account of the chain of principal events in Egyptian or Abyssinian history, . . . would convey an absolutely untrue idea" (*History of the East*, Introduction).

Happily, Rawlinson's notes in his edition of Herodotus correct most of the errors in the original. Lenormant and Chevalier's *History of the East* now replaces the corresponding parts of Rollin.

537. Of false statements **resulting from a violent partisan spirit** James Meline points out many examples occurring in Froude's *History of England.* (See a series of articles on Froude in the *Catholic World* for 1870.)

538. **Misquoting and mistranslating documents** is a method of falsification that comes under the head of false statements. In this connection it has been said " Mr. Froude does not seem to have fully grasped the meaning of inverted commas." (For examples of this defect see *Catholic World* for October, 1870, p. 73 ; and *Month* for 1879, p. 142.)

539. It is usual for great historians to give in **marginal notes** references to their authorities for every important statement. Prescott blames the earlier editions of Bancroft's *History of the United States* for discarding notes and abridging references, and he points out the evil results of this practice (*Miscellanies*, p. 327). The last edition of Bancroft has omitted references, and is now merely a popular book, no longer a work of great authority. (See articles on Bancroft in the *Catholic World* for 1883–84.)

540. How **documents may be distorted** from their real meaning by designing men is exemplified by the efforts of Gibbon to cast a doubt on the testimony of the Sacred Scriptures. Three Evangelists narrate that there was darkness over all the earth at the death of our Blessed Saviour. Gibbon, to invalidate their testimony, says among other things : " A distinct chapter of Pliny is designed for

eclipses of an extraordinary nature and unusual duration"
(chap. xv.)   Now, Pliny pretends to give only an example,
and the distinct chapter referred to is only this brief paragraph, which we quote entire :

"There happen wonderful and protracted eclipses" [notice the
plural number], "as was the one which occurred when Cæsar had
been slain, and while the war of Antony was carried on, at which
time the sun was pale for a whole year continuously" (Pliny, *Hist.
Nat.*, ii. 30).

§ 2. *Suppression of Facts.*

541. Witnesses before our courts of justice are made to
swear that they will tell "the truth, the whole truth, and
nothing but the truth."   The reason is that the **suppression of facts** may be, and often is, equivalent to a false
statement.   This suppression is another of the disingenu-
ous methods by which Gibbon attacks the Christian religion.   Prescott writes :

"He [Gibbon] has often slurred over in the text such particulars
as might reflect most credit on the character of the religion, or
shuffled them into a note at the bottom of the page, while all that
admits of a doubtful complexion in its early propagation is osten-
tatiously blazoned and set in contrast to the most amiable features
of paganism," etc. (Essay on *Conquest of Granada*).

It is a remarkable illustration of the power of prejudice
that Prescott, who has written this correct criticism of Gibbon, should have incurred a similar reproach in his writings.   He has described the conversion of Mexico to
Christianity in a manner analogous to Gibbon's method
of accounting for the early rise of Christianity in the
Roman Empire.   (See Spalding's *Miscellanea*, p. 293.)

542. Are there not some **details which an historian
may properly suppress?**   There certainly are; for as
history aims at useful instruction, whatever can in no

way contribute to this purpose is to be omitted ; for instance, the scandalous details of the voluptuous lives of Tiberius and Heliogabalus. But only details are to be suppressed, not important facts ; thus the life of David would be incomplete without the story of his fall into sin. Such events are important for the instruction of mankind, and as such they are related both by profane and sacred writers. It is not usually expedient, in writing the life of Luther, to quote freely from the shocking vulgarities of his *Table Talk ;* but it is a falsification of history to garble some of the extracts without warning the reader, as is done in Bohn's edition.

543. In encyclopædias, and similar works of reference, falsification by suppression of facts is often carried very far. Thus in the latest edition of the *Encyclopædia Britannica*, a work of high pretensions, the article on " Missions to the Heathens " suppresses and ignores almost all the facts regarding Catholic missions. (See a detailed criticism of the article in the *Dublin Review* for July, 1884.)

§ 3. *Partiality.*

544. It is not required, nor is it even desirable, that the historian shall feel no **speoial affeotion** for the nation whose history he writes. In fact, unless he can sincerely sympathize with the actors of his story he will scarcely do justice to their motives :

" Who would think," asks Prescott, " of looking to a Frenchman for a history of England ? to an Englishman for the best history of France ? Ill fares it with the nation that cannot find writers of genius to tell its own story. What foreign hand could have painted like Herodotus and Thucydides the achievements of the Greeks ? Who like Livy and Tacitus have portrayed the shifting character of the Roman in his rise, meridian, and fall ? Had the Greeks trusted their story to these same Romans, what would have been their fate with posterity ? Let the Carthaginians tell " (*Miscellanies,* " Bancroft ").

Washington Irving did not sympathize with the Span-iards in their struggle for independence from Moorish domination : the result is that his *Conquest of Granada* fails to bring out the true spirit of that heroic enterprise ; the work looks like the parody of a history.

545. But, on the other hand, **excessive sympathy** with a cause often leads to serious misrepresentations, and gross injustice towards its opponents. Livy is severely blamed for such partiality to Rome. Still, it must be remembered that Livy is not our only authority on the subject which he has treated. Several Greek historians support his state-ments concerning the virtues and the glory of the early Romans. The criticism passed on Livy by Macaulay in his " Essay on History" is exaggerated, as are many other statements in that unreliable essay (*supra* No. 51).

§ 4. *Prejudice or Hostility.*

546. We have seen that prejudice may readily prevent an author from discovering the truth ; but it often goes further, and under the form of **hostility** it leads the his-torian to make unjust attacks upon his opponents. This hostility sometimes manifests itself by direct charges, as when Prescott writes : "In that day the principle that the end justifies the means was fully recognized " (*History of Ferdinand and Isabella*, vol. i. p. 245).

547. False charges are often disguised under the form of **innuendoes.**

"Gibbon." says Prescott, "by a style of innuendo that conveys more than meets the ear, has contrived, with Iago-like duplicity, to breathe a taint of suspicion on the purity which he dares not openly assail " (" Essay on Irving ").

This unmanly system of warfare is not uncommon. After Irving has given us such a character of Ferdinand as the most reliable authorities prove him to have deserved, he continues thus : " It has been added, however, that he had more bigotry than religion, that his ambition was craving rather than magnanimous," etc. Irving does not say that such charges rested on good authority ; he merely breathes suspicion on a character which he appears unwilling to assail openly (*History of Columbus*, book ii. c. ii.) Another species of innuendo consists in suggesting unworthy motives where the actions related are honorable, as Irving does in attributing to Ferdinand unworthy motives for encouraging Columbus ; and he introduces these motives with a mere *perhaps* (c. iii.)

§ 5. *False Theories.*

548. **False theories** are a source of falsification which requires special attention, both because they are extensively used by late writers, and because they escape detection on the part of many readers. Macaulay gives a lucid explanation of them :

" The best historians of later times have been seduced from truth, not by their imagination, but by their reason. They far excel their predecessors in the art of deducing general principles from facts. But unhappily they have fallen into the error of distorting facts to suit general principles. They arrive at a theory from looking at some of the phenomena, and the remaining phenomena they strain or curtail to suit the theory For this purpose it is not necessary that they should assert what is absolutely false. . . . In every human character and transaction there is a mixture of good and evil : a little exaggeration, a little suppression, a judicious use of epithets, a watchful and searching scepticism with respect to the evidence on one side, a convenient credulity with respect to every report or tradition on the other, may easily make a saint of Laud or a tyrant of Henry the Fourth. This species of misrepresentation abounds in the most valuable works of modern historians " (*Essays*, " History ").

549. Macaulay **applies this criticism** to Hume and to

Gibbon, and especially to Mitford's *History of Greece.*
Orestes A. Brownson, in his *Quarterly Review* for 1852
(p. 423), applies it to several others :

"Herder, Kant, Hegel, Guizot, Cousin, Michelet, and even Carlyle and Macaulay," he says, "are instances in point, as all who are
familiar with their writings need not be informed. None of them
give us genuine history ; they merely give us their speculations on
what is not history, and what, according to those speculations,
ought to be history. It is the common error of the modern school
of so-called philosophical historians, and to which school Mr. Bancroft belongs, though he is not by any means the worst of the school,
to suppose that history may be reduced to the terms of a speculative
science, and be written, as it were, *a priori.* 'Give me the geographi-
cal position of a people,' says the brilliant and eloquent Cousin,
'and I will give you its history.'"

550. Brownson gives the following **examples of false
theories:**

"Herder finds in all history only his ideas of human progress ;
Kant finds nothing but his categories ; Hegel finds the significance
and end of all history, the operations of divine Providence, of all
mankind, and of all nature, to have been the establishment of the
Prussian monarchy ; Mr. Bancroft finds that the original purpose of
creation, of God and the universe, is fulfilled in the establishment
of American democracy."

The same article of Brownson's, in analyzing the entire
theory of Bancroft, shows conclusively that the philosophical speculations of that historian are not merely visionary,
but fraught with false principles of government and morality tending to the ruin of society. The article deserves
most careful study (Brownson's *Quarterly Review* for 1852,
"Bancroft").

551. **Carlyle's theory is:**
(*a*) That the world is ever tending to go wrong. From
time to time appear great minds that labor to set it right.
These are his "Heroes," who are not to be judged, but

whose conduct is law for us. Such are Oliver Cromwell, Mahomet, Napoleon I., Frederick the Great, as well as St. Paul, Shakspeare, Dante, Burns, Luther, and Calvin ; not Voltaire, who only pulled down. "It is from the heart of the world that he [the Hero] comes ; he is a portion of the primal reality of things" (Carlyle).

(*b*) The world is all wrong now: "God's laws are become a Great Happiness Principle, a Parliamentary expediency." "The Universe—a swine's trough," all scrambling for felicity.

(*c*) Religion is very necessary. It is moral rectitude as understood by Cromwell and the Puritans. They read their duty in themselves ; the Bible only aided them. At need they did violence to it. Carlyle is so much their brother that he excuses or admires their excesses. He sets them before us as models, and judges both past and present by them alone. "Carlyle's style has introduced into this country a thoroughly false method of writing history" (Justin MacCarthy).

552. Macaulay, in his *History of England*, disclaims all theory ; but, unconsciously perhaps, he inculcates the "Great Happiness Principle," which Carlyle condemns. By this standard everything is judged. Puritanism is good, the Establishment bad, Catholicity worst of all. This last did some good in the Dark Ages, when "the priests, with all their faults, were by far the wisest portion of society" ; it is now become "an unjust and noxious tyranny" (*Hist. of England*, chap. i.)

Hence he is more severe on blunders than on crimes. While "under Cromwell hell was the dread of being found guilty before the just Judge, now it is the dread of making a bad speculation or of transgressing etiquette" (Carlyle). Macaulay is the impersonation of the spirit of the world. (See also *Dublin Review* for April, 1886, " Studies of History.")

Article VI. The Plan of a History.

553. To erect a building that shall unite beauty with usefulness we need, besides sound material, a suitable **plan** drawn by a skilful architect. In the same manner the historian must conceive an artistic plan for the composition of his work. Now, everything artistic supposes unity of design. The events that make up a history must be bound together by some connecting principle, which enables the mind to see them in their bearing on one another, and to view them as the portions of one entire group.

554. This unity is easily attained **in particular histories** —that is, in those which narrate one event, such as the Conspiracy of Catiline, the French Revolution of 1789, etc.

But the difficulty is much greater in general or **universal histories,** which deal with various nations, each of which presents an independent series of events. In such works both utility and artistic beauty require that some leading idea shall combine those separate parts into a harmonious whole. The ancients, with their well-known perfection of taste, are here again our models.

555. Thus Herodotus, while embracing in his work all the nations known in his day, arranges the parts so as to develop this one idea: "that the whole empire of Persia, after subjugating and incorporating with itself all the nations of the East, was in its turn conquered by united Greece." His history resembles an heroic poem, in which one great enterprise or action is related. We find ourselves at once in the midst of the events, and we are gradually informed of all that preceded by long episodes appropriately introduced. Both in the main narration, which is the history of the Persian war, and in the various episodes or partial

histories of different lands, one philosophic thought is ever held before us—that of a Nemesis or avenging deity, which causes the exalted to be humbled.

556. **Polybius,** whom Blair pronounces the most successful of all ancient historians in respect to unity, wrote what he calls a *Universal History*—not, indeed, comprising all times, but all nations within a given period ; he maintains unity by professing to show "how. and by what sort of policy almost all the countries of the inhabited earth, in less than fifty-three years, passed into the power of Rome."

557. **Livy** exhibits "the power of Rome arising from humble beginnings and extending through gradual conquests to universal empire." Thus Livy begins at the centre and spreads to the circumference of Roman power, while Polybius begins at the circumference and unites all its parts with the centre.

558. **Thucydides,** on the contrary, in his *History of the Peloponnesian War*, has entirely neglected this source of light and beauty. Though his subject possessed the closest unity, as Dionysius of Halicarnassus observes, his account of it has none, but it is cut up into various campaigns, into winters and summers ; he leaves one enterprise or expedition unfinished, to carry us away to disconnected events in other parts of Greece. (See Dionys. Halic. Letter to Cneius Pompey.)

559. Among modern historians **Archibald Alison** is very successful in maintaining unity. He had a difficult task to perform, as he had undertaken to write the *History of Europe from the Commencement of the French Revolution in* 1789 *to the Restoration of the Bourbons in* 1815, which he afterwards continued to the accession of Louis Napoleon in 1852. His bond of unity is expressed in the following lines of his preface :

"Its earliest years [*i.e.* of the French Revolution] suggest at every page reflections on the evils of political fanaticism, and the terrible consequences of democratic fervor; the latter on the debasing effects of absolute despotism and the sanguinary march of military ambition."

Alison's is truly a learned work, but it bears a partisan character. To his mind the English constitution is the ideal of perfection politically, and the Church of England religiously ; everything else is measured by its approach to these two standards.

560. **The different parts** also of a large history must have their own principles of unity. For instance, one period of a nation's history may be marked by the steady growth of popular freedom, another by the constant increase of absolutism in the ruling power.

561. It is evident that the **selection of a false principle** or leading idea will cause misconceptions of many events, as if in the history of the sixteenth and seventeenth centuries the author should pretend to see the growth of liberty, whereas those centuries rather promoted the principles of absolutism. When the philosophic ideas which connect or underlie a history are made so prominent that the facts are not fully considered, but only in so far as they bear on the theory or the thesis, the work is then called a philosophical history, or the philosophy of history, of which species we are yet to treat.

ARTICLE VII. DEVELOPMENT OF THE FACTS.

562. **The facts should be so developed** as to secure two results—the *artistic beauty* of the narrative, and *proper instruction* for the reader.

§ 1. *The Artistic Beauty of the Narrative.*

563. The **artistic beauty of the narrative** is attained by

the observance of the precepts laid down for narration (*supra*, book iv. c. iii.)

As an example of the application of these precepts to a history, we shall here add **a criticism of Sallust's " Conspiracy of Catiline,"** confining our remarks to the artistic beauty of the narrative.

564. It is evident that not all the circumstances of that intricate plot, all that was said and done in Rome and elsewhere in connection with it, can be or need be narrated by the historian. He must "exhibit such parts of the truth as most nearly produce the effect of the whole." Let us suppose that we see Sallust at work. How does he go about it? He has formed to himself a clear conception of the events. He knows that the conspiracy did not arise suddenly and of itself, nor was it entirely the work of one designing man; but it was the natural outcome of **a combination of causes,** which had been some time developing before they produced so vast an effect.

565. He will, then, begin by showing us those causes at work. This, however, he does not attempt to do by a philosophical discussion, but by an exhibition of the facts. For the sake of unity he seizes upon **one prominent figure,** around which all the separate facts are made to cluster, as the parts in a group of statuary are gathered around one central figure. This prominent figure is Catiline. After his introduction, therefore, the historian at once makes us acquainted with that personage, who is to remain prominently before us during the whole narrative, like the hero of an epic poem.

566. This sketch, or **Character of Catiline,** is certainly a striking picture, perhaps overdrawn so far as truth is concerned, but artistically adapted to arouse interest from the opening of the story.

567. With this commanding figure before us, we are next

made to review the **history of Rome,** from its simple begin‑
nings to its full development, from the patriarchal virtues
of its early founders to the luxury and depravity of those
latter days. All this account is expressed in terms preg‑
nant with meaning, but very rapidly, especially the descrip‑
tion of former virtues, which forms the background to the
picture. Soon we see Rome abandoned to the designing
ambition of wicked men, the laws violated with impunity,
and wealth and lust replacing all higher aspirations.

568. As a natural consequence we see **the Roman youth
corrupt,** leading a life of extravagance and dissipation.
Here we have the materials which are to be kindled into
a vast conflagration. Now Catiline, whose commanding
figure has struck us from the beginning, steps forward to
apply the match. His methods of corrupting still further
the Roman nobility, the intended tools of his ambition, and
of next gaining them and binding them to himself, are most
vividly described. With this comes a brief sketch of Cati‑
line's former career, which makes the whole narrative more
probable.

569. With No. XVII. begins the narration of **the Con‑
spiracy** itself. So far great skill was required to keep unity
in view while tracing the various remote and proximate
cause of the events; but unity has been well maintained :
all is clear and interesting. Now the narrative becomes
more exciting; it reads like a novel or a tragedy. We see
the most desperate of the young Roman nobles assembled
at night around Catiline. We have his speech almost in
his own words—and an artful speech it is, showing the jus‑
tice and necessity of conspiring. For Sallust understood
human nature well : he knew that the most vicious men
will hide their wickedness from their own eyes under the
cloak of justice, or at least of a sad necessity. Then the
plan of action intended by Catiline is more fully devel‑

ɔped ; there are stirring scenes, as that of the conspirators pledging themselves to each other in cups of human blood.

570. But now a new personage, Furius, is introduced, whose foolish vanity must lead to the discovery of the criminal plot. All this is as naturally developed as in a well-conceived novel. Rome takes the alarm. **Cicero is made consul.** Here, however, it appears that private rancor in Sallust against the noble "Father of his country" prevented the historian from adding another great source of beauty and interest to his narrative. For as every element of evil had skilfully been gathered around Catiline, so now Cicero might and should have been made the central figure of the opposing group. Artistic beauty suggested it; truth required it; and the story would have gained from it in thrilling interest.

571. It will be a useful study to **compare** with Sallust's account of Catiline's Conspiracy the narrative of the Gunpowder Plot in Lingard's *History of England* (vol. vi. c. 1), or, better still, Father Gerard's *Narrative of the Gunpowder Plot*, which is more reliable.

§ 2. *Proper Instruction for the Reader.*

572. That a history may impart **proper instruction** to the reader, two rules must be observed :

Rule 1.—The facts must be narrated without false coloring, so that they may appear to the reader such as they really are.

Rule 2.—The historian should not be constantly interrupting his narrative to preach a sermon or point a moral; such practice would be inartistic, blending the historical with the didactic style of composition—as great a fault against good taste as the blending of two styles in architecture.

573. But **should the historian never show himself,** never

aid his readers directly to take the right view of the facts, by saying honestly what he himself thinks of them? This is the point on which critics and historians differ considerably, so that they may be divided into three distinct schools.

574. One school may be called the **Fatalistic School** of history. It wishes the historian not only to utter no judgment on the facts presented, approving some and condemning others, but not even to form such a judgment in his own mind. Writers of this school in reality admit no radical or essential difference between right and wrong ; or at most they consider this distinction as a matter of opinion only, which therefore the historian may leave to the taste of the reader. Of this school Thiers and Mignet are the leaders among the French. Bancroft is one of their imitators in this country. As scepticism is spreading, there is a tendency in many late historians to adopt the same course.

575. The second may be called the **Descriptive School.** It allows the historian to form his own judgment, but directs him never to utter it in so many words, but to describe or represent the facts in such a manner as to inculcate his own conclusions on the reader. This is, at present, a very popular school, adopted by some very good men and by many writers of unsound principles.

576. The third may be called the **Judicial School,** in which the historian, like a judge, after fully examining the evidence on both sides, boldly pronounces his judgment, approving and condemning as important occasions may require. This school is that of the ancients ; it is best exemplified in Tacitus, the prince of historians, who brands with ignominy the human monsters that bore the sceptre of the Roman Empire during so many calamitous years. To the same school belong, among the moderns, Bossuet in his

Discourse on Universal History, Alzog and Darras in their *Histories of the Church*, Ranke in his *History of the Popes*, and a multitude of others of the best historians.

577. The Fatalistic school is utterly unsound in principle and pernicious in practice. Of the two other schools **the Judicial** is, we think, **preferable** for several reasons:

1. It appears to be more honest on the part of the historian to state clearly his views on important events.

2. It is more useful; for the historian, who is supposed to be a man of maturity and wisdom, is better qualified to form such a judgment than ordinary readers, and thus can guide them aright.

3. It is the practice sanctioned by the approbation of ages.

578. 4. The only plausible objection brought against it— viz., that the historian may misjudge the facts—vanishes if we consider that the Descriptive school may mislead its readers as well, and that in a more pernicious manner. For in the Descriptive school the historian inculcates his private judgments by the coloring which he gives to the facts ; he does not lead the reader to judge for himself, but he forces his own conclusions on him.

579. 5. The Judicial school adds to the narrative the warmth of genuine passion, which, as the readers of Tacitus well know, contributes more to interest than any degree of ornament. In fact, without such honest warmth that defect is felt for which Prescott blames Gibbon when he says (" Essay on Irving ") :

" It is a consequence of this scepticism in Gibbon, as with Voltaire, that his writings are nowhere warmed with a generous moral sentiment. The most sublime of all spectacles, that of the martyr who suffers for conscience' sake, ... is contemplated by the historian with the smile, or rather sneer, of philosophic indifference. This is not only bad taste, as he is addressing a Christian audience,

but he thus voluntarily relinquishes one of the most powerful en-
gines for the movement of human passion, which is never so easily
excited as by deeds of suffering, self-devoted heroism."

Certainly, the Judicial manner of writing history may be
abused ; but every good thing may be abused, and the Descriptive manner is still more liable to this objection.

ARTICLE VIII. THE STYLE OF HISTORY.

580. As history is one of the noblest and most dignified
species of composition, all critics mention dignity as the
chief quality of **historical style.** But **dignity** does not
mean pomposity ; and such writers as Gibbon, Robertson, and Bancroft become less interesting by their excess of stateliness.   Prescott says :

" The historian of the *Decline and Fall* too rarely forgets his own
importance in that of his subject.   The consequence which he at-
taches to his personal labors is shown in a bloated dignity of expression and an ostentation of ornament that contrast whimsically
enough with the trifling topics and commonplace thoughts on which,
in the course of his long work, they are occasionally employed.   He
nowhere moves along with the easy freedom of nature, but seems to
leap, as it were, from triad to triad by a succession of strained, con-
vulsive efforts " (*Miscell.*, " Irving ").

In what, then, consists the dignity of style which history
requires ?

581. **Dignity consists, (*a*)** in a **proper gravity,** which Blair
explains thus :

" Gravity must always be maintained in the narration.   There
must be no meanness nor vulgarity in the style ; no quaint nor colloquial phrases ; no affectation of pertness or wit.   The smart or the
sneering manner of telling a story is inconsistent with the historical
character.   I do not say that the historian is never to let himself
down.   He may sometimes do it with propriety, in order to diver-
sify the strain of his narration, which, if it be perfectly uniform, is apt

to become tiresome. But he should be careful never to descend too far ; and on occasions when a light or ludicrous anecdote is proper to be recorded, it is generally better to throw it into a note than to hazard becoming too familiar by introducing it into the body of the work " (Lecture xxxvi.)

582. It consists, (*b*) in the use of such **ornaments of style** as will set off the thoughts to the best advantage, without, however, diverting the attention of the reader from the thoughts to the figures, from the march of the events to the harmonious flow of the sentences. History admits of a rich style, as rich as any other species of prose composition ; but no writing admits of bombast—*i.e.*, of more sound than sense, such as we find in the following lines of Bancroft (*Hist. of U. S.*, vol. i. p. 209) :

" It is one of the surprising results of moral power that language, composed of fleeting sounds, retains and transmits the remembrance of past occurrences long after every monument has passed away. Of the labors of the Indians on the soil of Virginia there remains nothing so respectable as would be a common ditch for the draining of lands ; the memorials of their former existence are found only in the names of their rivers and their mountains. Unchanging nature retains the appellations which were given by those whose villages have disappeared and whose tribes have become extinct."

The middle sentence would have been all-sufficient.

583. **Exactness** is a second quality of style in history. It consists in expressing just what the historian means, and not merely something like it. For instance, one of the sources of vagueness in the first sentence of the passage just quoted is the use of the word *moral* in a meaning which the word does not properly bear ; for ' moral ' regards law, or the distinction of right and wrong, which is not in question here.

584. Exactness should affect even the smallest words and the apparently insignificant portions of a sentence ; an ill-chosen or ill-placed adjective or adverb is often enough to

give a wrong notion to the reader which will accompany him through life.' But this quality is **particularly required** with regard to the names of men and places, the dates of events, and similar minutiæ, which perhaps make no great show in the work, but which must be distinctly and carefully noted if the events are to be rightly understood. It has often happened that an inexactness in such details has involved historical events in considerable confusion.

585. **Calmness** is a third quality which should belong to historical style. For the historian is like a judge who has examined a cause thoroughly, and who gives us the wise conclusions at which his mind has coolly and deliberately arrived. Strong passion is inimical to correctness of thought and expression. Macaulay, for example, is evidently too passionate on many occasions; and the sensational style of Carlyle would strip history of that calm dignity which so becomes its character. Still, we have seen that a certain glow of feeling is highly proper in the language of an honest historian, and we have quoted Prescott as censuring Gibbon and Voltaire for their apathy at the sight of heroic virtue (No. 579).

ARTICLE IX. VARIOUS SPECIES OF HISTORICAL WRITING.

586. The following are the **principal species** of historical writing : history proper ; annals, memoirs, and travels ; philosophical histories ; and biographies.

§ 1. *History proper.*

587. **History proper,** called by Polybius and by German critics 'Pragmatical,' embraces *general, particular,* and *special* histories.

588. **A general history** treats of several nations, as Alison's *History of Modern Europe*. If it embraces all nations and times it is properly called **universal.** General histo-

ries should (*a*) suppress minor details, so that the important events, names, and dates stand out prominently ; (*b*) observe due proportion among the parts—for instance, in a general history of the Church one country should not engross most of the attention of the writer.

589. **A particular history** treats of one nation, one province, one event, as Lingard's *History of England*, Prescott's *Conquest of Mexico*, etc. It enters more into detail, offers more picturesque passages, more dramatic scenes.

590. **A special history** relates events in as far only as they bear on one science, one art, one special consideration ; such is Bossuet's *History of the Variations of Protestantism*, any history of painting, commerce, literature, etc. The advantage of special histories is that they throw a concentrated light on one particular branch of study.

§ 2. *Annals, Memoirs, and Travels.*

591. **Annals or Chronicles** are not so much histories as a supply of materials for future histories. Being mere records of events penned down from day to day, they require no plan nor deep thought, but fidelity and distinctness throughout, and completeness with regard to all matters of importance. They need not be elegantly worded ; still, as Prescott observes, we find that some chronicles of the middle ages, in spite of their ill-formed and obsolete idiom, are read with more delight than many modern histories of high pretensions, because their narrative is more spirited (*Miscell.*, p. 107).

We may mention here the *Acta Sanctorum* of the Bollandists, S.J., a learned collection of biographies and of records from which the lives of the saints are usually written. Baronius' *Annales Ecclesiastici* contain the history of the Church from the first to the sixteenth century. Both these most valuable works rise far above the dignity of ordinary annals.

592. **Memoirs** relate such facts as have fallen under the personal observation of the writer. They descend from the stateliness of the historic style ; they should be sprightly and interesting, give useful information with regard to facts and characteristic traits of persons. Cardinal Wiseman's *Recollections of the Four Last Popes*, General Sherman's *Memoirs*, are examples in point. Cæsar's *Commentaries* of the Gallic and the Civil Wars are the most perfect memoirs in existence.

593. **Travels** may be ranked with memoirs as furnishing the materials for future histories. Such are the graphic narratives of the great American missionary Father De Smet, Livingstone's African and Kane's Arctic Explorations, Vetromile's Travels in the Holy Land, etc.

§ 3. *Philosophical Histories.*

594. **Philosophical histories** are those in which the principles derived from the facts are made more prominent than the facts themselves. When the work is so taken up with theories that it resembles an essay rather than a narrative, it is called a **philosophy of history**.

595. Philosophical histories are of comparatively recent origin. The first in time, and so far the grandest in conception, is Bossuet's **Discourse on Universal History**, the English version of which is unfortunately garbled, omitting whatever is distinctively Catholic. The work enables us to realize the definition which Bunsen gives of history, as "that most sacred epic or dramatic poem, of which God is the author, humanity the hero, and the historian the philosophical interpreter." Bossuet's idea is to unveil the workings of Providence in the government of mankind.

596. **Voltaire,** in his *Essai sur les Mœurs* and in his *His-*

tory of Louis XIV., exhibits his anti-Christian theories, which made Prescott say : " He resembled the allegorical agents of Milton, paving the way across the gulf of Chaos for the spirits of mischief to enter more easily upon the earth " (*Miscell.*, p. 99).

597. **Montesquieu,** in his *Grandeur et Décadence des Romains*, used the facts of history simply as the arguments of a thesis, or, as Prescott calls it, " the ingredients from which the spirit was to be extracted.   But this was not always the spirit of truth " (*Ib.* p. 100).

598. **Buckle's** *History of Civilization* is but a fragment of what was intended to be a voluminous work.   It is brilliant in style but weak in logic ; its spirit is infidel.

599. **Guizot** wrote his *History of Civilization* in a Christian spirit.   It is full of novel views, of sagacious inductions, of pathetic eloquence, but also of capital errors.   It pays some glowing tributes to the Catholic Church; but the author, being an alien, often fails to understand this divine institution, and grossly misconceives its legislation.

600. The most valuable Philosophy of History is **Balmes'** noble work, *Protestantism and Catholicity compared in their Effects on the Civilization of Europe.*   It analyzes the history of modern times, and discusses all the vital questions which have agitated the civilized world in the last three centuries.   It combines varied information, lofty views, sound principles, close reasoning, all expressed in a noble style, whose eloquence is preserved in the English translation.

§ 4. *Biography.*

601. **Biography** is the history of the life and character of a particular person.   Such writings present two **advantages :**

 1. They **throw light upon general history;** for it is a

common saying that the history of the world is to a great extent the record of the great men of the world. Such men exert a powerful influence upon all around them, and usually contribute greatly to shape the events of the age in which they live, and even of future ages. Their influence, however, has been exaggerated by some writers, particularly by Carlyle in his lectures on Heroes. The great events of the world's history have generally deeper and wider causes than the character of one or two individuals. Still, it is true that Almighty God raises up great geniuses at proper times to accomplish His designs of mercy or justice on the nations. Thus He raised Cyrus for the establishment, and Alexander for the overthrow, of the Persian empire, and both these conquerors for the protection of His chosen people (Josephus, *Antiq.*, xi. c. 8 ; Daniel viii.)

602. 2. Biographies **aid the reader to understand human nature** more thoroughly when he studies it in the passions, the virtues, and the foibles of remarkable characters. He will there find that man, as such, is in many respects a feeble and very defective being, elevated, however, at times by the principles which he imbibes, and by the natural or supernatural strength of will and intellect with which he carries these principles into effect.

603. Knowing now the two advantages to be aimed at, we shall readily discover the **rules which the biographer must follow.**

Rule 1.—Only very remarkable men and women should be made the **subjects** of biographies—such persons as have widely influenced public events, or such as afford the reader special opportunities for studying the workings of human nature or the operations of divine grace.

Rule 2.—The writer should clearly trace the **influence** which the subject of his biography exercised over persons

or events, avoiding the common mistake of introducing ir-
relevant facts with which he had but little to do.

Rule 3.—He must exhibit the true **character** of his hero :
the motives of his conduct, the grasp of his intellect, the
principles which he has adopted, the promptings of his
passions, the power or the weakness of his will, the causes
that have contributed to the development of his virtues or
his vices. We may refer to Father Morris' *Life of St.
Thomas Becket* as a model in this respect. Characters are
often better represented by mentioning sayings, incidents,
etc., than by the description of battles and other public
exploits. Boswell's *Life of Johnson* is replete with familiar
traits.

Rule 4.—The facts narrated, even the familiar traits
and incidents, must be drawn from **authentic sources** or
from personal knowledge. Of late the practice has gained
ground of quoting liberally in biographies from the letters
and other writings of the persons concerned ; and the results of this innovation are very gratifying. Thus Father
Coleridge gives us the **Life and Letters** of St. Francis
Xavier, Father Bowden those of F. W. Faber. Bouhours
had already written in French an excellent biography of
St. Xavier, which the poet Dryden thought it worth his
while to translate into English. It seemed difficult to surpass this masterpiece, but extensive quotations from the
Saint's own letters have enabled Coleridge to overcome the
difficulty.

604. **A danger to be guarded against** in biographies is
an excess of admiration or hatred for the character described. Carlyle idolizes his hero Oliver Cromwell ;
Abbott extols Napoleon I., while Scott undervalues the
qualities of this great genius. No human work is perfect.

605. Still, **literature is rich in successful biographies**; the

Latin *Lives* of Cornelius Nepos and the **Greek** *Lives* of Plutarch are deservedly admired. The latter gains much interest for his biographies by presenting them in pairs, comparing a Grecian with a Roman character ; but fidelity to truth is often wanting. Xenophon's *Cyropædia* is highly praised for its literary qualities, but not for the truth of its narrative. Tacitus' *Life of Agricola* is a work unsurpassed in merit.

606. **Of French** biographies we may mention with special praise Audin's Lives of Luther, Calvin, Henry VIII., and Leo X.; Baunard's *Life of Madame Barat*, the foundress of the Ladies of the Sacred Heart, and his *Life of Madame Duchesne.* (See also *American Catholic Quarterly Review*, 1878, p. 321, on Pope Alexander VI.)

607. In **English** model biographies are numerous ; in particular, Miss Strickland's *Lives of the Queens of England and of Scotland*, Johnson's *Lives of the Poets*, Alban Butler's *Lives of the Saints*, Sparks' *American Biographies*, Clarke's *Deceased Bishops of the Catholic Church in the United States*, Kathleen O'Meara's *Life of Ozanam*, Thompson's *Lives of St. Aloysius and St. Stanislaus.* The *Life of Washington*, by Washington Irving, is probably the most elaborate and most successful biography written in the English language.

608. There are many modern works of considerable historical and literary value which comprise not merely the life, but the **life and times** together, of some distinguished personage. In such books the hero must never be lost sight of ; for unity requires that only those events be introduced which have some real connection with the leading character. All must be made to cluster around him, without, however, attributing to him more influence than he really exercised. Among the most valuable works of this kind are Hurter's *Life of Innocent III.*, Voigt's *Life of*

Gregory VII., Hübner's *Sixtus V.*, Hefele's *Ximenes*, Montalembert's *Life and Times of St. Elizabeth of Hungary.*

609. In conclusion we may remark that while in many species of literature the highest point of perfection appears to have been reached, and a decline to have set in, history has been remarkably improved within this century, and there seems to be, in the minds of many, an earnest determination to establish on earth the reign of historic truth.

BOOK V.

VERSIFICATION.

CHAPTER I.

HISTORY AND NATURE OF VERSIFICATION.

ARTICLE I. ITS RISE AND IMPORTANCE.

610. Verse has been from time immemorial the usual dress of poetry. We can easily believe that **in ancient times** poetic effusions were frequent. These effusions were the expression of uncommon emotion. They were the voice of lamentation or of triumph, an appeal to martial feeling, or an invitation to high festivity. In early days uncultivated tribes, like those of the present time, were strongly influenced by the manner of expression ; and the manner of expression was suggested by the sentiment that held mastery at the moment. As, therefore, in those days passions were often more violent and more variable than now, when education is more general and control of feeling more complete, in like manner the expression was then more lively and more in accordance with the first impulses of nature. Hence the disposition to express strong emotion in an unusual form. A wail, for example, over the dead, low and tender at one moment, then loud and impas-

sioned, various in cadence as the degrees of passion or the bursts of feeling were various, was more natural and impressive than a wordy passage of prose could be.

611. Exultation likewise, and festive rejoicing, and stirring calls to arms found vent in unusual tones. We ourselves are often moved by a plaintive or a merry air to a state of feeling similar to that of him who executes it. **Poetry and Music** were thus naturally allied. The bard who made the song was the same in ancient times as the musician who sang it in accord with his instrument. Assuredly he adapted it to the step of the music. Hence the presumptive cause of the peculiar form which poetic composition adopted.

612. Moreover, verse was in early ages **almost a necessity.** It was a medium of communication which could not be dispensed with. Whatever was traditional was preserved by the memory alone; for writing was not yet invented. But as it was difficult to learn so many events by heart when recounted in prose, recourse was had to the poet's art, which aided the memory, pleased the fancy, and rendered the task delightful. The son studied the history of tribes and nations in the verses which he learned from his father. The priest knew the rites of the sacrifice from verse, and recited or chanted his prayers in verse. The science of war, the science of medicine, the laws of the land and of religion, the praises of heroes, and the rhapsodies of prophecy, all were communicated by the same means.

613. But **the form** in which they were communicated was not the same. One kind of subjects was calm and deliberate in its tenor, hence the strain of the verse was regular; another kind was light and gay, and a suitable strain was adapted to it; another was mournful, and a slow and solemn movement in the poetry and music was observed. The

supplication to the Deity and the wild, almost incoherent language of the prophet were embalmed, as we shall see, in a form irregular and broken. This accounts for the various kinds of verse taught in prosodies.

ARTICLE II. ITS INFLUENCE AT THE PRESENT DAY.

614. The **influence of verse in modern times** cannot be denied. It has power to elevate or degrade the multitude, to breathe into their hearts a healthy, moral tone, or imbue them with moral depravity and irreligion. One of these two effects it will inevitably produce, according as it is used to adorn thoughts truly poetical or to insinuate the venom of baneful thoughts. The Scotch statesman, Andrew Fletcher, said long ago . "The popular songs of a country are of more importance than its laws"; and O'Connell said : "Let me write the ballads of a country, and I care not who makes the laws." A national anthem is produced to make men patriotic ; songs are distributed among the troops to make them brave ; sacred melodies are given to the people to humanize them and turn their minds heavenward ; and these efforts are often singularly successful.

615. On the other hand, the minstrel and comedian have scarcely sung their song, however vile or nonsensical it may be, before it is caught up and repeated with eagerness by the whole nation, often with a demoralizing effect. To be able to counteract this latter evil with the same instruments, or to discern and appreciate more fully the artistic merits of a poetical production, will amply **repay the labor of studying** the art of versification. All may not be able to write beautiful poetry, but every cultivated mind should be able properly to appreciate it.

ARTICLE III. THE NATURE OF THE ART.

616. We have said that **poetry and music** were originally united. Later, for evident reasons, they separated. Not every one whom nature endowed with poetic abilities could play on an instrument, and not every one familiar with the instrument was inspired with a poet's feeling. But poetry retained in its ordinary mode of structure, after the separation, many of the features received from music. It retained notably the musical count or beat, which to the accord of various sounds adds a melodious flow and an ingenious and an apt turn of expression. In these, judiciously handled, lies the art of poetic numbers.

617. Independent of the meaning conveyed by the language, there is in verse not only a diction peculiar to it and capable of arousing desired emotions, but, besides, a charming **melody** which arrests the ear and, far more than prose can do, affects the soul. We find a pleasure in listening to tones of varied movement, when there is **harmony** in the variation, for the same reason that music harmonious and accordant is pleasurable. The aim of versification ìs to present the most beautiful variations with perfect, or almost perfect, uniformity. And in proportion as verses blend these two qualities they are successful and delight the ear. It is for this reason that the lips are wont to repeat, with undiminished pleasure, the same idea embodied in the same expression. Do we not often hum to ourselves snatches of song, whether serious or humorous, without disgust or fatigue? Here is a specimen of a serio-comic. After reading it once or twice we shall find, in moments of sadness or gayety, one or other of its stanzas drumming in our head:

618. The Last Leaf.

1. They say that in his prime,
Ere the pruning-knife of time
   Cut him down,
Not a better man was found
By the crier on his round
   Through the town.

2. But now he walks the streets,
And he looks at all he meets,
   Sad and wan ;
And he shakes his feeble head
Till it seems as if he said,
   " They are gone."

3. The mossy marbles rest
On the lips that he has prest
   In their bloom,
And the names he loved to hear
Have been carved for many a
   year
   On the tomb.

4. My old grandma has said
(Poor old lady! she is dead
   Long ago)
That he had a Roman nose,
And his cheek was like a rose
   In the snow.

5. But now he's old and thin,
And his nose hangs on his chin
   Like a staff ;
And a crook is in his back,
And a melancholy crack
   In his laugh.

6. I know it is a sin
For me to sit and grin
   At him here ;
But the old three-cornered hat,
And the breeches, and all that,
   Are so queer.

7. And if I should live to be
The last leaf on the tree
   In the spring,
Let them laugh as I do now
At the old forsaken bough
   Where I cling.—*Holmes.*

619. Here there is a charming but **uniform variation.**
Express these thoughts in prosaic terms, and the effect is
destroyed. The second, third, and seventh stanzas contain
sentiments worthy of a passing reflection, but even they
would, in prose, pass away to return no more.

620. On the other hand, many of the metrical compositions of the day, though containing ideas truly poetic, are
thrown aside as worthless because they **lack the two qualities** insisted on above.

621. Listen now to the chime of—

> "1. Those evening bells ! those evening bells !
>   How many a tale their music tells
>   Of youth and home, and that sweet time
>   When last I heard their evening chime.
>
> "2. Those joyous hours are passed away,
>   And many a heart that then was gay
>   Within the tomb now darkly dwells,
>   And hears no more those evening bells.
>
> "3. And so 'twill be when I am gone :
>   Those evening bells will still ring on,
>   While other bards shall walk these dells
>   And sing your praise, sweet evening bells."
>
> —*Moore.*

This idea expressed in prose becomes tame; expressed in bad verse it is almost insupportable.

622. To show more forcibly the **influence of numbers** on the mind and heart two more examples are given. These quotations are lengthy, but well adapted to several purposes—viz., to guide the taste, to drill the student in criticism, and to accustom him to note the beat of the verse. The words italicized should be uttered slowly and feelingly. There is a melancholy pleasure conveyed in the solemn tread of the following. It is the picture of the leper, whom the laws of his country send into solitude. The metre will keep pace with his movement :

623. "THE LEPER.

> " And he went forth—*alone !* Not one of all
>   *The many whom he loved*, nor she whose name
>   Was woven in the fibres of the heart
>   Breaking within him now, *to come and speak*
>   Comfort unto him. *Yea, he went his way*
>   Sick and heart-broken and *alone—to die !*
>   *For God had cursed the leper.*

" It was noon,

And Helon knelt beside a stagnant pool
In the lone wilderness, *and bathed his brow,*
Hot with the burning leprosy, *and touched*
The loathsome water to his fevered lips,
Praying that he might be *so blest—to die !*
Footsteps approached, *and, with no strength to flee.*
He drew the covering closer on his lip,
Crying, '*Unclean ! Unclean !*' And, in the folds
Of the coarse sackcloth *shrouding up his face,*
He fell upon the earth till they should pass.
Nearer the stranger came, *and, bending o'er*
The leper's prostrate form, pronounced his name—
'*Helon !*' *The voice was like the master tone*
Of a rich instrument—*most strangely sweet ;*
And the dull pulses of disease awoke
And for a moment *beat beneath the hot*
And leprous scales with a restoring thrill.
'*Helon ! Arise !*' And he *forgot his curse,*
And rose and stood before Him."

—*Willis.*

624. In the succeeding lines the rapid step of the verse makes us feel more sensibly the torrent of the speaker's eloquence. Italics are here unnecessary : the quick step reigns throughout :

" In stature majestic, apart from the throng
He stood in his beauty, the theme of my song !
His cheek pale with fervor, the blue orbs above
Lit up with the splendors of youth and of love ;
Yet the heart-glowing raptures that beamed from those eyes
Seemed saddened by sorrow and chastened by sighs—
As if the young heart in its bloom had grown cold,
With its loves unrequited, its sorrows untold.

" Such language as his I may never recall ;
But his theme was Salvation—Salvation to all ;
And the souls of a thousand in ecstasy hung
On the manna-like sweetness that dropped from his tongue.

Nor alone on the ear his wild eloquence stole ;
Enforced by each gesture, it sank to the soul,
Till it seemed that an angel had brightened the sod
And brought to each bosom a message from God.

He spoke of the Saviour—what pictures he drew !
The scene of His sufferings rose clear on my view :
The cross—the rude cross where He suffered and diea ;
The gush of bright crimson that flowed from His side ;
The cup of His sorrow, the wormwood and gall ;
The darkness that mantled the earth like a pall ;
The garland of thorns and the demon-like crews
Who knelt as they scoffed him—' Hail, King of the Jews !'

He spake, and it seemed that his statue-like form
Expanded and glowed as his spirit grew warm—
His tone so impassioned, so melting his air,
As, touched with compassion, he ended in prayer;
His hands, clasped above the blue orbs, alone
Still pleading for sins that were never his own ;
While that mouth, where such sweetness ineffable clung
Still spoke though expression had died on his tongue.

' O God ! what emotions the speaker awoke !
A mortal he seemed, yet a deity spoke ;
A man, yet so far from humanity riven !
On earth, yet so closely connected with Heaven !
How oft in my fancy I've pictured him there,
As he stood in that triumph of passion and prayer,
With his eyes closed in rapture, their transient eclipse
Made bright by the smiles that illumined his lips.

" There's a charm in delivery, a magical art,
.That thrills like a kiss from the lip to the heart ;
'Tis the glance, the expression, the well-chosen word,
By whose magic the depths of the spirit are stirred ;
The smile, the mute gesture, the soul-startling pause,
The eye's sweet expression that melts while it awes,
The lip's soft persuasion, its musical tone—
Oh ! such was the charm of that eloquent one ! "
                                        —*Amelia Welby.*

CHAPTER II.

STRUCTURE OF VERSE.

625. A poem in verse is composed of lines, feet, and syllables. These are **essentials**; but there are often **accidental** modifications, some of which belong to one poem, some or all to another, but all of which tend to increase the melody and the harmony of the composition. Thus *syllables* are arranged into *feet*, feet into *cæsural members*, cæsural members into *lines* or *verses*, verses into *groups* or stanzas, stanzas into *pieces of poetry*.

To understand fully the part which these have respectively in the construction of numbers, let us study each in particular; and first the essentials—syllables, feet, and lines.

ARTICLE I. THE SYLLABLE.

626. Every **syllable** in a sentence may be viewed in two ways—either with regard to the relative amount of *time* occupied in pronouncing it, or with regard to the relative *force* with which it is pronounced. For the slightest attention to speech will show that some syllables take more time for utterance than others, and that some are uttered more forcibly than others.

Relatively, therefore, some syllables are long and some are short, and the relative time passed in uttering the syllable is called the syllable's **quantity.** Relatively, also, some are forcibly, some are feebly uttered, and the relative force exerted in its pronunciation is called the syllable's accentuation. On its quantity and its accentuation the adaptation of a syllable for poetic purposes mainly depends.

§ 1. *Accentuation.*

627. Accentuation is the chief source of rhythmical effect in English verse. It is better adapted to the genius of our tongue than quantity ; for the accent is in general determined, whilst the quantity is not.

628. Accent is the peculiar stress laid upon a syllable to distinguish it from others ; example, *ób*duracy, en*lígh*ten, res*érve*. As accent requires a greater force of sound in uttering the syllable or letter on which it falls, a line in which syllables with the accent and syllables without it alternate affords in reading a pleasing cadence.

Every word of two syllables has an accent on one of them ; this is called the **primary** accent. Words of three syllables or more have frequently an additional accent, called the **secondary**, less forcible, however, than the primary.

629. Monosyllables have no accent upon them, since the object of the accent is to distinguish a syllable or syllables of the same word. They may, however, receive an emphasis upon them when they are the words most important to the sense. In this case emphasis has the force of accent. In the subjoined lines emphasis and primary and secondary accent are exemplified. The emphatic words are italicized, the accents are marked thus ' " :

> *Boys* will antic'-ipa"te, lav'-ish and dis'-sipa"te
> *All* that your bu'-sy pate hoar'-ded with care.

§ 2. *Quantity.*

630. The time occupied by each syllable in modern languages is determined in a great degree by the usage of the

ancient tongues, from which the modern are derived. The
ancients invented and perfected the system of quantity. It
is expedient, therefore, in explaining **quantity** to refer to
this principle as the ancients understood and employed it.
In the Latin and Greek, with the poetry of which we are
most conversant, every syllable was· heard ; none were
slurred over or lost to the ear. To prevent a disagreeable
drawl in speech the sound of the vowel was sometimes uttered briefly, sometimes prolonged. The quantity of every
vocal sound was governed by fixed rules, according to the
nature or position of the vowel. By a certain admixture
of brief and protracted sounds a musical result was obtained and time was kept. A couple of lines will illustrate it : *

Īnsŏnŭērĕ căvāe, gĕmĭtūmqŭe dĕdĕrĕ căvērnae.—*Virgil.*

Sēd fŭgĭt īntĕrĕā, fŭgĭt īrrĕpărābĭlĕ tēmpūs.—*Id.*

631. The **proportion of a long syllable to a short one**
was that of two to one; that is, the long syllable occupied
in pronunciation twice the time of a short one. Thus in
the second line the first sound, *sēd*, is protracted as long as
it takes to pronounce the two following in *fŭgĭt*. Had
every syllable been long the result would have been a
sluggish, heavy monotony, repugnant to the fine musical ear
of the Greek and Roman. Had every one been short its
frisky, precipitate steps would have ill-comported with the
dignity and the majestic sonorousness of the ancient tongues.
But by an ingenious blending of the two quantities the
metrical effect was most happy.

632. In the **English** language the force of quantity in
the arrangement of sounds is readily felt, though not so

* The bar, or *makron* (‾), denotes a long syllable ; the curve, or *breve* (‿), a
short syllable.

easily managed as in the classics. Compare, for instance, the following lines as to the time employed in uttering them :

1. Dark clouds rise, loud peals rend heaven.
2. An infinitesimal.

The two have the same number of syllables, but the former occupies at least twice the time of the latter. Combine long and short sounds, and the metrical result or the melodious flow of the verse is at once perceived :

> Ĭn h̄ōpe ănd f̄ēar, Ĭn t̄oīl ănd p̄aīn,
>   Thĕ wēarў̆ d̄āy hăve m̄ortăls p̄ast;
> Nŏw drēams ŏf b̄līss bĕ yōurs tŏ reīgn,
>   Ănd āll yŏur spēlls ăroūnd thĕm c̄ast.
> —*Mrs. Hemans.*

633. But in English the quantity, or relative time of utterance, is **by no means determinate** or constant. In the example just given many of the words may be prolonged or hurried rapidly over ; *day* and *have* in the second line, *your* and *them* in the last, may be uttered in a manner to change the quantity which the verse requires. Sometimes, in fact, the syllable is so precipitately passed over as to occupy no appreciable portion of time ; whilst long syllables occupy times so unequal in utterance as to defy every effort to obtain a strict equality or uniformity in respect to quantity. Thus in

"Graves of the good,"

the word *good* is long, and is equal to the two words *of the ;* whilst the three words *of the good* are pronounced in as short a space of time as the single monosyllable *graves,* thus rendering the quantity of the word *graves* equal to that of four short syllables.

634. The majority of syllables in our vocabulary may be uttered with greater or less rapidity or prolongation. And the rhythm of a poem founded on quantity alone (could accent be disregarded, as in the classics) would be left to the mercy of the reader. From these remarks it is evident that quantity, with us, is **not the leading principle** of metrical strains. It is a principle, however, and cannot be neglected without injury to melody. The contrary opinion and usage have rendered the expression of the most beautiful thoughts harsh and unpleasant. For although, in general, English quantity is uncertain, there are, notwithstanding, some syllables of fixed length, and they cannot be pronounced as short; others are short, and they cannot be made long in utterance unless by a particular emphasis, *e.g.*:

The waves surge high and their chasms yawn deep.

635. A common error in dealing with quantity is occasioned by confounding the words *long* and *short*, as used by orthoëpists to denote the peculiar sound of a vowel, with the same words used by prosodians in denoting the time of the entire syllable. Many consider the syllable short because the vowel has the short sound; but very often when the vowel is short the syllable is long, and sometimes when the vowel has the long sound the syllable is short. The quantity of a syllable depends upon the manner of uttering it. Thus in *far, fern, bird, come, fur,* the vowel is short, but the pronunciation is retarded by the consonants connected with it; hence the syllable is long.

636. Comprehensive **rules for the regulation of quantity** cannot be given. The following items are taken from Kerl:

1. A syllable having a long vowel or diphthongal sound,

especially when closed by one or more consonant sounds,
is long ; as, *dry, warm, proud, flashed ; round* us *roars* the
tempest *louder*.

2. A syllable having a short vowel sound, but closed or
followed by consonants in such a way as to retard pronunciation, is generally long ; as,

> When *Ajax strives* some *rock's vast weight* to *throw*.

3. A syllable ending in a short vowel sound is short; *e.g.*,

> *Thĕ, ă, ŭo, sălăry, chă-ri-ty*.

4. A syllable next to an accented syllable of the same
word is often made short by the greater stress on the accented syllable ; *e.g.*, hómewărd, púnĭshment.

5. An unimportant monosyllable ending in a single consonant, preceded by a single short vowel, and joined immediately to the more important word to which it relates, is
short: ex., ăt war.

6. A few words in the language may be pronounced
either as one syllable or as two ; ex., *our, flower, heaven, lyre*.

§ 3. *Influence of quantity and accent.*

637. We have spoken of **quantity and accent as distinct
principles** of metrical numbers. It must not be imagined
that to use or not use them is left to the free choice of the
writer. A poem cannot be written without the influence of
both acting upon the melody. When both are duly consulted the effect is most pleasing ; for variety is obtain d,
not in the duration of sound alone, but also in the stress of
voice. If one, however, of these two predominates, a particular emotion is excited. It is noticed that greater attention to quantity affects the sentiment and the tenderer feelings of the soul. Attention to accent affects the sterner

qualities of the mind. A line made from quantity is often more beautiful ; a line made from accentuation is stronger, sterner. The very words *beauty* and *strength* exemplify the theory : the word *beauty* being composed mostly of vowels, which lengthen the sound ; the word *strength* being composed of seven consonants, which sharpen the sound in the same way as an accent.

638. Here are two **examples** in which the influence of **quantity** is most sensible :

> " There is a calm for those who weep,
> A rest for weary pilgrims found ;
> They softly lie and sweetly sleep
> Low in the ground.

> " The storm that wrecks the winter's sky
> No more disturbs their deep repose
> Than summer evening's latest sigh
> That shuts the rose."—*Montgomery.*

639. Here is a strain more rapid, but rich with quantity :

> " This world is all a fleeting show,
> For man's illusion given ;
> The smiles of joy, the tears of woe—
> Deceitful shine, deceitful flow :
> There's nothing true but Heaven.

> " And false the light on glory's plume
> As fading hues of even ;
> And Love, and Hope, and Beauty's bloom
> Are flowers gathered for the tomb :
> There's nothing bright but Heaven.

> " Poor wanderers of a stormy day,
> From wave to wave we're driven ;
> And Fancy's flash and Reason's ray
> Serve but to light the troubled day :
> There's nothing calm but Heaven."—*Moore.*

640. The following piece is not given as an example of

good taste. It is quoted to illustrate the different effect produced when **accent** is more attended to :

> " In their ragged regimentals
>   Stood the old Continentals,
>   Yielding not ;
>   When the grenadiers were lunging,
>   And like hail fell the plunging
>   Cannon-shot ;
>   When the files
>   Of the isles
> From the smoky heights encampment bore the banner of the rampant
>   ' Unicorn,'
> And grummer, grummer, grummer rolled the roll of the drummer
>   Through the morn," etc.
>   —*Knickerbocker.*

641. In the following it will be seen that **emphasis on monosyllables** excites emotions similar to those aroused by heavy accentuation :

> " Though the *rock* of my *last* hope is shivered,
>   And its fragments are *sunk* in the *wave ;*
> Though I *feel* that my *soul* is delivered
>   To *pain*, it shall not be its *slave.*
> There is many a pang to pursue me—
>   They may *crush*, but they *shall* not contemn ;
> They may torture, but *shall* not subdue me ;
>   'Tis of thee that I think, not of *them.*"—*Byron.*

642. *Note.*—After these observations on quantity and accent we shall, for greater convenience, in future apply the term *long* to syllables either accented or of a prolonged sound ; the term *short* to syllables neither accented nor prolonged in utterance. The *macron* and *breve* will indicate the long and short syllable.

ARTICLE II. THE FOOT.

643. We have said that long and short syllables combined in certain proportions produce a rhythm or cadence sensible to the most obtuse ear. This rhythm is the measured tread or musical beat of the expression, like the regular pulsations of the blood or like the tread of a procession stepping in unison. A full beat is produced by a group of syllables called a **foot;** it is also known by the name of *metre* or *measure* (μετρον—*mensura,* measure). Thus in the line,

> Slŏwlў thĕ | mĭst ĭn thĕ | mĕădŏw wăs | crĕĕpĭng,

we perceive the pulsation or beat four times, produced by as many groups of syllables; hence there are four feet in the line.

In each of the following lines there are two feet:

> Wăvĭng hĕr | gōldĕn vĕil
> Ŏvĕr thĕ | sĭlĕnt dăle.—*Holmes.*

There are four beats in the following:

> Even in | the ves | per's heaven | ly tone
> They seemed | to hear | a dy | ing groan,
> And bade | the pas | sing knell | to toll
> For wel | fare of | a part | ing soul.—*Walter Scott.*

The next contains three and a half beats alternating with three:

> " Ă sīgh | o'er thĕ dāys | ŏf mў chīld | hŏŏd,
> Ă tĕăr | fŏr thĕ beău | tĭfŭl pāst ;
> Nŏ trŭst | ĭn the hōpes | ŏf thĕ fū | tŭre,
> Nŏ hōpes | ŏf ă jŏy | thăt wĭll lāst.
> Ĭ līve | ĕncīr | clĕd bў phān | tŏms,
> Ănd clīng | tŏ ă lōve | thăt mŭst flēē ;
> Ĭ ne'er | wăs sŏ săd | ănd sŏ lōne | lў,
> Ŏh ! lōne | lў ăs lōne | lў căn bĕ.

" 'Pŏor wăīf, | whăt nēĕd | ŏf rĕpīn | ĭng ?'
Sāĭd ă vŏīce | frŏm thĕ cā | verns below :
'Ĭf thĕ hĕărts | thŏu hăst lōved | ăre tŏo nār | rŏw
Tŏ ĕmbrăce | thĕe now | in thy woe,
Lŏŏk ūp | tŏ Hīm | whŏse ăffĕc | tiŏn
Ĭs brŏăd | ănd ĭmmēnse | ăs thĕ sēa,
Ănd thў sŏūl, | sŏ dĕspōn | dent ănd lōne | lў,
Shăll bĕ hāp | pў ăs hăp | pў căn bē.' "
                                   —*Lesperance.*

644. *Note.*—After reading these various exercises the student will more easily understand why a group of syllables
is called a **foot.** Some ascribe it to the fact that it is the
standard of metrical measure. Others say it is because it
corresponds to the beat in music, which was indicated by
raising and dropping the foot. It is more probable because the voice trips along the verse, making a foot or step
in each group.

§ 1. *Combinations of syllables into feet.*

645. A foot may be composed of two syllables or of three.

1. **Two syllables.** A foot of two long syllables ($\bar{\ }\,\bar{\ }$) is
called a *spondee*—so called because at the σπονδαί, or
libations in ancient times, slow, solemn melodies were used,
chiefly in this metre.

2. A foot of two short syllables ($\breve{\ }\,\breve{\ }$) is called a *pyrrhic*—
much used in the πυρρίχη, or war-song.

3. A foot of one long and one short syllable ($\bar{\ }\,\breve{\ }$) is called
a *trochee*—from τρέχειν, to run.

4. A foot with the first syllable short and the second
long ($\breve{\ }\,\bar{\ }$) is an *iambus*—ἴαμβος, the peculiar measure used
in the earliest satires ; ἰάπτειν, to satirize.

646. Feet of **three syllables** may arise from eight various
combinations :

1. The *Molossus*—from the name of an old author ; as, s̄eā-b̄eāt s̄trand.
2. The *Tribrach*—τρεῖς, three ; βραχύς, short ; as, ĭs tŏ thĕ.
3. The *Bacchic*—used in hymns to Bacchus ; as, tĭll d̄aȳlīght.
4. The *Antibacchic*—ἀντί, opposed to, viz., the Bacchic ; as, s̄wēet ēchŏ.
5. The *Amphimacer*—ἀμφί, on both sides; μακρόν, a long ; as, d̄awnĭng st̄ar.
6. The *Amphibrach*—ἀμφί, on both sides ; βραχύς, a short ; as, rĕm̄embrănce.
7. The *Dactylic*—δάκτυλος, a finger, having a long joint and two short joints ; as, P̄urĭfȳ.
8. The *Anapest*—ἀνά, back ; παίω, strike—*i.e.*, dactyl struck back ; as, Ĭntĕrdīct.

647. Sometimes **one single syllable** is so emphasized as to occupy the time of a foot. To do justice to the piece the sound must be prolonged. Of this kind are lines in Hood's "Song of the Shirt" and numbers of pieces written in imitation. Whenever used, such a syllable is indicative of deep feeling, strong passion, or solemn thought.

> " ' *Halt !*'—the dust-brown ranks stood fast ;
>   ' *Fire !*'—out blazed the rifle's blast."—*Whittier.*

§ 2. *Principal and secondary feet.*

648. Feet are either *principal* or *secondary*. **Principal feet** are those of which a poem may be wholly or chiefly formed. **Secondary feet** are certain measures sometimes blended in a poem with principal feet. A poem cannot be composed of secondary feet. There are only four principal feet. Two are of two syllables, the *trochee* and *iambus ;* two are of three syllables, the *dactyl* and *anapest.* The various others are secondary.

649. Iambuses, trochees, anapests, and dactyls produce the greatest perceptible effect in the metrical art. Read a

line or several successive lines of iambic measures, or of trochaic, dactylic, or anapestic, and you will easily perceive that a poem in any of these measures would be agreeable. Here are some **iambuses** from " Cassandra " (the prophetess of Troy, maddened because she was unheeded) :

> " Go, age ! and let thy withered cheek
>   Be wet once more with freezing tears,
>   And bid thy trembling sorrow speak
>   In accents of departed years.
>
> " Go, child ! and pour thy sinless prayer
>   Before the everlasting throne ;
>   And He who sits in glory there
>   May stoop to hear thy silent tone.
>
> " Ye will not hear, ye will not know ;
>   Ye scorn the maniac's idle song ;
>   Ye care not !—but the voice of woe
>   Shall thunder loud and echo long."—*Holmes.*

650. In the following there are numerous **trochees**.

" THE MARTYRDOM.

" *Angels.* Bearing lilies in our bosom,
          Holy Agnes, we have flown,
        Missioned from the Heaven of Heavens
          Unto thee, and thee alone.
We are coming, we are flying.   Lo ! behold thy happy dying.

> " When a Christian lies expiring,
>   Angel choirs with plumes outspread
>   Bend above his death-bed, singing
>   That, when Death's mild sleep is fled,
> There may be no harsh transition while he greets the heavenly
>   vision."—*Aubrey de Vere.*

651. In the two examples just given quite a difference is perceptible, though the trochee which is most prominent

in the latter is but an iambus reversed ; the one is quick and lively, the other grand and stately.

In the next the **dactyl** is very frequent:

> " Leave us not—leave us not,
> Say not adieu ;
> Have we not been to thee
> Tender and true?
> Take not thy sunny smile
> Far from our hearth ;
> With that sweet light will fade
> Summer and mirth.
> Leave us not—leave us not ;
> Can thy heart roam ?
> Wilt thou not pine to hear
> Voices from home ?"—*Hemans.*

652. " The Sister of Charity " will give us the **anapest,** or dactyl reversed.   The dactyl is a quicker measure than the trochee ; and the anapest has a more majestic step than the iambus.   It is not, however, so well suited to every subject :

> ' She once was a lady of honor and wealth;
> Bright glowed in her features the roses of health ;
> Her vesture was blended of silk and of gold,
> And her motion shook perfume from every fold.
> Joy revelled around her, love shone at her side,
> And gay was her smile as the glance of a bride ;
> And light was her step in the mirth-sounding hall
> When she heard of the daughters of Vincent de Paul.

> " She felt in her spirit the summons of grace
> That called her to live for her suffering race ;
> And, heedless of pleasure, of comfort, of home,
> Rose quickly like Mary, and answered, ' I come.'
> She put from her person the trappings of pride,
> And passed from her home with the joy of a bride ;
> Nor wept at the threshold as onward she moved—
> For her heart was on fire in the cause it approved.

" Lost ever to fashion, to vanity lost,
    That beauty that once was the song and the toast ;
    No more in the ball-room that figure we meet,
    But gliding at dusk to the wretch's retreat.
    Forgot in the halls is that high-sounding name,
    For the Sister of Charity blushes at fame ;
    Forgot are the claims of her riches and birth,
    For she barters for Heaven the glory of earth.

" Those feet that to music could gracefully move
    Now bear her alone on the mission of love ;
    Those hands that once dangled the perfume and gem
    Are tending the helpless or lifted for them ;
    That voice that once echoed the song of the vain
    Now whispers relief to the bosom of pain ;
    And the hair that was shining with diamond and pearl
    Is wet with the tears of the penitent girl.

" Her down-bed—a pallet ; her trinkets – a bead ;
    Her lustre—one taper, that serves her to read ;
    Her sculpture—the crucifix nailed by her bed ;
    Her paintings—one print of the thorn-crownèd head ;
    Her cushion—the pavement that wearies her knees ;
    Her music—the psalm, or the sigh of disease :
    The delicate lady lives mortified there,
    And the feast is forsaken for fasting and prayer.

" Yet not to the service of heart and of mind
    Are the cares of the Heaven-minded virgin confined :
    Like Him whom she loves, to the mansions of grief
    She hastes with the tidings of joy and relief ;
    She strengthens the weary, she comforts the weak,
    And soft is her voice in the ear of the sick ;
    Where want and affliction on mortals attend,
    The Sister of Charity *there* is a friend.

" Unshrinking where pestilence scatters his breath,
    Like an angel she moves 'mid the vapors of death ;
    Where rings the loud musket and flashes the sword
    Unfearing she walks—for she follows her Lord.

> How sweetly she bends o'er each plague-tainted face
> With looks that are lighted with holiest grace !
> How kindly she dresses each suffering limb !
> For she sees in the wounded the image of Him.
>
> " Behold her, ye worldly ! behold her, ye vain !
> Who shrink from the pathway of virtue and pain ;
> Who yield up to pleasure your nights and your days,
> Forgetful of service, forgetful of praise.
> Ye lazy philosophers, self-seeking men ;
> Ye fireside philanthropists, great at the pen ;
> How stands in the balance your eloquence, weighed
> With the life and the deeds of that high-born maid ?"
>
> *—Gerald Griffin.*

ARTICLE III. THE VERSE.

653. A **verse** is a line consisting of a certain number of feet.

Note.—The term *verse* is often improperly used to designate a number of lines. Its true meaning is a single line, composed of feet. The word is derived from *vertere*, to turn, because the pen reverts at the close of each line to begin a new one.

To **scan** a verse is to resolve it into its several divisions.

To **versify** means to make verses ; whence the art of versification is the art of making verses.

§ 1. *Species and length of the verse.*

654. Lines or verses receive their specific name from the foot which predominates in them. Thus they are called *Iambic, Trochaic, Anapestic,* or *Dactylic,* according as the iambus, trochee, anapest, or dactyl is wholly or principally employed in them. Examples have been given of each.

655. With regard to the **length of verses** the greatest variety is admitted. They may consist of one, two, three feet, or more ; they may even include in their limits seven or eight feet. Lines of less than three feet, however, are generally found in combination with lines of greater length. They frequently have, in this conjunction, a beautiful effect. A lengthy piece composed of lines less than three feet has an unpleasant sound. Cardinal Newman seems to have understood this in his " Dream of Gerontius," where the demons speak without melody ; the angels speak melodiously. (See *Verses on Various Occasions*, p. 293, etc.)

656. The **length of a verse is indicated** by a Greek numeral compounded with the term *meter* (μέτρον, a measure or standard of measure).

A line of one foot is called a *monometer* (μόνον, one, *i.e.*, measure).

A line of two feet is called a *dimeter* (δίς, twice, *i.e.*, the measure).

A line of three feet is called a *trimeter* (τρίς, thrice).

A line of four feet is called a *tetrameter* (τέτρα, four).

In the same way *pentameters* (five feet), *hexameters* (six feet), *heptameters* (seven feet), *octometers* (eight feet), are formed respectively from πέντε, ἕξ, ἑπτά, ὀκτά.

It is easy to understand from the foregoing what is an iambic monometer, an iambic dimeter, or an iambic pentameter ; also what is a trochaic monometer or dimeter, a dactylic or anapestic monometer, dimeter, trimeter, etc. The first term gives the species of verse, the second its length.

§ 2. *Acatalectic, catalectic, and hypermeter.*

657. It very often happens that verses are not exact monometers, nor exact dimeters, trimeters, etc. They are frequently longer than a dimeter and yet shorter than a trimeter, or longer than a trimeter and too short for a tetrameter, etc.

If the line consists of full round feet, neither lacking a syllable of completion nor having one too much, the line is said to be **acatalectic** (καταληκτικός, stopping short or incomplete, and α privative, *i.e.*, not incomplete).

If it lacks one syllable of completion the verse is said to be **catalectic** (καταληκτικός, incomplete) ; if it contains one syllable over an exact measure it is styled **hypermeter** (ὑπέρ, above ; μέτρον, the measure).

658. In iambic and trochaic measures it is optional to call a foot and a half a *monometer hypermeter* or a *dimeter catalectic ;* two feet and a half a *dimeter hypermeter* or a *trimeter catalectic*, etc., etc.

But in dactylic and anapestic measures a monometer hypermeter contains one syllable less than a dimeter catalectic ; a dimeter hypermeter one syllable less than a trimeter catalectic, etc.

Thus :

<blockquote>

"Făr frŏm oŭr | hĕārth ⟩ are dactylic monometer
   Sūmmĕr ănd | mĭrth." ⟨   hypermeters.
               —*Mrs. Hemans.*

</blockquote>

But

<blockquote>

"Swēĕt wăs Ĭts | blēssĭñg, ⟩ are dactylic dimeter
   Kĭnd Ĭts că | rēssĭñg." ⟨   catalectics.
               —*Mrs. Cockburn.*

</blockquote>

§ 3. *Combining and dividing verses.*

659. It is sometimes useful to make **one verse out of two,** or to make **two out of one.** Short lines begin and close before the ear can readily detect the correspondence of the parts and the harmony of the construction. But if two such lines be combined the result is more beautiful.

Example :

" No fear more,
  No tear more
To stain my lifeless face ;
  Enclasped
  And grasped
Within thy cold embrace."
	is oftener
	written
		" No fear more, no tear
		   more
		To stain my lifeless face ;
		Enclasped and grasped
		Within thy cold embrace."
		          —*Burns.*

660. A heavy and monotonous line may be rendered sprightly and agreeable by division. The hexameter, if written by one skilled in melodious strains, may be changed into two trimeters, or into one tetrameter and one dimeter ; the heptameter into a tetrameter and trimeter, or into a pentameter and dimeter.

Examples:

" Look on the children of our poor, on many an English child ;
Better that it had died secure by yonder river wild.
Flung careless on the waves of life, from childhood's earliest
    time
They struggle one perpetual strife with hunger and with crime."
                                          —Landon.

The same verse of a different length :

Lock on the children of our poor,
  On many an English child ;
Better that it had died secure
  By yonder river wild.

Flung careless on the waves of
  life,
  From childhood's earliest time
They struggle one perpetual
  strife
With hunger and with crime.

661. This example of an **octometer catalectic** trochaic is capable of two constructions—thus :

" And the only word there spoken was the whispered word ' Le-
    nore !'
This I whispered, and an echo murmured back the word ' Le-
    nore !'
                Merely this and nothing more."
                                      —Poe.

      And the only word there spoken
      Was the whispered word " Lenore !"
      This I whispered, and an echo
      Murmured back the word " Lenore !"
            Merely this and nothing more.

· § 4. *The blending of various feet in the same verse.*

662. In verse, as in every other art, strict uniformity may become monotonous, and the regular return of an alternate long and short syllable will tire the ear. To avoid this an occasional variation in the form is allowed; and a secondary foot, or a principal foot of a different species from that which predominates, may be introduced.

Verses composed of only one species of feet are said to be **pure**; those in which two or more species are employed are said to be **mixed.**

Rules can hardly be given to fix what is allowed and what should be avoided in mingling various feet. A delicate ear will, after some practice, be the safest guide.

663. The following **liberties** are taken by the best writers:
I. **Spondees are admitted** into iambic and trochaic verse
Examples:

Iambic: "I had a dream, a strange | *wīld drēam.* |
　　　"*Păle grēw* | the youthful warrior that | *pāle face* | to meet."
　Trochaic: "Sixty pillars, | *ēach ōne* | shining
　　　　　With a wreath of rubies twining,
　　　　　Bear the roof; the | *snōw-whīte* | floor
　　　　　Is with | *smāll stārs* | studded o'er."

It is frequently found in *anapestic* measure.
Example:

　　"| *Swēet vāle* | of Avoca, how calm could I rest."

664. II. The **Pyrrhic** is occasionally employed in iambic and trochaic measure.
Examples:

　　Iambic: "Goest thou to build an early name,
　　　　Ŏr eār | *ĭy ĭn* | the task to die?"—*Bryant.*

Trochaic: " | *Thĕn thĕ* | forms of | *thĕ dĕ* ' parted
Enter | *ăt thĕ* | open door."—*Longfellow.*

Note.—The syllables italicized exemplify the remark ; other syllables scored, but not in italics, betray some liberty in the use of other species of feet.

665. III. A **Pyrrhic in the first and a Spondee in the second** place of iambic verse, when occasionally adopted, give a fine variety.

Example :

" The watch-dog's voice that bay'd the whispering wind,
Ănd thĕ | *loŭd laŭgh* | that spoke the vacant mind."

—*Goldsmith.*

666. IV. The **Tribrach** is found in iambic strains.
Example :

" His country's suf | *fĕrĭngs ănd* | his children's shame
Streamed o'er his mem | *ŏrў lĭke* | a forest flame."

—*Holmes.*

667. V. The **Molossus** rarely, but the **Amphimacer** and the **Bacchic** foot frequently, enter the anapestic verse.
Example :

" Wert thou all that I wish | *thēe, grēat, glōr* | ious, and free,
First flower of the earth and first gem of the sea !
I might hail | *thēe wĭth prōud* | er, with happier brow,
Bŭt ăh ! could I love thee more deeply than now?
| *Nŏ ! thў chāins* | as they rankle, thy blood as it runs,
Bŭt māke | *thēe mōre pāin* | fully dear to thy sons,
Whōse hēarts, like the young of the des | *ĕrt bīrd's nēst,* |
Drĭnk lōve in each life | *drŏp thăt flōws* | from thy breast."

—*Moore.*

668. VI. The **Antibacchic** foot occurs in dactylic verse. The last foot in dactylic measure is often occupied by an **Amphimacer** ; the reason of this is to secure a rhyme more easily, as we shall see. The **Amphibrach** is rarely found.

The following to the skylark will afford examples of the three last named :

> ' Bird of the wilderness,
>> Blithesome and cumberless,
> Sweet be thy | *mātīn o'er* | moorland and lea ;
>> Emblem of happiness,
>>> Blest in thy | *dwelling place :* |
> Oh ! to abide in the desert with thee !
>> Wild is thy | *lay and loud,* |
>> Far in the | *downy cloud ;* |
> | *Love gives it* | energy, | *love gave it* | birth ;
>> Where on thy | *dewy wing,* |
>> Where art thou journeying ?
> *Thy lay is in heaven, thy love is on earth.*"—*Jas. Hogg.*

This last verse may be divided into three amphibrachs and one iambus, or into one iambus and three anapests.

669. We have spoken of the intermixture of secondary feet in a verse ; a yet more beautiful result is obtained by blending judiciously the **various principal feet.** Thus : I. **Iambic verses** admit the trochee into every foot of the line except the second and last, where the trochee would be inharmonious. The common and happiest place of the trochee is the first :

> " But one *still watched* no self-encircled woes,
> | *Chased from* | his lids the ang | *el of* | repose ;
>> He watched, he wept—for thoughts of bitter years
> | *Bowed his* | dark lashes, wet with burning tears."—*Holmes.*

670. II. **Trochees** admit the dactyl. In the following (by Longfellow) two pyrrhics, one spondee, and one dactyl are found. The iambus in the second verse is injurious to the melody :

> " *In the court-yard of the* castle, bound with | *many an* | iron band,
>> Stands the mighty linden planted by Queen Cunigunde's hand."

671. III. **Dactylic** verse admits trochees ; other species
are often introduced, but the result is less happy. The
difficulty of constructing them renders pure dactylic verses
very rare :

> " | *Rīng oŭt* | merrily,
> | *Loūdlў,* | cheerily,
> Blīthe ōld | bēlls frŏm thĕ | *stēeplĕ* | *tōwĕr !* |
> Hopefully, fearfully,
> Joyfully, tearfully,
> Moveth the bride from the | *maīdĕn* | *bōwĕr*." |

672. IV. A very ordinary and a very successful variety
is found in mixing **iambuses and anapests.** The anapest
dropped into an iambic verse gives it a sprightly motion :

Example :

> "Fūll măn | *ȳ ă gēm* | of purest ray serene
>   The dark, unfathomed caves of ocean bear;
> Fūll măn | *y ă flōwer* | is born to blush unseen,
>   And waste its sweetness on the desert air."—*Gray.*

673. A regular return of the iambus and anapest has a
vigorous, racy, and agreeable effect :

> " *'Tis a bird* I love, *with its brood*ing note,
>   *And the trem*bling throb *in its mott*led throat ;
>   *There's a hum*an look *in its swell*ing breast
>   *And the gen*tle curve *of its low*ly crest ;
>   *And I of*ten stop *with the fear* I feel,
>   He runs so close *to the rap*id wheel."— *Willis.*

674. An anapest at the opening of an iambic line is
frequent ; it saves the piece from a dreary monotony :

> " *Thou art come* from forests dark and deep, thou mighty, rushing wind,
>   *And thou bear*est all their unisons in one full swell combined ;
>   *Thou art come* from cities lighted up fŏr thĕ cōnqueror passing by,
>   *Thou art waft*ing from their streets a sound of haughty revelry ;

Thou art come from kingly tombs and shrines, from ancient minsters
   vast,
Through the dark eye of a thousand years thy lonely wing hath
   passed;
Thou hast caught the anthem's billowy swell, the stately dirge's tone,
For a chief with a sword and shield and helm *to his place* of slumber
   gone."—*Mrs. Hemans.*

675. An iambus at the opening of an anapestic verse is
very commonly found, and is in uncommonly good taste:

" *The robe* and the ermine, by few they are won ;
   How many sink down ere the race be half run !
   What struggles, what hopes, what despair, may have been
   Where sweep those dark branches of shadowy green !
   What crowds are around us—what misery is there,
   Could the heart, like the face which conceals it, lie bare ! "
                                        —*Miss Landon.*

ARTICLE IV. STRUCTURE OF THE STANZA.

676. **Verses may be arranged** in simple succession or in
groups. Nearly all long poems of a solemn or historic
character take the former system—such are epics, essays,
dramas, etc. In the latter method are indited shorter
pieces, and those especially of a highly imaginative or a
deeply tender nature. Of this kind are songs, elegiac
verses, etc. Some very long pieces are found in this
shape. When the verses are of a uniform species and
length they are more frequently put down in regular
succession ; but when they combine measures of various
lengths or species they are separated into groups.

677. A complete group of verses adjusted together constitutes the **Stanza** (from *stare,* to stand or stop—because
the sense is usually expressed in the limits of the group,
and a period is at the close).

Stanzas may be of **infinite variety,** according to the taste of the writer. The number of lines and the various measures combined in them are determined by no rules. Hence we find stanzas of varied and fantastic shapes. Here are two out of eight stanzas on " The Brevity of Life " :

<pre>
            Behold !...............................1 foot.
        How short a span.......................2 feet.
       Was long enough of old........................3 feet.
     To measure out the life of man.......................4 feet.
   In those well-tempered days his time was then...........5 feet.
Surveyed, cast up, and found but threescore years and ten....6 feet.
</pre>

<pre>
            Alas !
         And what is that ?
       They come and slide and pass
     Before my pen can tell thee what.
   The posts of time are swift, which having run
Their seven short stages o'er, their short-lived task is done.
                                    —*Francis Quarles.*
</pre>

678. Numbers of other shapes, fanciful and odd, have been given to stanzas; they are compositions generally without melody, often without sense. Their chief merit lies in the fact that they are *difficiles nugæ*—trifles, it is true, but difficult trifles. The ·**simpler kinds** of stanza are commonly more agreeable than intricate and ingenious inventions. The ear is well pleased by a regular and quick return of like measures. **Unusual combinations** of verses are successful when they are the dress of lofty and unusually stirring thoughts.

679. **Verses of more than five feet** are generally grouped in stanzas of four, sometimes of six or eight. Here is a stanza of four heptameters, which, however, could be enlarged, for the reason that each verse is divided into a tetrameter and trimeter, thus rendering it fluent :

" My speech is faltering and low—the world is fading fast—
The sands of life are few and slow—this day will be my last.
I've something for thine ear ; bend close—list to my failing word ;
Lay what I utter to thy soul, and start not when 'tis heard."

—*Cook.*

Here are **dimeters**:

" 1. And it is meant
　　To weave a tent
Of summer twilight over,
　　With warp and woof,
　　And all sun-proof—
A cool and fragrant cover.

" 2. And from the earth
　　A stream of mirth
Into the spirit rises,
　　While sudden spring
　　From off her wing
Is scattering sweet surprises.

" 3. And every hour
　　In vernal shower
The heart finds sweet ablution,
　　While it receives
　　'Mid buds and leaves
A very absolution."—*Rev. F. W. Faber.*

The same could be changed into a beautiful stanza of twelve tetrameters and trimeters :

" And it is meant to weave a tent
　　Of summer twilight over,
With warp and woof, and all sun-proof—
　　A cool and fragrant cover," etc.

It would please less if put into a stanza of six heptameters, such as :

' And it is meant to weave a tent of summer twilight over,
With warp and woof, and all sun-proof a cool and fragrant cover.'

680. **Stanzas of another form**:
Amidst the variety of stanzas here given we notice : 1, that the stanzas of each piece are similar ; 2, that each stanza contains a separate thought, distinct from the others, and therefore thrown into a distinct form :

"To the Sea.

" What hidest thou in thy treasure-caves and cells,
   Thou hollow-sounding and mysterious main ?
Pale, glistening pearls, and rainbow-colored shells,
   Bright things which gleam unrecked-of and in vain.
Keep, keep thy riches, melancholy sea—
       We ask not such of thee.

" Yet more ! the billows and the depths have more !
   High hearts and brave are gathered to thy breast !
They hear not now the booming waters roar ;
   The battle-thunders will not break their rest :
Keep thy red gold and gems, thou stormy grave !
      Give back the true and brave."
          —*Felicia Hemans.*

681. "Stanzas written at my Mother's Grave

" The trembling dewdrops fall
Upon the shutting flowers ; like souls at rest
   The stars shine gloriously : and all
      Save me is blest.

" Mother, I love thy grave !
The violet, with its blossoms blue and mild,
   Waves o'er thy head : when shall it wave
      Above thy child ?

" Where is thy spirit flown ?
I gaze above—thy look is imaged there ;
   I listen, and thy gentle tone
      Is on the air.

" Oh, come ! while here I press
My brow upon thy grave, and in those mild
   And thrilling words of tenderness
      Bless—bless thy child."
        —*Geo. D. Prentice.*

682. THE HEART'S SONG.

1. In the silent midnight watches,
    List—thy bosom door !
How it knocketh, knocketh, knocketh,
    Knocketh evermore !
Say not 'tis thy pulse's beating—
    'Tis thy heart of sin ;
'Tis thy Saviour knocks and crieth :
    " Rise and let me in ! "

2. Death comes down with reck-
    less footsteps
    To the hall and hut ,
Think you Death will stand
    a-knocking
    Where the door is shut ?
Jesus waiteth, waiteth, waiteth,
    But the door is fast ! .
Grieved, away the Saviour goeth:
    Death breaks in at last.

3 Then 'tis thine to stand en-
    treating
    Christ to let thee in ;
At the gate of heaven beating,
    Wailing for thy sin.
Nay, alas ! thou foolish virgin,
    Hast thou then forgot
Jesus waited long to know thee,
    But He knows thee not ?
                            —*Coxe.*

683. A NAME IN THE SAND.

1. Alone I walked the ocean
    strand ;
A pearly shell was in my hand ;
I stooped and wrote upon the
    sand
    My name, the year, the day.
As onward from the spot I passed
One lingering look behind I cast: .
A wave came rolling high and fast,
    And washed my lines away.

2. And so, methought, 'twill
    shortly be
With every mark on earth from
    me :
A wave of dark Oblivion's sea
    Will sweep across the place
Where I have trod the sandy shore
Of time, and been to be no more ;
Of me, my day, the name I bore,
    To leave nor track nor trace.

3. And yet with Him who counts
    the sands,
And holds the waters in His
    hands,
I know a lasting record stands,
    Inscribed against my name—
Of all this mortal part hath
    wrought,
Of all this thinking soul has
    thought,
And from these fleeting moments
    caught
    Of glory or of shame.
                    —*Hannah Gould.*

In the well-known poem, " Lamentation of David over the Body of Absalom," by Willis, both systems, successive lines and stanzas, are employed.

684. A more labored arrangement is that of the *Acrostic.*
The **acrostic** is a stanza in which the initial letters of the
different verses, taken in the order in which they proceed,
make up a word or phrase, usually the name ot a person,
an epoch, a virtue, or some motto :

> " *R*ome on her hill is standing still,
> *O*ld as the hill is her truth ;
> *M*any a gentile reviles her the while,
> *E*xhausting his age on her youth."

685. When both the initial letters and the letters at the
middle of each verse constitute a word or sentence it is a
double acrostic:

> " *J*esus, to Thee and Thy *M*other I offer
> *E*ach hope of my heart and its *A*rdent affection i
> *S*hattered by shipwreck, a *R*emnant I proffer ;
> *U*nder Thy guidance and *I*n Thy protection
> *S*hield it and shelter it *A*t resurrection."

686. Here is an ingenious Latin acrostic, bearing the
Holy Name at the beginning, at the end, at the middle,
and in the centre :

> " *I*nter cuncta micans *I*gniti sidera coel*I*,
> *E*xpellit tenebras *E* toto Phœbus ut orb*E* ;
> *S*ic cæcas removet *IESVS* caligine umbra*S.*
> *V*ivificansque simul *V*ero præcordia mot*V*,
> *S*olem justitiæ *S*ese probat esse beatu*S.*"

ARTICLE V. RHYME.

687. **Rhyme** is an element not essential to poetry, but
found in the greater part of English verse.

The return of similar or identical sounds, like an accord
in music, gives to verse a new beauty. This repetition of
sounds, whether they be the same or only like sounds, is to
some, it is true, an empty jingle, an unmeaning, expression-
less trick, unworthy of attention ; but on the majority it

has a strange and a powerful effect. Ballads become famous with a little rhythm and a good deal of rhyme.

 1. The fondness of the ear for this feature is observed in the simplest form of it, called *alliteration :*

§ 1. *Alliteration and Repetition.*

688. **Alliteration** is the use of such words as begin with or contain the same letter :

> 1. " *Sl*ow*ly* and *s*ad*ly* we *l*aid him down,
>   *F*rom the *f*ield of his *f*ame *f*resh and gory."—*Wolfe.*
>
> 2. " I *l*ove the *l*yric of the soaring *l*ark."—*Bungar.*
>
> 3. " And *f*ast be*f*ore *th*eir *fath*er's men."—*Campbell.*
>
> 4. " *H*is *h*orsemen *h*ard be*h*ind us ride."
>
> 5. " What this *g*rim, ungainly, *g*hastly, *g*aunt, and ominous bird."—*Poe.*

Note.—Alliteration is most successful when most natural and least studied. It seems spontaneous in the following, where the aspirate expresses sensibly the panting of heavy labor :

> " Up the *h*igh *h*ill *h*e *h*eaves a *h*uge round stone."—*Pope.*

689. 2. Allied to Alliteration is the **Repetition** of syllables and entire words :

> 1. " *Un*wept, *un*honored, and *un*sung."
>
> 2. " *Un*heed*ing* and *unheeded.*"
>
> 3. " The *light laugh* is *laugh*ed and the *sweet song* is *sung.*"
>   —*Landon.*
>
> 4. " Trea*son* and poi*son* are *named* with his *name.*"—*Id.*
>
> 5. " *Flow gently*, sweet Afton, among thy green braes ;
>   *Flow gently*, I'll *sing* thee a *song* in thy praise."
>   —*Burns.*

6. " *Scenes of woe* and *scenes of pleasure*,
   Scenes that former thoughts renew ;
  Scenes of woe and *scenes of pleasure*,
   Now a sad and last adieu."—*Richard Gall.*

7. " ' *One* body, *one* spirit,' ' *one* Lord,'
   And ' *one* faith ' for all ages was given ;
   ' *One* baptism ' in blessed accord
   With *one* God and ' *one* Father ' in Heaven ;
   ' *One* Church,' the sole pillar and ground
   Of the truth, an unmovable rock ;
   ' *One* shepherd ' by all to be owned,
   And ' *one* Fold ' for that primitive flock."
           —Anon. in *Lyra Catholica.*

§ 2. *Nature and laws of rhyme.*

690. In **rhyme,** properly so called, the sounds must not be identical, as in alliteration, but merely *similar.*

Thus, 'flows,' 'rose ;' 'by,' 'dry,' contain similar sounds.

There are **two kinds** of rhyme, the *perfect* and the *imperfect.*

A rhyme is **perfect** when the resemblance is entire and genuine :

" No grandeur of prospect astonished the *sight*,
  No abruptness sublime mingled awe with de*light.*
  Here the wild flower blossomed, the elm proudly *waved,*
  And pure was the current the green bank that *laved.*"
           —*Halleck.*

691. To **secure a perfect rhyme** the following circumstances must concur :

1. Similarity or identity in the vowel sounds of accented syllables.

2. Similarity or identity in the consonant sounds that follow the vowel, if any. These two rules will insure resemblance ; but a third is necessary to prevent identity of sound :

3. Diversity in the consonant sounds that precede the vowels, if any; and there must be a consonant preceding one of the vowels.   In the examples given we have identity of vowel sounds, identity of consonants affixed, and diversity of consonants prefixed to the vowels.

It is not necessary to have the same vowels or consonants following those vowels; thus the following words, though they have not the same vowels or consonants, form perfect rhymes : beaux, rose, flows, sews, etc.; and many words that have the same spelling do not rhyme : tough, plough, dough, cough, etc.

692. Rhymes are called **imperfect** or allowable when the resemblance is slight; such is the case :

1. When the vowel sounds are alike, but are not in an accented syllable :

> " Awake, my soul ! awake, mine eyes !
>   Awake, my drowsy fácul*ties* ! "—*Thos. Flatman.*

> " Sleep ! downy sleep ! come close mine eyes,
>   Tired with beholding váni*ties*."—*Id.*

2. When the vowel sounds are dissimilar; as, 'wood,' 'abode,' etc.:

> " But the spirit that ruled o'er the thick-tangled *wood*,
>   And deep in its gloom fixed his murky *abode*."—*Halleck.*

> " While the noise of the war-whoop still rang in his *ears*,
>   And the fresh-bleeding scalp as a trophy he *bears*."—*Id.*

3. When the vowels are followed by dissimilar consonant sounds :

> " A peopled city made a desert *place* ;
>   All that I saw, and part of which I *was*."—*Dryden.*

4. When the vowel is immediately preceded by the same consonant sound :

> " Seasons and months began the long proce*ss*ion,
>   And measured o'er the year in bright suc*cess*ion."
>   —*Mrs. Barbauld.*

> " Vile man is so per*verse*,
>   'Tis too rough work for *verse*."—*Baxter.*

693. The best authors have occasionally used imperfect rhymes ; in fact, it requires too much labor at times to hunt up similar sounds. There are, however, some liberties taken which haste will not justify :

> " Some heart's deep language, where the glow
>   Of quenchless faith sur*vives ;*
>   For every feature said, ' I know
>   That my Redeemer *lives.*' "—*Mrs. Hemans.*

> " Ye stars ! bright legions that before all *time*
>   Camped in yon plain of sapphire, what can TELL
>   Your burning myriads, but the eye of *Him*
>   Who bade through Heaven your golden chariots WHEEL ? "
>   —*Geo. Croly.*

694. There are a few words which have two pronunciations, one for prose and one for poetry. Thus the word ' wind ' (a current of air) forms a perfect rhyme with mind, find, behind, etc., according to its poetic pronunciation :

> " When genial gales the frozen air un*bind*,
>   The screaming legions wheel and mount the *wind*."
>   —*Beattie.*

So also the word ' wound ' (a hurt), more usually pronounced in prose like pruned, forms in verse a perfect rhyme with found, bound, etc.:

> " But round my heart the ties are *bound*,
>   That heart transpierced with many a *wound*."—*Burns.*

§ 3. *Single, double, and triple rhymes.*

695. A rhyme, to be pleasing, must fall on a long sylla-

ble ; for this engages the attention of the mind.   If, therefore, the verse closes with an exact iambus or anapest, the rhyme is on the ultimate syllable of the verse ; if it closes with an exact trochee the rhyme is on the penultimate syllable ; if the last foot is a dactyl the rhyme is on the antepenultimate.

696. When the rhyme is on the ultimate it is called a **single rhyme** :

> " As a beam o'er the face of the waters may *glow*
>   While the tide runs in darkness and coldness be*low*,
>   So the cheek may be tinged with a warm, sunny *smile*,
>   Though the cold heart to ruin runs darkly the *while*."
>
> —*Moore.*

697. The **double rhyme** belongs to the trochaic acatalectic.   It will be noted in the double rhyme that the penultimate syllables only are similar in sound, and that the ultimate syllables are identical in sound—as, 'healing,' 'dealing'; the last syllables have the same sound, the next to the last have like sounds :

LITTLE NELL.

" Spring, with breezes cool and airy,
Opened on a little *fairy*,
Ever restless, making *merry*;
She, with pouting lips of *cherry*,
Lisped the words she could not *master*,
Vexed that she might speak no *faster*—
Laughing, playing, running, *dancing*,
Mischief all her joys en*hancing*.

" Autumn came! the leaves were *falling*,
Death the little one was *calling* ;
Pale and wan she grew, and *weakly*,
Bearing all her pains so *meekly*
That to us she seemed still *dearer*
As the trial-hour drew *nearer*.
But she left us hopeless, *lonely*,
Watching by her semblance *only*,
And a little grave they *made* her,
In the churchyard cold they *laid* her."—*Rebecca Nichols.*

See also Dryden's " Ode in honor of St. Cecilia"; *e.g.:*

> " Softly sweet, in Lydian measures,
> Soon he sooth'd his soul to pleasures.
> War, he sung, is toil and trouble ;
> Honor but an empty bubble ;
> Never ending, still beginning,
> Fighting still, and still destroying.
> If the world be worth the winning,
> Think, O think it worth enjoying! "

698. The **triple rhyme** is the rarest. It requires a long syllable in the antepenultimate—a condition which it is hard to satisfy. In this rhyme the ultimate and penultimate must be identical ; as, 'charity' rhymes with 'parity,' 'vanity' with 'humanity,' etc.

> " Touch her not *scorn ful ly,*
> Think of her *mourn ful ly,*
> Make no deep *scru ti ny*
> Into her *mu ti ny.*"—*Hood.*

The difficulty in finding triple rhymes is the main reason why dactylic verse generally closes with an amphimacer or trochee, or a single hypermeter.

699. The following stanza embraces the single, the double, and the triple rhyme. It would be excusable if all the stanzas of the piece were similarly constructed ; the other stanzas, however, of the same piece, "The Bridge of Sighs," vary widely :

> " Perishing *gloomily,*
> Spurred by con*tumely,*
> Cold inhum*anity,*
> Burning ins*anity*
> Into her *rest.*
> Cross her hands *humbly,*
> As if praying *dumbly,*
> Over her br*east.*"—*Hood.*

NOTE.—Catalectics and hypermeters follow the rule of acatalectics—the rhyme is on the long syllable.

§ 4. *Position of the rhyme in verse.*

700. At the **dawn of English verse** rhyme was unknown, but alliteration was indulged in. Gradually the recurrence of a letter at intervals in the course of the verse extended to syllables, then to a syllable at the close of the verse, where, being last heard, it would produce a deeper impression. It is far more striking at that point than a mere repetition of sounds elsewhere would prove.

Example:

> " Ah ! fleeting spirit, wandering *fire,*
>   That long hast warmed my tender *breast,*
> Must thou no more this frame *inspire,*
>   No more a pleasing, cheerful *guest ?*
> Whither, ah ! whither art thou *flying,*
>   To what dark, undiscovered *shore ?*
> Thou seem'st all trembling, shivering, *dying,*
>   And wit and humor are no *more.*"
>   —Pope's translation of *Adrian's Versicles.*

701. The **middle** of the verse is sometimes accordant with the **close.**

Example:

Single rhyme :   " I sift the *snow* on the mountain *below,*
>   And the great pines groan aghast ;
>   And all the *night* 'tis my pillow *white,*
>   While I sleep in the arms of the blast."— *Shelley.*

Double rhyme :   " Sublime on the *towers* of my skyey *bowers*
>   Lightning, my pilot, sits ;
>   . In a cavern *under* is fretted the *thunder—*
>   It struggles and frets at fits."— *Id.*

Triple rhyme :
> " Boys will an*ticipate,* lavish, and *dissipate*
>   All that your busy pate hoarded with care ;
> And in their *foolishness,* passion, and *mulishness*
>   Charge you with churlishness, spurning your prayer."

702. In some poems lines rhyme in close succession ; in others the rhyme falls upon alternate verses ; in others various systems, with or without a rule, prevail. **Succes- sive rhymes** are the more common :

> " Slowly and softly it flittereth *down*,
>   Veiling the earth's sombre mantle of *brown*.
>   Lightly it drifteth in eddying *whirls*,
>   Crowning each brow with a chaplet of *pearls*."—*Una.*

703. 1. If only two successive lines end similarly (as above), the two constitute the **couplet**, sometimes styled a **distich** (δίς, στίχος, two lines).

2. If three lines, and only three, rhyme together, they form the **triplet.**

Example :

> " For Iris had no mother to enfold her,
>   Nor ever leaned upon a sister's shoulder,
>   Telling the twilight thoughts that nature told her."
>   —*Holmes.*

It was the practice formerly to throw a triplet among couplets irregularly and without method. The practice is discontinued, except in the Ode, where greater freedom prevails.

704. When four successive lines rhyme together they form a **quatrain;** as :

> " I cast my eager, straining eye
>   From sky to sand, from sand to sky—
>   No, no relief ! My hound and I
>   Were all that broke the vacancy."—*Eliza Cook.*

705. **Alternate rhymes.** More frequently the first rhymes with the third, the second with the fourth ; as :

" See how the rose and eglantine are threading
Through all the openings in the acacia leaves ;
The massive chestnuts their white flowers are shedding
On the still moat ; the red verbena weaves
Mats for the lawn we are so rudely treading :
Naught in the garden save Carl Ritter grieves."—*Faber.*

The position of the rhyming verses relatively to each other is left to the fancy or taste of the poet. Hence we have the greatest variety of systems.

ARTICLE VI. SYSTEMS OF RHYMING VERSES IN GENERAL USE.

706. The forms or **systems** in which rhyming verses are usually arranged are :

(*A*) The *short metre*, the *common metre*, and the *long metre.*

(*B*) The *triplet stanza*, the *rhythm royal*, the *ottava rima*, and *terza rima.*

(*C*) The *Spenserian stanza* and the *sonnet.*

(*D*) The *ode.*

When a system of verses occurs as a distinct portion of a poem it is called a **stanza.**

§ 1. *The short, common, and long metres.*

707. In each of these three the stanza consists of **four iambic verses,** ordinarily with alternate rhymes. The verses, however, of these three metres differ respectively in length.

(*a*) The **short metre** has a trimeter for the first, second, and fourth line, and a tetrameter for the third. **Example :**

" 1. You, old forsaken nests,
Returning spring shall cheer ;
And thence the unfledged robin breathe
His greeting wild and clear ;

> " 2. And from yon clustering vine,
>   That wreathes the casement round,
>   The humming-bird's unresting wing
>   Send forth a whirring sound."—*Lydia Sigourney.*

708. (*b*) The **common metre** has a tetrameter for the first and third, a trimeter for the second and *fourth* verse. It is called the *ballad measure*, because ballads were frequently written in this form.

Example :

> " 1. My harp has one unchanging theme,
>   One strain that still comes o'er
>   Its languid chord, as 'twere a dream
>   Of joy that's now no more.

> " 2. In vain I try with livelier air
>   To wake the trembling string;
>   That voice of other times is there,
>   And saddens all I sing."—*Moore.*

709. Another species of measure very common in ballads is an alternate trimeter hypermeter and a trimeter. It is sometimes styled the *Continental.*

Example:

> " The night was dark and fearful,
>   The blast swept wailing by ;
> A watcher, pale and tearful,
>   Looked forth with anxious eye.
> How wistfully she gazes !
>   No gleam of morn is there !
> And then her heart upraises
>   Its agony of prayer.

> " Within that dwelling lonely,
>   Where want and darkness
>   reign,
> Her precious child, her only,
>   Lay moaning in his pain ;

> And death alone can free him,
>   She feels that this must be ;
> ' But oh ! for morn to see him
>   Smile once again on me !'

> " A hundred lights are gleaming
>   In yonder mansion fair,
> And merry feet are dancing—
>   They need not morning there ;
> O young and lovely creatures !
>   One lamp from out your store
> Would give that poor boy's fea-
>   tures
>   To her fond gaze once more.

"The morning sun is shining—
  She needeth not its ray:
Beside her dead reclining,
  That pale, dead mother lay!

A smile her lips was wreathing,
  A smile of hope and love,
As though she still were breath-
  ing,
   ' There's light for us above.' "
        —*Sarah J. Hale.*

710. (*c*) In the **long metre** every verse is an iambic tetrameter.

1st Example—Rhymes *alternately :*

"1. The monarch of a world
    wert thou,
  And I a slave on bended knee,
Though tyrant chains my form
    might bow,   {thee.
  My soul shall never stoop to

"2. Until my hour shall come,
    my heart
  I will possess secure and free ;
Though snared to ruin by thine
    art,
  I would sooner break than bend
    to thee."—*Frances Osgood.*

2d Example—Rhymes *successively:*

"1. There's nothing bright above,
    below,
From flowers that bloom to stars
    that glow,
But in its light my soul can see
Some feature cf the Deity.

"2. There's nothing dark below,
    above,
But in its glow I trace Thy love ;
And meekly wait that moment
    when
Thy touch shall turn all bright
    again."—*Moore.*

§ 2. *The triplet stanza, elegiac stanza, rhythm royal, ottava rima, terza rima.*

711. (*a*) We have seen that when three lines rhyme together they constitute a **triplet.** The pieces in which they are found are generally made up of verses written in close succession, not arranged into stanzas. The term triplet, however, is also applied to stanzas formed of only three lines. The verses may contain any number of feet. The triplet is here aptly chosen to clothe thoughts on "The Shortness of Life." It is the shortest of stanzas, and yet it expresses the thought in full :

" 1. And what's a life ? A weary pilgrimage
    Whose glory in one day doth fill the stage
    With childhood, manhood, and decrepit age.

" 2. And what's a life ? The flourishing array
    Of the proud summer meadow, which to-day
    Wears her green plush, and is to-morrow hay."
—Francis Quarles.

712. (*b*) The **elegiac stanza** is formed of four iambic pentameters. These usually rhyme alternately :

" 1. We saw thee shine in youth, and beauty's pride,
    And virtue's light that beams beyond the spheres ;
    But, like the sun eclipsed at morning-tide,
    Thou left'st us darkling in a world of tears.

" 2. The parent's heart that nestled fond in thee,
    That heart how sunk—a prey to grief and care !
    So decked the woodbine sweet yon aged tree,
    So, from it ravished, leaves it bleak and bare."—*Burns.*

713. (*c*) The stanza known as **rhythm royal** consists of seven heroics. The first verse rhymes with the third, the second with the fourth and fifth, the sixth with the seventh.

Example :

" Too many blissful moments there I've known,
    Too many hopes have there met their decay,
    Too many feelings now for ever gone,
    To wish that thou wouldst e'er again display
    The joyful coloring of thy prime array ;
    Buried with thee let them remain a blot,
    With thee their sweets, their bitterness forgot."
—Margaret Blennerhasset.

714. (*d*) The **ottava rima** contains eight heroics. The first rhymes with the third and fifth, the second with the fourth and sixth, the seventh with the eighth. It is an Italian measure.

Example—" **Richard II.**," the morning before his murder :

> " O happy man ! says he, that lo ! I see
> Grazing his cattle in those pleasant fields,
> If he but knew his good. How blessed he
> That feels not what affliction greatness yields !
> Other than what he is he would not be,
> Nor change his state with him that sceptre wields.
> Thine, thine is that true life : that is to live,
> To rest secure and not rise up to grieve."
>   *—Daniel.*

715. The **terza rima** (*terza*, triple ; *rima*, rhyme) is taken from the Italian. It was the strain of the Troubadours * in olden times. The piece is not separated into stanzas, but is prolonged at the option of the writer. The first rhymes with the third ; after that the even lines rhyme together three by three, and the odd lines rhyme together three by three. The piece must, of course, finish with the last triplet incomplete. A couplet closes it. The *Divina Commedia* of Dante is written in this metre. English poets have used it with happy effect.

Example:

> " The storms yet sleep, the clouds still keep their station,
> The unborn earthquake yet is in the womb,
> The bloody chaos yet expects creation,
> But all things are disposing for thy doom.
> The elements await but for the word,
> ' Let there be darkness !' and thou grow'st a tomb !
> Yes, thou, so beautiful, shalt feel the sword,
> Thou, Italy ! so fair that Paradise,

---

* The Troubadours (Fr. *trouver*, to invent or compose) were a class of poets who flourished during the eleventh, twelfth, and thirteenth centuries, in Provence, the south of France, and north of Italy. Their songs, which were chiefly of the Lyric kind, went under the name of Provençal poetry. They delighted in rhymes, and in a peculiar dialect formed from the Latin, the Greek, and the old French tongues. Many of the most beautiful conceptions found in later verses are taken from their strains. The Church, to prevent immoral influences arising from the abuse of the art, gave in many places a sacred bent to their minstrelsy, the effects of which are still apparent in religious songs. They sang the mysteries of Christ's life and passion, and the beautiful traditions of the Church.

Revived in thee, blooms forth to man restored ;
  Ah ! must the sons of Adam lose it twice ?
Thou, Italy ! whose ever-golden fields,
  Ploughed by the sunbeams, solely would suffice
For the world's granary ; thou, whose sky Heaven gilds
  With brighter stars, and robes with deeper blue ;
Thou ! in whose pleasant places Summer builds
  Her palace, in whose cradle Empire grew,
And formed the Eternal City's ornaments
  From spoils of kings whom freemen overthrew,
Birthplace of heroes! sanctuary of saints!
  Where earthly first, then heavenly glory made
Her home ; thou, all which fondest Fancy paints,
  And finds her prior vision but portrayed
In feeble colors, etc , ...
  Thou, thou must wither to each tyrant's will."—*Byron.*

§ 3. *The Spenserian stanza and the sonnet.*

716. (*a*) The **Spenserian stanza** is composed of eight heroics and one Alexandrine. The first verse rhymes with the third, the second with the fourth, fifth, and seventh, the sixth with the eight and ninth. The stanza takes its name from Edmund Spenser, whose *Faerie Queene* is composed in this form. We quote its opening lines :

" A gentle knight was pricking on the plaine,
  Ycladd in mightie armes and silver shielde
  Wherein the old dints of deep woundes did remaine,
  The cruel markes of many a bloody fielde.
  Yet armes till that time did he never wield ;
  His angry steede did chide his foaming bitt,
  As much disdayning to the curb to yield ;
  Full jolly knight he seemed, and faire did sitt,
  As one for knightly giusts and fierce encounters fitt."

717. There is a large number of very lengthy pieces written in this stanza ; among them are Thomson's "Castle of Indolence," Beattie's " Minstrel," Byron's " Childe

Harold," Campbell's " Gertrude of Wyoming." Of all the various kinds of stanza it seems best adapted to prolonged poems :

> " There is a pleasure in the pathless woods,
>   There is a rapture on the lonely shore,
>   There is society where none intrudes,
>   By the deep sea, and music in its roar.
>   I love not man the less, but nature more,
>   From these our interviews, in which I steal
>   From all I may be or have been before
>   To mingle with the universe, and feel
>   What I can ne'er express, yet cannot all conceal."
>   *—Byron.*

718. (*b*) The **sonnet** (*sonetto*, a little song) is likewise an Italian system of verse. It is composed of fourteen heroic verses, in which the first, fourth, fifth, and eighth inter-rhyme together ; the second, third, sixth, and seventh ; the ninth, eleventh, and thirteenth ; the tenth, twelfth, and fourteenth. It contains, therefore, two quatrains and two triplets. The rhymes of the last six lines, however, are often differently arranged.

719. The sonnet is not used in long poems ; it is a complete poem in itself, comprising in its fourteen lines some short, vivid description or the expression of a lively sentiment :

> " Low hung the moon when first I stood in Rome ;
>   Midway she seemed attracted from her sphere,
>   On those twin Fountains shining broad and clear
>   Whose floods, not mindless of their mountain home,
>   Rise there in clouds of rainbow, mist, and foam.
>   That hour fulfilled the dream of many a year :
>   Through that thin mist, with joy akin to fear,
>   The steps I saw, the pillars, last the dome.
>   A spiritual Empire there embodied stood :
>   The Roman Church there met me face to face :

Ages, sealed up, of evil and of good
Slept in that circling colonnade's embrace.
Alone I stood, a stranger and alone,
Changed by that stony miracle to stone."—*Aubrey de Vere.*

§ 4. *The ode.*

720. The most irregular strain in the language is the **ode.**
It observes no regularity, either in the length of verse or
system of rhyming. The only point to be noted is that it
usually adopts the iambic species of feet. The verses are
sometimes arranged into stanzas ; but the stanzas, like the
verses, are confined to no fixed length and to no similarity of construction. It supposes an imagination strongly
moved and spurning the conventional forms of art.

721. Here is part of an ode to

"THE HOLY NAME OF JESUS.

" Fair, flowery Name ! in none but Thee
    And Thy nectareal fragrancy
        Hourly there meets
A universal synod of all sweets ;
    By whom it is definèd thus,
        That no perfume
        For ever shall presume
    To pass for odoriferous
But such alone whose sacred pedigree
Can prove itself some kin, sweet Name, to Thee.
    Sweet Name ! in Thy each syllable
    A thousand blest Arabias dwell.
Oh ! that it were as it was wont to be,
When Thy old friends, of fire all full of Thee,
Fought against frowns with smiles ! gave glorious chase
To persecutions, and against the face
Of death and fiercest dangers durst, with brave
And sober pace, march on to meet a grave !
On their bold breasts above the world they bore Thee,

And to the teeth of hell stood up to teach Thee ;
In centre of their inmost souls they wore Thee,
Where rack and torments strove in vain to reach Thee.
  Each wound of theirs was Thy new morning,
  And reinthroned Thee in Thy rosy nest,
With blush of Thine own blood Thy day adorning ;
  It was the wit of love o'erflowed the bounds
  Of wrath, and made the way through all these wounds.

    " Welcome, dear, all-adorèd Name !
      For sure there is no knee
        That knows not Thee ;
    Or, if there be such sons of shame,
      Alas ! what will they do
      When stubborn rocks shall bow,
  And hills hang down their heaven-saluting heads,
      To seek for humble beds
  Of dust, where, in the bashful shades of night,
  Next to their own low nothing they may lie,
And couch before the dazzling light of Thy dread Majesty ?
    They that by love's mild dictate now
      Will not adore Thee
  Shall then with just confusion bow
    And break before Thee."—*Richard Crashaw.*

ARTICLE VII. BLANK VERSE.

722. Verse without rhyme is called **blank verse.** It is especially appropriate where deep passion, lofty emotions, or sublime descriptions are involved. But when one beauty is removed the remaining properties of the verses must be of a superior character. When the music is no longer there the **law of compensation** requires for blank verse a greater depth of feeling, a greater beauty of thought, a grander or more delicate finish of language, and finer touches of the imagination. This is the more reasonably expected since the poet is free from the labor of finding a rhyme.

723. As blank verse is better suited to grave, solemn subjects, so it is most successful when written in a **stately metre**—not light and frisky, as trochees, dactyls, iambic dimeters or trimeters, etc., nor yet long and monotonous, as the hexameter, heptameter, etc. It is best adapted, therefore, to the heroic verse, which partakes of the solemn, and will afford the most beautiful and majestic strains. The following are the opening lines of Milton's "Paradise Lost":

> "Of man's first disobedience and the fruit
> Of that forbidden tree, whose mortal taste
> Brought death into the world, and all our woe,
> With loss of Eden, till one greater Man
> Restore us, and regain the blissful seat,
> Sing, Heavenly Muse, that on the secret top
> Of Oreb or of Sinai didst inspire
> That shepherd, who first taught the chosen seed
> In the beginning how the heavens and earth
> Rose out of chaos."

724. Some critics say that "Thalaba, the Destroyer" is the only successful effort at **varied measures in blank verse.** It owes its success in great part to its varied imagery and its "wild and wondrous tale." Beautiful imagery will often cover a multitude of defects. The tale of the Destroyer opens thus:

> "How beautiful is night !
> A dewy freshness fills the silent air ;
> No mist obscures, nor cloud, nor speck, nor stain
> Breaks the serene of heaven.
> In full-orbed glory yonder moon divine
> Rolls through the dark-blue depths ;
> Beneath her steady ray
> The desert-circle spreads,
> Like the round ocean, girdled with the sky.
> How beautiful is night !"—*Southey.*

725. At first view it appears easy to write in blank verse; yet the majority of writers find success in it more difficult than in rhyme; it requires more taste and genius.

726. Blank verse is **not allowed at random** among rhyming verses; nor is a rhyme admissible in blank verse. There is one exception to this rule: where it seems to enter into the author's plan—when, viz., a notable change in the measure or strain occurs, or when, in the midst of the description or narration in blank verse, a speaker is introduced as chanting in rhyme.

Example:

> " And up she raised her bright blue eyes,
>   And fiercely she smiled on him :
>
> " 'I thank thee, I thank thee, Hodeirah's son !
>   I thank thee for doing what can't be undone—
>   For binding thyself in the chain I have spun.'
>
> " Then from his head she wrench'd
>   A lock of his raven hair,
>   And cast it in the fire,
>   And cried aloud as it burnt :
>
> " ' Sister, sister ! hear my voice !
>   Sister ! sister ! come and rejoice
>   The thread is spun,
>   The prize is won,
>   The work is done,
>   For I have made captive Hodeirah's son.' "—*Southey.*

ARTICLE VIII. PAUSES IN VERSE.

727. The study of **poetic pauses** is highly conducive to beauty in the expression of poetic thought. The pauses which the sense demands are the same in verse as in prose. But there are certain other stops or rests not employed in prose, but admitted into metrical strains. Their purpose

is to increase the harmony of the verse. These rests are called the *final*, the *cæsural*, and the *semi-cæsural* pauses. They are used where the sense will allow a suspension of the voice, and where such suspension will improve the metrical beauty. The final pause should rarely, and the cæsural pauses never, separate words very closely connected in construction. The reason of this is because the metre should never interfere with the sense.

§ 1. *The final pause.*

728. The **final pause** is a slight suspension of the voice at the close of each verse. It marks the limit of the metre; and where no other·mark is given this pause is very important. When it is not properly attended to it is often difficult to tell by the ear the character of the verse, or even to distinguish verse from poetic prose. This is especially the case in blank verse. When rhyme is employed the consonance of sounds usually suffices. Thus it is easy to tell the metre in the annexed couplets, though there is no pause in the sense.

Example:

> " But past is all his fame ; the very spot
> Where many a time he triumphed is forgot."—*Goldsmith.*

If you take away the rhyme the ear will depend upon the suspension of the voice to bound the line.

729. The slow tones of **blank verse** will easily admit a slight suspension of the voice at the end of the line, even when the sense would immediately join the closing with the succeeding line. As its language is more stately, it is read more deliberately and with a more frequent suspension of sound. Hence the final pause is not apt to injure the sense.

Example :

> " When thoughts
> Of the last bitter hour come like a blight
> Over thy spirit, and sad images
> Of the stern agony, and shroud, and pall,
> And breathless darkness, and the narrow house
> Make thee to shudder and grow sick at heart—
> Go forth under the open sky, and list
> To nature's teachings, while from all around,
> Earth, and her waters, and the depths of air,
> Comes a still voice : ' Yet a few days, and thee
> The all-beholding sun shall see no more
> In all his course ; nor yet in the cold ground,
> Where thy pale form was laid with many tears,
> Nor in the embrace of ocean, shall exist
> Thy image."—*Bryant.*

Note.—The pause does not imply a falling of the voice, but merely its suspension.

§ 2. *The cæsural pause.*

730. In most poetry the sentences are so constructed as to admit a pause, or slight suspension of the voice, at certain intervals.

This pause is called the *Cæsura* (from *cædere*, to divide), or **cæsural pause,** because it divides the line. The parts into which the line separates are called *cæsural members.*

Example :

> " Oh ! breathe not his name, | let it sleep in the shade,
> Where, cold and unhonored, | his relics are laid ;
> Sad, silent, and dark | be the tears that we shed,
> As the night-dew that falls | on the grass o'er his head.

> " But the night-dew that falls, | though in silence it weeps,
> Shall brighten with verdure | the grave where he sleeps ;
> And the tear that we shed, | though in secret it rolls,
> Shall long keep his memory | green in our souls."—*Moore.*

731. The cæsural pause unites several **advantages** :

1. The close of the line is the part where the interest of the hearer is greatest ; a fresh breath somewhere about the middle assists the reader to bring out the close with a happy effect. The cæsura gives breathing-time.

2. The harmony of the verse is enhanced by dividing it into sections, as sections may be divided into feet or parts of feet, and feet into syllables.

3. By grouping together more immediately the words which the sense requires to be connected, the cæsura assists the intelligence.

4. It gives prominence to a certain idea which the word immediately before it or immediately after it expresses.

732. The following will **exemplify** the first three advantages :

> " How oft have I thought, when the last light has faded
>   From off the clear waves of some soft-flowing stream,
>   That, like its bright waters, my last hopes were shaded
>   By darkness, uncheered by the hope of a beam !
>
> " Oh ! could I but fly from this false world for ever,
>   Where those whom I trust are the first to betray,
>   From the cold and the fickle my young heart I'd sever
>   Ere they steal all its bloom and its sweetness away.
>
> " I'd seek in some orb of the blessed above me
>   The peace that on earth I can never receive :
>   The spirits that dwell in that bright orb would love me,
>   For they are too gentle to wound or deceive.
>
> " Oh ! why should the hearts of the purest be shaken
>   While calmly reposing 'neath love's sunny beam ?
>   If they slumber so sweetly, why should they awaken
>   To muse o'er the past and to weep o'er a dream ?"
>   —*Amelia Welby.*

733. The next will illustrate particularly the fourth advantage :

" My barb ! my glorious steed !
Methinks my soul would mount upon its track
More fleetly, could I die upon thy back !
    How would thy thrilling speed
Quicken my pulse ! O Allah ! I get wild !
Would that I were once more a desert child !

    " Nay, nay—I had forgot !
My mother ! My star mother ! Ha ! my breath
Stifles !—more air ! Ben Khorat !—this is—death !
    Touch me !—I feel you not !
Dying !—Farewell ! Good master !—room !—more room !
Abra ! I loved thee ! Star ! bright star ! I—come."
                                                —*Willis.*

§ 3. *The semi-cæsural pause.*

734. There frequently occurs, especially in a long line, a secondary cæsura, called the **semi-cæsural pause.** Thus twice, or even three times, the suspension of the voice subdivides the verse. The semi-cæsural pause, however, is less prolonged than the cæsural. In the following extract the parallels mark the cæsural, the single lines the semi-cæsural rest.

A writer had compared Ireland in her sufferings to Judea, and the Irish to the sons of Juda. This poem contains Moore's reflections on the subject. It is replete with Scriptural allusions, and terms once applied to the land of the outcast Hebrews. It is addressed to the city of David :

" Yes, sad one of Sion ! | If closely resembling
    In shame | and in sorrow | thy withered-up heart,
If drinking deep, | deep | of the same ' cup of trembling,'
    Could make us | thy children, | our parent | thou art.
Like thee | doth our nation | lie conquered and broken,
    And fallen from her head | is the once royal crown ;
In her streets, | in her halls, | Desolation | hath spoken,
    And ' while it is day yet, | her sun | hath gone down ';

Like thine | doth her exiles, | 'mid dreams of returning,
  Die far | from the home | it were life | to behold ;
Like thine | do her sons, | in the day of their mourning,
  Remember the bright things | that blessed them of old.
Ah ! well may we call her, | like thee, | ' the forsaken ':
  Her boldest | are vanquished, | her proudest | are slaves ;
And the harps | of her minstrels, | when gayest | they waken,
  Have tones | 'mid their mirth | like the wind over graves."
                              —*Moore.*

735. **In rhyming verses** the cæsural pause falls generally about the middle of the verse ; the semi-cæsura about the middle of the cæsural members. In the example just given, and in the two found in Nos. 730 and 732, it would be difficult to omit these pauses without injury to melody. We are more inclined to place the cæsura about the middle, on account of our predilection for grace and symmetry. We like to see measure answering to measure, member to member, in due proportion. The flow of the verse, besides, is smoothest when these parts correspond. For this reason good poets generally so construct their sentences as to admit a pause in the sense at that point where a metrical pause would be most available ; and it may be laid down as infallible that there is nothing in which the artistic skill of the poet is evinced more forcibly, nothing on which the polish and melody of the composition depends more, than on the clever management of the cæsural members and their adaptation to the sense.

736. But strict uniformity in the position of the pause cloys the taste. A sprinkling of **variety**, without detracting from the polish of the verse, will add at times the beauty of novelty to the execution.

737. **In blank verse** the pause is far less uniform. The majestic motion of the strain is arrested by the cæsura, not so much to refine the melody or enhance the metrical cadence, as to improve the expression and heighten the

grandeur of the thought. Thus, in "Satan's soliloquy," the expression of highly wrought passion and depth of feeling is rendered more intense by the irregular but judicious fall of the pause :

> " So farewell hope, | and with hope | farewell fear !
> Farewell remorse : | all good to me is lost.
> Evil, | be thou my good: | by thee at least
> Divided empire with Heaven's King I hold—
> By thee ! and more than half, perhaps, will reign ;
> As man ere long, | and this new world, | shall know."
>
> —*Milton.*

738. Here, by force of the cæsura, we are made more sensible of the fiend's emotion as each succeeding passion gains the ascendency. Anguish and despair tremble through the first lines, checking his speech ; then a paroxysm of rage hurries him impetuously along, till at the close haughty resolve and defiance are breathed heavily between his lips. The pauses give dignity to the language, manifest the grandeur of the thought, and inspire awe into the soul.

739. Note the startling effect of it in the "description of Moloch " :

> " His trust was | with the Eternal to be deemed
> Equal in strength, | and rather than be less
> Cared not | to be at all ; | with that care lost
> Went all his fear | ; of God, | of hell, | or worse,
> He reck'd not."

740. The study of effect in the fall of the cæsura is important, as upon it depends often the sweetness, the vivacity, or the majesty of the expression. In poetry where no high or strong emotions are to be stirred, but where the pleasurable feelings are addressed, where simple beauty is to be displayed or a shade of pathos to be cast, the place of the cæsura is generally uniform.

BOOK VI.

NATURE AND VARIETIES OF POETRY.

741. The study of poetry affords considerable **advantages**:

1. It contributes sensibly to that **liberal culture** which has ever been so highly appreciated in civilized communities. This culture consists in a detachment of the heart from the gross pleasures of sense, an appreciation of mental and spiritual excellence.

742. 2. It affords powerful **aids towards success in other literary compositions**:

(*a*) It stores the memory with beautiful images;

(*b*) It excites the imagination to suggest illustrations and even proofs to the orator;

(*c*) It makes the heart sensitive to beauty, and intensifies all the passions which an orator may employ to advantage;

(*a*) It perfects the judgment or taste, which must preside over all works of art;

(*e*) It furnishes the most pleasing and energetic expression of thought. Therefore poetry has always been studied in connection with eloquence.

743. 3. It yields exquisite and elevating **pleasure**, which ennobles him who can enjoy it, and especially him who, by the composition of poetry, can impart it to others. · Hence the ancients revered the poet as a special favorite of the gods, and attributed his art to celestial inspiration.

744. The study of poetry **may be abused** in two ways :

1. By **excessive fondness** of the art, allowing the pleasure found in its pursuit to interfere with the performance of important duties. Many persons, by too great a love of fiction, have become unprofitable members of society.

2. By **perversion of poetic talent**: the poet is, as it were, the priest of nature, the interpreter to the common mind of its more hidden teachings, the guide of mankind to a higher sphere of happiness. But many poets, like Ovid of old in his *Amores*, and Swinburne to-day, have made themselves the priests of Venus instead, or, like Byron and Shelley, they have taught the creature to rise in rebellion against the Creator.

CHAPTER I.

THE NATURE OF POETRY.

745. **Poetry is the antithesis of prose.** Some consider this opposition to consist in the outward form only, calling poetry whatever is in verse, and prose whatever is not in verse. Others consider the thought only, and call a piece, whether in verse or not, poetry when the thoughts have a peculiar charm or elevation different from the thoughts of common life. The peculiarity of this charm lies in a plastic or creative power which the mind exhibits in the conception of such thoughts. Hence the name poetry, from ποιέω, to make or create. Most critics, however, understand by poetry such literary productions as express poetic thoughts in verse.

746. Hence **poetry may be thus defined**: A composition in metrical language, produced by a creative imagination, and affording intellectual pleasure by exciting elevated, agreeable, and pathetic emotions. Poetry, then, contains three elements.

747. 1. **Metrical language.** Many a passage of glowing pathos in oratory, of graphic description or tender narrative in real or fictitious histories, etc., have all the conditions of poetry except versification. We do not call these poetry. The valuable work of Macpherson called *Ossian's Poems* does not pretend to be a collection but a translation of poems which were metrical in their original Gaelic ; the translation has all the qualities of poetry except verse.

748. 2. **A creative imagination.** To *create* means to

make things out of nothing. This no man can do. He cannot even conceive any new object except by combining in his mind images formerly admitted there. For instance, having seen a 'horse' and 'wings,' he can combine these notions and imagine a 'winged horse.' This combination is poetic creation, which Shakspeare describes in a poetic strain :

> " The poet's eye, in a fine frenzy rolling,
>   Doth glance from heaven to earth, from earth to heaven ;
>   And, as imagination bodies forth
>   The forms of things unknown, the poet's pen
>   Turns them to shapes, and gives to airy nothing
>   A local habitation and a name."

749. 3. **Intellectual pleasure.** Pleasure is the immediate end of poetry, as of all the fine arts. This pleasure results from the excellence of the thoughts and the language ; for, as Coleridge says, "Poetry is the flower of all human knowledge, thought, human passions, emotions, and language." Still, pleasure is not its ultimate end ; war-songs, didactic pieces, sacred odes, and, in fact, all kinds of poetical compositions, can and should be referred to a further end, more worthy of man than mere transient pleasure.

750. The power within man which retains and recalls images formerly conceived is his **memory** ; the power which combines them anew, producing, as it were, new creations, is the fancy or imagination. These last two terms are often used as perfect synonyms ; but it is more correct to make a distinction between their meanings. What this distinction is critics are not agreed ; many state it as follows : **Fancy** moves on lighter wings ; its comparisons are founded rather on accidental qualities and relations, on associations more remote—hence the term *fanciful ;* it supposes a less serious frame of mind. Poe's " Bells " is one of its productions. **Imagination** traces comparisons founded on more

inherent qualities or on real effects ; it supposes more earnestness ; its images are more select, delightful, grand, or terrible ; its passion is genuine. Campbell's " Exile of Erin," for example, is one of its creations.

751. The whole process of poetic creation is excellently described by Akenside in his " Pleasures of the Imagination." We shall here briefly examine what are the various classes of objects which poetry creates.

Poetry is creative:

752. 1. Of an entire **plot** or story—*e.g.*, Parnell's " Hermit," Virgil's "Æneid," Shakspeare's tragedies, Newman's " Dream of Gerontius," Scott's " Lady of the Lake," Longfellow's " Evangeline."

753. 2. Of particular **characters**—*e.g.*, Macbeth, Lady Macbeth, Hamlet, Falstaff, Hiawatha. Shakspeare is remarkable for the variety and distinctness of his characters ; but Homer excels all other poets in this respect : mortals and immortals alike are so painted by his unrivalled brush that their forms and characters become as distinct to us as those of our familiar friends.

754. 3. Of peculiar **kinds of beings**—*e.g.*, of nymphs, satyrs, sirens, witches, ghosts ; or of personified moral qualities, as of ' Envy ' in Ovid, or of ' Death ' and ' Sin ' in Milton.

755. 4. Of peculiar **scenes**—*e.g.*, ' The Gates of Hell ' in Milton ; the ' Hell ' of Virgil and Dante ; the interview between ' Hector and Andromache ' in Homer ; Thomson's " Castle of Indolence," the ' dagger-scene ' in " Macbeth," ' Jupiter and Thetis ' in Homer.

756. 5. Of numberless **images**, bolder, more pleasing, more significant, more elevated than prose usually employs, and more copiously accumulated—*e.g.*, " The care that sat on the faded cheek of Satan " ; " The sound that tore Hell's concave " ; " Thoughts that wander through eternity " ;

the curses of Lear that " stamped wrinkles on the brow of youth"; Hamlet "benetted round with villanies"; "The power winged with red lightning and impetuous rage."

It presents the moon as a " Vestal," night as " clothed in a starry train," the sun as " a giant rejoicing in his strength.' It dictates such lines as the following :

> " So when the last and dreadful hour
> This crumbling pageant shall devour,
> The trumpet shall be heard on high,
> And music shall untune the sky."—*Dryden.*

757. 6. Of special **phraseology**—*e.g.:*

> " By them stood
> Orcus and Hades, and the dreadful name
> Of Demonorgan " (=Demonorgan of dreadful name).

" Notes that wing their heavenly ways."

" But the day-star attracted his eye's sad devotion."

758. 7. Of a happy **utterance of thoughts and feelings·**

> " Nature to advantage dressed
> What oft was thought but ne'er so well expressed."

Example of *feeling :* Burns' "To a Mountain Daisy."
Example of *thought :* Pope's " Essay on Man."
See a combination of creations in Thomson's " Hymn on a Review of the Seasons" and in Collins' "Ode on the Passions."

759. A poem **need not be a creation throughout**: its creation is the essence of the drink, the gold of the coin ; but a drink need not be all essence, nor currency pure gold. The most imaginative writers are not always the most pleasant to read. Poetic phraseology, in particular, is often absent ; as when King Lear exclaims : " Pray do not mock me."

760. Since poetry deals so extensively with creation and imagination, it may be asked whether **poetry is truthful**. We answer that poetry does not express the literal truth, but suggests it. Its original conceptions are not to be judged by the ordinary rules of logic. It combines something with the reality ; it sees into the core and secret relations of things, and is suggestive — *like the breath of an oracle*, says Barry Cornwall, thus exemplifying his meaning; prose would have said, like the *words* of an oracle. " Darkness visible," " In the lowest deep, another deep," etc., are expressions which logic may quarrel with, but poetry delights in them.

CHAPTER II.

POETIC DICTION.

761. The **poetic diction** of the English language is extensive and rich. Many words and forms of expression are restricted to poetry, or at least recognized as peculiar to poetic language. Orators sometimes use them, but they are then understood to borrow the graces of poetry to beautify their thoughts.

762. The **licenses** granted to the poet, as well as the restrictions laid upon him, are learned best in the study of the best authors. The following are some of the liberties they use :

1. Frequent *omissions of words :*

(*a*) Of the *article :*

> " Like [a] shipwrecked mariner on [a] desert coast."

(*b*) Of *pronouns :*

> " For is there aught in sleep [which] can charm the wise ?"

> " [He] Who does the best his circumstances allow."

(*c*) Of *verbs :*

> " Does well, acts nobly. Angels could [do] no more."

> " To whom thus Adam [spoke]."

2. *Frequent inversions :*

> " Where echo walks steep hills among."

> " A transient calm the happy scenes bestow."

> " Heaven trembles, roar the mountains, thunders all the ground."

" When first thy sire to send on earth
    Virtue, his darling child, designed,
  To thee he gave the heavenly birth,
    And bade thee form her infant mind."

" Come, Nymph demure with mantle blue."

" His praise, ye brooks, attune, ye trembling rills."

" His prayer, he saith, this holy man."

" Who dares think one thing, and another tell,
  My soul detests him, as the gates of hell."

                    " Now storming fury rose,
  And clamor such as heard in Heaven till now
  Was never."

3. *Intransitive verbs are made transitive :*

" Still in harmonious intercourse they lived
  The rural day and talked the flowing heart."

" I fly these wicked tents devoted."

4. *The first and third person imperative are used:*

" Go we to yonder hill."

" Perish he who calls me traitor."

5. *The nominative is repeated :*

" The night it was still, and the moon it shone
    Serenely on the sea,
  And the waves at the foot of the rifted rock
    They murmured pleasantly."—*Kirke White.*

6. *Or is used for either, and nor for neither :*

" Nor pain nor joy shall rend us."

" Or by the lazy Scheldt or wandering Po."—*Goldsmith.*

7. *Adjectives are joined to nouns which they do not qualify :*

" The ploughman homeward plods his weary way."

8. *Adjectives are used for adverbs:*

> " Slow moves the solemn train."

9. *Newly compounded epithets are used:*

> " In hollow-sounding dales."—*Thomson.*
>
> " Sphere-descended maid."—*Collins.*

10. *Foreign idioms are sometimes used:*

> " To some she gave
> To search the story of eternal thought."
>
> " Never since created man
> Met such embodied force."

11. *A syllable is omitted or added:*
Amaze, for amazement ; 'gan, for began ; wail, for be-wail ; e'er, for ever ; lone, for lonely ; morn, for morning dread, for dreadful ; darkling, for dark ; disport, bedim, etc.; yon, for yonder; eve, for evening; font, for foun-tain, etc.

12. *Antiquated words and phrases* are used, and words purely poetical :
Haply, inly, oft, blithe, dun, fell, lithe, rife, twain, fain, withouten, whilom, passing rich, passing strange, etc. Yore, sheen, behests, core, benison, bourne, ire, ken, meed, wel-kin, ingle, the whiles, in sooth, etc.

Ween, wot, ken, ycleped, to weet, what likes me best, etc.

CHAPTER III.

VARIETIES OF POETRY.

763. Poetry is either **subjective** or **objective.** The former utters the thoughts or the feelings that exist in the poet's soul ; the latter represents what is outside of him, whether the poet speaks in his own person or in the person of others. Hence we have four species of poetry :

When the poet utters his thoughts, he gives us *didactic* poetry ; when he utters his feelings, he gives us *lyric* poetry ; when he states in his own person what is outside of him, *narrative or descriptive ;* when he speaks in the person of others, *dramatic* poetry. We shall treat of these four species in so many articles, and we shall add a fifth article on some accidental variations of poetical composition.

ARTICLE I. NARRATIVE AND DESCRIPTIVE POETRY.

§ 1. *Narrative and Descriptive Poetry in General.*

764. The ancients did not cultivate **descriptive poetry as a distinct species:** their descriptions occur only incidentally as parts of other compositions. Dante wrote the first great work of the descriptive kind—viz., his wonderful account of "Heaven, Hell, and Purgatory," a work of the highest literary merit. Thomson in his "Seasons," Milton in his "Allegro " and "Penseroso," and many others have made description the chief object of their poetical writings, and they have produced real masterpieces.

765. **As parts of Narrations, Dramas, Odes, etc.,** both an-

cients and moderns have composed an endless variety of poetic descriptions, which, besides being very beautiful in themselves, are likewise useful models for the imitation of students. (See description of night, No. 131.)

Here is a description of the scenery presented by the Mississippi in its frequent inundations :

" All the soft, damp air was full of delicate perfume
From the young willows in bloom on either bank of the river—
Faint, delicious fragrance, trancing the indolent senses
In a luxurious dream of the river and land of the lotus.
Not yet out of the west the roses of sunset were withered ;
In the deep blue above light clouds of gold and of crimson
Floated in slumber serene, and the restless river beneath them
Rushed away to the sea with a vision of rest in its bosom.
Far on the eastern shore lay dimly the swamps of the cypress ;
Dimly before us the islands grew from the river's expanses—
Beautiful, wood-grown isles, with the gleam of the swart inundation
Seen through the swaying boughs and slender trunks of their willows.
And on the shore beside us the cotton-trees rose in the evening,
Phantom-like, yearningly, wearily, with the inscrutable sadness
Of the mute races of trees. While hoarsely the steam from her
    'scape-pipes
Shouted, then whispered a moment, then shouted again to the silence.
Trembling through all her frame with the mighty pulse of her en-
    gines,
Slowly the boat ascended the swollen and broad Mississippi."
                                    —Howells.

766. In poetry as well as in prose, even when description is the direct object of the composition, **life and action** should be constantly introduced to keep it from languishing. Notice the happy effect of the reference to the steamboat in the lines just quoted.

767. On the other hand, **narration** is adorned by introducing frequent brief descriptions, and by presenting the actions narrated so graphically that they appear like to a succession of pictures.

Notice the vividness of the following descriptive narration :

" In his story a moment the pilot paused, while we listened
To the salute of a boat that, rounding the point of an island,
Flamed toward us with fires that seemed to burn from the waters—
Stately and vast and swift, and borne on the heart of the current.
Then, with the mighty voice of a giant challenged to battle,
Rose the responsive whistle, and all the echoes of island,
Swamp-land, glade, and brake replied with a myriad clamor
Like wild birds that are suddenly startled from slumber at midnight,
Then were at peace once more ; and we heard the harsh cries of the
       peacocks
Perched on a tree by a cabin-door, where the white-headed settler's
White-headed children stood to look at the boat as it passed them."
          —*Howells.*

768. In most other productions of art, good taste requires that the different species be kept separate from each
other ; but with regard to narration and description, especially in poetry, a great secret of success lies in the art of
blending them constantly together, so that every action is
painted and every scene presented as full of action and
emotion.

769. As an example of poetic narration we quote the
greater portion of Longfellow's " The Monk Felix " :

" One morning, all alone,
  Out of his convent of gray stone
  Into the forest older, darker, grayer,
  His lips moving as if in prayer,
  His head sunken upon his breast
  As in a dream of rest,
  Walked the Monk Felix. All about
  The broad, sweet sunshine lay without,
  Filling the summer air ;
  And within the woodlands as he trod,
  The twilight was like the Truce of God
  With worldly woe and care;

Under him lay the golden moss ;
And above him the boughs of hemlock-trees
Waved, and made the sign of the cross,
And whispered their Benedicites ;
And from the ground
Rose an odor sweet and fragrant
Of the wild flowers and the vagrant
Vines that wandered,
Seeking the sunshine, round and round.

" These he heeded not, but pondered
On the volume in his hand,
A volume of Saint Augustine,
Wherein he read of the unseen
Splendors of God's great town
In the unknown land ;
And, with his eyes cast down
In humility, he said
' I believe, O God !
What herein I have read,
But, alas ! I do not understand !

" And lo ! he heard
The sudden singing of a bird,
A snow-white bird, that from a cloud
Dropped down,
And among the branches brown
Sat singing
So sweet, and clear, and loud,
It seemed a thousand harp-strings ringing
And the Monk Felix closed his book,
And long, long
With rapturous look
He listened to the song,
And hardly breathed or stirred,
Until he saw, as in a vision,
The land Elysian,
And in the heavenly city heard
Angelic feet
Fall on the golden flagging of the street,

And he would fain
Have caught the wondrous bird,
But strove in vain ;
For it flew away, away,
Far over hill and dell,
And instead of its sweet singing
He heard the convent bell
Suddenly in the silence ringing
For the service of noonday.
And he retraced
His pathway homeward sadly and in haste.

" In the convent there was a change !
He looked for each well-known face,
But the faces were new and strange ;
New figures sat in the oaken stalls,
New voices chanted in the choir ;
Yet the place was the same place,
The same dusky walls
Of cold, gray stone,
The same cloisters and belfry and spire.
   .   .   .   .

. . . Such had been the power
Of that celestial and immortal song,
A hundred years had passed,
And had not seemed so long
As a single hour."

770. See specimens of poetic descriptions *supra* Nos. 7, 8, 9, 15, 46, 131, 238, 271 ; see also Bryant's description of the Indian Summer. As specimens of narration read Miles' "Inkerman," Longfellow's "Evangeline," Macaulay's "Lays of Ancient Rome," Campbell's "Gertrude of Wyoming," Scott's "Lady of the Lake," etc. In Latin see Ovid's charming stories of "The Death of Icarus" and "Baucis and Philemon" (*Metamorph.* l. viii.)

771. The **fables** of Phædrus in Latin and of La Fontaine in French are brief narratives to which there is no paral-

lel in English literature. Their style is simple, lively, and rapid ; the stories are brief, and the moral is very obvious. Gay, Wilkie, and others have attempted fables, but their productions are wordy and want sprightliness.

§ 2. *Epic poetry.*

772. **Epic poetry** is the recital of some illustrious enterprise in a poetical form. It is considered as the highest effort of poetic talent, on account of the loftiness of its conceptions, the dignity of its character, and the difficulty of its execution. Few epic poems have gained general admiration. Those most highly prized are Homer's " Iliad " and " Odyssey," Virgil's " Æneid," Milton's " Paradise Lost," and Tasso's " Jerusalem Delivered."

773. All poetry aims at giving pleasure : epic poetry does so by the exhibition of heroic qualities, which it holds up for admiration. Admiration may be called the **character- istic mark** of epic poetry, while that of tragedy is compassion ; of comedy, ridicule ; of lyric poetry, sentiment ; of didactic, good sense ; of pastoral poetry the prevailing idea is innocence and simplicity. Epic poetry is more calm, self-possessed than lyric or dramatic ; it requires more than any other kind of poetry a grave, equable, and sustained dignity.

774. **Its action or subject must have three properties:**

1. **Unity,** which requires that all the parts make up one well-connected story, that all tend to the accomplishment of one grand undertaking or achievement ; for example, the subject of

Homer's " Iliad " is the wrath of Achilles ;

Homer's " Odyssey," the return of Ulysses to Ithaca ;

Virgil's " Æneid," the establishment of Æneas in Italy ;

Tasso's " Jerusalem Delivered," the taking of Jerusalem ;

Milton's " Paradise Lost," the fall of Adam and Eve ;

Lucan's " Pharsalia," Cæsar's triumph over Roman liberty ;

Statius' " Thebaïd," the vengeance of Œdipus ;

Camoëns' " Luciad," Vasco da Gama's expedition ;

Klopstock's " Messiad," the redemption of mankind ;

Milton's " Paradise Regained," the same.

775. **Episodes** are such incidents as are introduced for variety's sake, connected with the main story, but not necessary to it. They are departures from unity, but they atone for this imperfection by the happy variety which they introduce and the superior beauties which they exhibit. For, being ornaments, they are always expected to contain some special excellences, for the sake of which they are admitted. They should : (*a*) Fit in well, and be naturally introduced into the story ; (*b*) Vary the character of the narrative ; (*c*) Be very elegant ; (*d*) Conclude with some thought that leads naturally to the continuation of the main subject. The interview between Hector and Andromache in the sixth book of the " Iliad," the descent of Æneas into hell in the sixth, and the expedition of Nisus and Euryalus in the ninth book of the " Æneid " are episodes of remarkable beauty.

776. 2. The action should be **great**—*i.e.*, sufficiently important and splendid to command attention and to justify the magnificence of the style.

3. It should be **interesting,** so as to keep up the attention of the reader throughout the long narrative. The chief **sources of interest** are :

(*a*) The *choice of a story* and of characters that enlist the sympathies of readers ; for instance, great benefactors of humanity or of the particular nation for which the poem is written.

(*b*) The skilful *management of the plot*, so that the hero is made to pass through many affecting incidents before he succeeds or fails at last in his undertaking. A favorable termination is more gratifying to the reader, and is usual in epics : the " Paradise Lost " is an exception, from the necessity of the case, not from the author's choice.

(*c*) The masterly *drawing of characters.* In this respect Homer is unrivalled ; Virgil has only Æneas and the boy Iulus ; Tasso has displayed great skill : his characters are varied, some very noble, and all well supported.

777. By machinery we mean the gods and goddesses and other preternatural beings introduced by many epic poets. No machinery is necessary ; when any is used it should be such as the readers would consider proper and conformable to their belief. Camoëns shocks all common sense by blending pagan superstitions with Christian faith.

778. Selections from the " Iliad" :

Book I., II. The plot is unfolded.
  "   IV., V. Battles.
  "   VI. Lines 370–529. Episode of Hector and Andromache.
  "   VIII. 1–75. Jupiter's power.
             392–408. The gates of heaven.
  "   IX. 485–515. Speech of Phœnix.
  "   XV. 1–200. Jupiter awakens.
  "   XVI. Patroclus fights and perishes.
  "   XVII. 412–450. The horses grieve.
  "   XVIII. Achilles, Vulcan, and Thetis.
  "   XIX. Achilles and Agamemnon are reconciled
  "   XX. The gods join the combat.
  "   XXII. Hector is slain.
  "   XXIV. Priam and Achilles.

779. *From the "Æneid"*:

Book   I. Wreck of Æneas' fleet.
"   II. Æneas relates the fall of Troy.
"   V. Æneas in Sicily.
"   VI. 236–755. Visits the lower regions.
"   IX. Episode of Nisus and Euryalus.
"   X. 789–908. Death of Lausus and his fathei

780. *From the "Jerusalem Delivered"*:

Canto   I. entire. Godfrey elected.
"   III. 1–16. Arrival at Jerusalem.
     58–end. Christian camp.
"   IV. 1–28. Satan's plans—Armida.
"   VI. 1–54. Single combat.
"   VII. 23–end. Tancred decoyed.
"   IX. entire. A night attack.
"   X. 57–end. The returning knights.
"   XI. entire. Storming Jerusalem.
"   XIV. 1–52. Rinaldo recalled.
"   XVII. 1–35. The Egyptian army.
"   XIX. 1–56. Argantes slain.
"   XX. 1–121. The great battle.
     137–end. Conclusion.

781. *From the "Paradise Lost"*:

Book   I. entire. Pandemonium.
"   II. 643–925. Gates of Hell—Chaos.
"   III. 56–143. God the Father and Son.
"   IV. 355–440. Satan in Paradise.
     788–873. Satan discovered.
"   V. 136–246. Morning hymn.
     577–672. Satan's sin related.
"   VI. entire. War in heaven related.

Book VII. entire. The creation of this earth related.
" IX. 494–1010. The fall of man.
" X. 1–965. Consequences of the fall.
" XI. 1–555. Expulsion from Paradise.
" XII. 552–end. Departure from Paradise.

ARTICLE II. DIDACTIC POETRY.

782. The **Didactic** (from $\delta\iota\delta\acute{\alpha}\sigma\varkappa\varepsilon\iota\nu$, to teach) is a species of poetry intended to convey instruction. As instruction is naturally uninteresting to many, it must be rendered interesting by skilful treatment. Hence judgment and poetic talent are required in the selection of the subject as well as of the details. Especially needful is poetic thought clothed in poetic diction ; there should be pleasing ornament and variety. The style should be simple, clear, dignified, neat, or even elegant. The episodes or digressions should be ornate, not too long, naturally introduced and naturally dismissed.

783. Didactic poetry is usually written in heroic verse. **Example** from a " Treatise on Health " :

" O comfortable streams ! with eager lips
   And trembling hand the languid thirsty quaff
   New life in you ; fresh vigor fills their veins.
   No warmer cups the rural sages knew ;
   None warmer sought the sires of humankind.
   Happy in temperate peace, their equal days
   Felt not the alternate fits of feverish mirth
   And sick dejection. Still serene and pleased
   They knew no pains but what the tender soul
   With pleasure yields to, and would ne'er forget.
   Blest with divine immunity from ails,
   Long centuries they lived ; their only fate
   Was ripe old age, and rather sleep than death.
   Oh ! could those worthies from the world of gods
   Return to visit their degenerate sons,

> How would they scorn the joys of modern time,
> With all our art and toil improved to pain !
> Too happy they ! but wealth brought luxury,
> And luxury on sloth begot disease."—*Armstrong.*

784. The highest species of didactic poetry is a **regular treatise** on some instructive and important subject. Such were, among the ancients, Lucretius' treatise " De Rerum Naturâ," Virgil's " Georgics," and Horace's "Art of Poetry." Among the moderns Vida has composed an elegant " Art of Poetry " in Latin, Boileau in French, Pope an " Art of Criticism " and an " Essay on Man " in English ; all these, as well as Armstrong's poem on " Health," Akenside's on the " Pleasures of the Imagination," are works of superior merit.

§ 1. *Poetical epistles.*

785. Poetical epistles and satires may be classed under the head of didactic poetry. **Epistles**, it is true, may belong to various species of writings, according to the matter treated in them. The reason why they are classed with didactic poetry is that many didactic compositions, such as the " Art of Poetry " of Horace, have been written in the form of a letter. When they are letters properly so called they are usually letters of friendship ; their matter is sometimes serious, sometimes light and pleasant.

786. They **differ from prose** letters in *thought* and in *language*.

1. The **thoughts** should be choice while they are natural ; what is ordinary should derive an additional charm from the delicacy, liveliness, or energy of the expression.

2. The **language** should be (*a*) Adorned with figures of the more modest kind, and (*b*) Metrical, but in an easy measure. It may be quite musical ; usually it is but slightly

inverted, so as to keep the air of conversation. Sometimes the language is as elevated as that of the ode.

787. Their **principal beauty** lies in delicacy, liveliness, sweetness, refinement of thought and expression. (See *Spectator*, No. 618, "On Poetical Epistles.")

Models: Southey's "To a Friend"; Pope's "To Earl of Oxford," "To James Craggs," "To Lady Montagu"; Horace's "Epode I.," "Epistles," b. i. Ep. 2, 8, 9, 10, 20.

788. **A Letter of Condolence** (Horace, *Odes*, b. i. 24):

TO VIRGIL.

" What cheek would blush to greet the falling tear ?
   And who shall bid our loving tribute cease,
Our sad lamenting o'er a bard so dear ?
   O tragic Muse ! on whom thy loving sire
Bestowed the harp and mellow voice of song,
   My aching heart to mournful themes inspire !
And doth Cremona's bard for ever sleep ?
   Eternal slumber close his weary lids ?
Ah ! when shall meekness find his modest peer ?
   Or spotless faith discover one so pure ?
Or truth unsullied meet his equal here ?
   Around the sleeper good men bowed the head
Yet none, O Virgil ! mourned his fate like thee.
   Thy rare devotion cannot wake the dead ;
His life was loaned on other terms than these.
   Although thy finger sweeps the magic lyre
With greater skill than charmed the listening trees
   When minstrel ardor thrilled the bard of Thrace,
The blood no more shall warm his empty shade
   Or paint the whiteness of that marble face.
The soul by Hermes sent to gloom profound
   With wand relentless is for ever lost.
A bitter thought, and hard to bear, my friend ;
   Yet patience lightens every earthly lot
Beyond the power of mortal grief to mend."—*Pierce.*

789. Compare with the preceding Tennyson's " Letter to
J. S." :

I.

" The wind that beats the mountain blows
   More softly round the open wold,
And gently comes the world to those
   That are cast in gentle mould.

II.

" And me this knowledge bolder made,
   Or else I had not dared to flow
In these words toward you, and invade
   Even with a verse your holy woe.

III.

" 'Tis strange that those we lean on most,
   Those in whose laps our limbs are nursed,
Fall into shadow, soonest lost ;
   Those we love first are taken first.

IV.

" God gives us love.   Something to love
   He lends us ; but when love is grown
To ripeness, that on which it throve
   Falls off, and love is left alone.

V.

" This is the curse of time.   Alas !
   In grief I am not all unlearned ;
Once through mine own doors Death did pass—
   One went, who never hath returned.

.   .   .   .

XV.

" I wrote I know not what.   In truth,
   How *should* I soothe you anyway,
Who miss the brother of your youth ?
   Yet something I did wish to say:

XVI.

" For he too was a friend to me :
    Both are my friends, and my true breast
Bleedeth for both ; yet it may be
    That only silence suiteth best.

XVII.

" Words weaker than your grief would make
    Grief more.   'T were better I should cease,
Although myself could almost take
    The place of him that sleeps in peace."

  . . . .

790. We miss, however, in the two epistles just quoted the beauty of **Christian sentiment.**   How much more consoling are the following lines of Longfellow:

" RESIGNATION.

" There is no flock, however watched and tended,
    But one dead lamb is there ;
There is no fireside, howsoe'er defended,
    But has one vacant chair !

" The air is full of farewells to the dying
    And mournings for the dead ;
The heart of Rachel, for her children crying,
    Will not be comforted.

" Let us be patient !   These severe afflictions
    Not from the ground arise,
But oftentimes celestial benedictions
    Assume this dark disguise.

" We see but dimly through the mists and vapors ;
    Amid these earthly damps
What seem to us but sad, funereal tapers
    May be heaven's distant lamps.

"There is no death ! What seems so is transition ;
    This life of mortal breath
Is but a suburb of the life Elysian,
    Whose portal we call Death.

"She is not dead, the child of our affection,
    But gone unto that school
Where she no longer needs our poor protection,
    And Christ Himself doth rule.

"In that great cloister's stillness and seclusion,
    By guardian angels led,
Safe from temptation, safe from sin's pollution,
    She lives whom we call dead.

"Day after day we think what she is doing
    In those bright realms of air ;
Year after year, her tender steps pursuing,
    Behold her grown more fair.

"Thus do we walk with her, and keep unbroken
    The bonds which nature gives,
Thinking that our remembrance, though unspoken,
    May reach her where she lives.

"Not as a child shall we again behold her ;
    For when with raptures wild
In our embraces we again enfold her,
    She will not be a child,

"But a fair maiden, in her Father's mansion,
    Clothed with celestial grace ;
And beautiful with all the soul's expansion
    Shall we behold her face.

"And though, at times, impetuous with emotion
    And anguish long suppressed,
The swelling heart heaves moaning like the ocean,
    That cannot be at rest,

> " We will be patient, and assuage the feeling
>   We may not wholly stay ;
>   By silence sanctifying, not concealing,
>   The grief that must have way."

§ 2. *Satires.*

791. A **Satire** holds up to ridicule the faults and follies of mankind. It aims at reforming them, and hence it is classed with didactic poems. It is the comedy of didactic verse. If well managed it is productive of good. If managed with awkwardness or bitterness it excites rancor but produces no reformation.

792. Here is a satire on "Love of Praise " :

> " What will not men attempt for sacred praise!
>   The love of praise, howe'er concealed by art,
>   Reigns more or less, and glows in every heart.
>   The proud, to gain it, toils on toils endure ;
>   The modest shun it but to make it sure ;
>   O'er globes and sceptres how on thrones it swells ;
>   Now trims the midnight lamp in college cells :
>   'Tis Tory, Whig ; it plots, prays, preaches, pleads,
>   Harangues in senates, squeaks in masquerades ;
>   Here to Steele's humor makes a bold pretence,
>   There bolder aims at Pultney's eloquence ;
>   It aids the dancer's heel, the writer's head,
>   And heaps the plain with mountains of the dead ;
>   Nor ends with life, but nods in sable plumes,
>   Adorns our hearse and flatters on our tombs."— *Young.*

See also Saxe's " Satire on Progress."

793. The **Lampoon** or **Pasquinade** is directed against an individual, and aims solely at irritating. The **epigram** is a short but pungent piece. To be successful it must be brief and elegant, and discover suddenly at the conclusion a brilliant turn. Here is a specimen of the lampoon and epigram united—" To a noble Lord G—— " :

> " Spare me thy vengeance, G——,
>   In quiet let me live ;
> I ask no kindness at thy hand,
>   *For thou hast none to give."—Robert Burns.*

An epigram—" Woman's Will " :

> " Men dying make their wills, but wives
>   Escape a work so sad ;
> Why should they make what all their lives
>   The gentle dames have had ? "—*Saxe.*

ARTICLE III. LYRIC POETRY.

794. **Lyric poetry** expresses the sentiments of the heart. It occurs usually in the form of brief compositions, because passion soon exhausts itself. The lyric may, however, be prolonged by the judicious introduction of narration and description, and by the combination of various passions in one poem, as is well exemplified in Dryden's celebrated " Ode on Alexander's Feast."

795. Still, **unity** must be kept in view : it will result from the plan of the narration or description, or, better still, from the subordination of all the sentiments to the expression of one leading emotion ; in the poem just referred to admiration for the power of music is the link of unity.

796. Lyrics may be classified under three **heads**: *odes, psalms,* and *elegies.* In a wider meaning the name 'ode' is applied to any lyric ; for an 'ode' means originally a song, and it was sung to the accompaniment of the 'lyre.' 'Psalm' is the term applied to a sacred song, and in particular to the collection of one hundred and fifty inspired songs in the Sacred Scriptures. 'Elegies' (from $\acute{\varepsilon}\lambda\acute{\varepsilon}\gamma\varepsilon\iota\nu$, to say woe!) are plaintive lyrics. We shall first take the term 'ode' in its widest meaning, and afterwards treat of psalms and elegies in particular.

§1. *The Ode.*

797. The **versification** of the ode has been explained and exemplified in the treatise on Versification (b. v. c. iii. art. vi. § 4).

798. The **nature** of the ode is the outpouring of emotion by means of poetic thought and language. Here is Dryden's "Song for St. Cecilia's Day," considered one of the most beautiful odes in the English language:

I.

' From harmony, from heavenly harmony,
  This universal frame began :
  When Nature underneath a heap
   Of jarring atoms lay,
   And could not heave her head,
  The tuneful voice was heard from high,
   Arise, ye more than dead !
  Then cold and hot, and moist and dry,
  In order to their stations leap,
   And Music's power obey.
 From harmony, from heavenly harmony,
  This universal frame began ;
  From harmony to harmony,
 Through all the compass of the notes it ran,
 The diapason closing full in Man.

II.

" What passion cannot music raise and quell!
  When Jubal struck the chorded shell,
   His listening brethren stood around,
  And, wondering, on their faces fell
   To worship that celestial sound.
 Less than a God they thought there could not dwell
  Within the hollow of that shell,
  That spoke so sweetly and so well.
 What passion cannot music raise and quell?

III.

" The trumpet's loud clangor
    Excites us to arms,
  With shrill notes of anger
    And mortal alarms.
The double double double beat
    Of the thundering drum
    Cries, Hark ! the foes come ;
Charge, charge ! 'tis too late to retreat.

IV.

 " The soft complaining flute
In dying notes discovers
The woes of hopeless lovers,
Whose dirge is whispered by the warbling lute.

V.

 " Sharp violins proclaim
Their jealous pangs, and desperation,
Fury, frantic indignation,
Depth of pains, and height of passion
  For the fair, disdainful dame.

VI.

" But oh ! what art can teach,
  What human voice can reach,
  The sacred organ's praise ?
Notes inspiring holy love,
Notes that wing their heavenly ways
  To mend the choirs above.

VII.

" Orpheus could lead the savage race ;
  And trees uprooted left their place,
    Sequacious of the lyre.
But bright Cecilia raised their wonder higher :
When to her organ vocal breath was given,
  An angel heard and straight appeared,
    Mistaking earth for heaven.

"GRAND CHORUS.

" As from the power of sacred lays
    The spheres began to move,
And sung the great Creator's praise
    To all the bless'd above ;
So when the last and dreadful hour
This crumbling pageant shall devour,
The trumpet shall be heard on high,
The dead shall live, the living die,
And Music shall untune the sky."

799. It will be noticed that the lyric poet, in passing from one passion to another, does not express the transition in words. The imagination, warmed by the sentiments, readily supplies the link, provided there be truly some natural association of thought or feeling. When the transition is very bold it is called a **saltus lyricus**—in the language of Wordsworth, "a bound of graceful hardihood." Lyrics remarkable for such hardihood are called Pindaric odes ; but unfortunately the hardihood in them is not always graceful. The reason why we admire such bounds in the Greek poet Pindar is that he used them judiciously to extricate himself from a special difficulty. Pindar was a kind of poet-laureate in his day ; he was expected to sing the victories of the Olympian and Pythian games. The heroes were different, but the theme was ever the same. With 'graceful hardihood' he would 'bound' away from one subject to another. A 'lyric bound' is a license, and, like all licenses, it is not beautiful in itself ; but we admire the judicious use made of it to avoid an unpleasantness or introduce some beauty which would otherwise be lost.

800. The **style of lyric poetry** should be finished and ornate, characterized by dignity or sweetness, as the subject or the occasion may require. Grandeur and solemnity are expected in *sacred* odes ; enthusiasm and magnificence

in *heroic* odes—*i.e*, in those which proclaim the praises of heroes ; those of the *philosophic* or moral kind, inculcating virtue and wisdom, require an equable flow of thought and language ; the *social* or festive ode, also called 'Anacreontic,' should be marked by neatness and tenderness.

801. Lyrics, like all literary productions, should be **perspicuous** in thought and language. Some readers imagine that incomprehensible utterances contain very deep and wise thought. They are ever ready to exclaim with Peona in the "Endymion":

> " Brother, 'tis vain to hide
> That thou dost know of things mysterious,
> Immortal, starry."

802. They find frequent occasion for such blind admiration, especially in the poetry of this century. J. B. Selkirk, in his *Ethics and Æsthetics of Modern Poetry*, justly remarks :

" Although obscurity is no new grievance against the poets, we doubt much if there ever was a time in which the charge could be more justly made than our own, or in which the indictment could be more circumstantially supported in detail by direct reference to examples."

He traces the beginning of this mysticism to the writings, poetry and prose, of Coleridge.

803. Ralph Waldo Emerson in this country has carried this **obscurity** so far that many of his sayings are like riddles : they

> " Dodge
> Conception to the very bourne of heaven,
> Then leave the naked brain."

Many labor hard to find the clue to his philosophy. There is no clue : with Emerson, and with most anti-Christian sceptics of the present day, there is no philosophy at all in their works.   He says of himself in a letter to Rev. H. Ware (1838):

"I could not give an account of myself if challenged. I could not possibly give you one of the 'arguments' you cruelly hint at on which any doctrine of mine stands; for I do not know what arguments are in reference to any expression of a thought. I delight in telling what I think, but if you ask me how I dare say so, or why it is so, I am the most helpless of mortal men."—*Life of Emerson*, by O. W. Holmes, p. 126.

804. **Horace** has always been considered as the greatest of uninspired lyric poets.   In enthusiasm and magnificence he is surpassed by Pindar, in sweetness by Anacreon, but he surpasses all in the combination of varied beauties.   He possessed a happy, rich, and lively imagination, and the choicest language, with an exquisite ear for the music of verse; above all, a delicate tact which made him find favor with the greatest men of his age, while he maintained in his writings a certain spirit of independence.   He gave the highest polish to most of his pieces.   His immorality, however, in many places offends Christian modesty; he should be read with wise discretion.

805. We insert a list of **selections**:

1. *Neat odes:* Book i. 1. Mæcenas atavis. B. i. 10. Mercuri facunde.   B. ii. 6. Septimi Gades.   B. ii. 20. Non usisata.   B. iii. 30. Exegi monumentum.

2. *Expressive of affection:* B. i. 3. Sic te Diva potens. B. i. 24. Quis desiderio.   B. ii. 7. O sæpe mecum.   B. ii. 9. Non semper imbres.   B. ii. 17. Cur me querelis.   Ep. 1. Ibis Liburnis.

3. *Grand:* B. i. 2. Jam satis terris.   B. i. 15. Pastor quum traheret (compare "Lochiel's Warning," by Campbell).   B. i. 37. Nunc est bibendum.   B. iii. 3. Justum ac

tenacem. B. iv. 2. Pindarum quisque. B. iv. 4. Qualem ministrum.

4. *Sweet :* B. i. 26. Musis amicus. B. i. 38. Persicos odi. B. iii. 29. Tyrrhena regum. B. iv. 3. Quem tu Melpomene. B. iv. 7. Diffugere nives. Ep. 2. Beatus ille.

5. *Moral or philosophical :* B. i. 14. O navis referent. B. ii. 15. Jam pauca aratro. B. ii. 2. Nullus argento. B. ii. 3. Æquam memento. B. ii. 10. Rectius vives. B. ii. 14. Eheu fugaces. B. ii. 16. Otium divos. B. ii. 18. Non ebur neque aureum. B. iii. 5. Cœlo tonantem. Ep. 7. Quoquo scelesti.

6. *Sacred :* Carmen sæculare.

(See a judicious essay on Horace in *Blackwood's Magazine*, April, 1868.)

806. Many **Latin hymns** occurring in the Breviary are lyrics of superior merit. In style they present four chief species ; of each we shall mention some examples :

1. *The tender :* Salvete flores. Jesu dulcis memoriæ. Jesu decus angelicum. Jesu corona virginum. Salutis humanæ sator.

2. *The noble and grand :* O sola magnarum. Vexilla Regis. Lustra sex. Pange lingua. Verbum Supernum (the stanza "se nascens dedit socium," etc., so pleased Rousseau that he would have given all his poetry to be its author). Cœlestis urbs.

3. *The devout :* O sol salutis. Stabat Mater. Veni Creator. Ave Maris Stella.

4. *The festive :* Aurora cœlum. Te Joseph celebrent. Sanctorum meritis.

807. Here is Caswall's translation of St. Bernard's " Jesu Decus Angelicum " :

" O Jesu ! Thou the beauty art
Of angel worlds above ;
Thy name is music to the heart,
Enchanting it with love.

" Celestial sweetness unalloyed !
    Who eat Thee hunger still ;
    Who drink of Thee still feel a void
        Which naught but Thou canst fill.

" O my sweet Jesu ! hear the sighs
    Which unto Thee I send ;
    To Thee mine inmost spirit cries,
        My being's hope and end !

" Stay with us, Lord, and with Thy light
    Illume the soul's abyss ;
    Scatter the darkness of our night,
        And fill the world with bliss.

" O Jesu ! spotless Virgin flower !
    Our life and joy ! to Thee
    Be praise, beatitude, and power
        Through all eternity."

Translations of all the hymns mentioned above are found in the *Lyra Catholica* and in the translation of the Breviary by the Marquis of Bute. (See also Newman's *Verses on Various Occasions* and the *Hymns and Poems* of Father Faber.)

808. We add an example of an ode which assumes the form of a **sonnet**:

"THE BLESSED VIRGIN.

" Mother ! whose virgin bosom was uncrost
    With the least shade of thought to sin allied ;
    Woman ! above all women glorified,
    Our tainted nature's solitary boast ;
    Purer than foam on central ocean tost ;
    Brighter than eastern skies at daybreak strewn
    With fancied roses, than the unblemished moon
    Before her wane begins on heaven's blue coast ;
    Thy image falls to earth.   Yet some, I ween,

Not unforgiven the suppliant knee might bend,
As to a visible power, in which did blend
All that was mixed and reconciled in thee
Of mother's love with maiden purity,
Of high with low, celestial with terrene ! "
—Wordsworth.

809. Some of the most perfect odes in existence are found in the **choruses of the Greek and the French tragedies.** Sir Bulwer-Lytton renders the beginning of a chorus in *Œdipus at Colonos* as follows:

Strophe I.

" Well did Fate thy wanderings lead,
    Stranger, to this land of fame,
Birthplace of the generous steed,
    Graced by white Colonos' name.
Frequent in the dewy glade,
    Here the nightingale is dwelling ;
Through embowering ivy's shade
    Here her plaintive notes are swelling.
Through yon grove, from footsteps pure,
    Where unnumbered fruits are blushing—
From the summer sun secure,
    Screened from wintry whirlwinds rushing ;
Where, with his fostering nymphs, amid the grove,
The sportive Bacchus joys to revel or to rove."

Antistrophe I.

" Bathed in heaven's ambrosial dew,
    Here the fair narcissus flowers,
Graced each morn with clusters new,
    Ancient crown of mightiest Powers ;
Here the golden crocus blows,
    Here exhaustless fountains gushing
Where the cool Cephisus flows
    Restless o'er the plains are rushing ;

> Ever as the crystal flood
>   Winds in pure, transparent lightness,
> Fresher herbage decks the sod,
>   Flowers spring forth in lovelier brightness.
> Here dance the Muses, and the Queen of Love
> Oft guides her golden car through this enchanting grove."

§ 2. *The Psalms.*

810. No profane lyric poetry equals the **lyrical portions of Holy Scripture.** The principal of these are the Psalms, the Canticle of Canticles, the Magnificat of the Blessed Virgin Mary, the Benedictus of St. Zachary, the Canticle of Moses after crossing the Red Sea. The canticle of Mary, the sister of Aaron, mentioned in the book of Genesis (xv. 21), is thus developed by Moore in imitation of Moses' Canticle :

> " Sound the loud timbrel o'er Egypt's dark sea !
>   Jehovah has triumphed !—His people are free !
>   Sing,—for the pride of the tyrant is broken,
>   His chariots, his horsemen, all splendid and brave ;
>   How vain was their boasting !   The Lord hath but spoken,
>   And chariots and horsemen are sunk in the wave.
>   Sound the loud timbrel o'er Egypt's dark sea !
>   Jehovah has triumphed !—His people are free.

> " Praise to the Conqueror, praise to the Lord :
>   His word was our arrow, His breath was our sword !
>   Who shall return to tell Egypt the story
>   Of those she sent forth in the hour of her pride ?
>   For the Lord hath looked out from the pillar of His glory,
>   And all her brave thousands are dashed in the tide.
>   Sound the loud timbrel o'er Egypt's dark sea !
>   Jehovah has triumphed !—His people are free."

811. **The Psalms contain** the loftiest inspiration concerning God and the mysteries of His grace to men ; concerning

the life and death of our Blessed Saviour, the praises and the rewards of virtue, the humiliation and ruin of the proud sinner, the mercies of the Lord, the wonderful history of His chosen people ; David's own eventful life, with its faults, its trials, and its unfailing hope.   (See Archbishop F. P. Kenrick's introduction to his translation of the Psalms.)

§ 3. *Elegies.*

812. **An elegy,** as explained above, is an ode expressive of sorrow, but the name is often extended to signify any ode that expresses gentle emotions.   Being a composition of a temperate character, it admits no boldness of metre, thought, or language, nor any sudden transitions or *saltus lyrici.*   Its style is easy, equable, careful, finished.   Gray's " Elegy in a Country Church-Yard " is probably the most perfect elegy in the English language.   The selections quoted above under epistles (788, 789, 790) are of the elegiac kind.

813. We add here two brief selections containing much thought in few words :

"The Lost Love.

" She dwelt among the untrodden ways
 Beside the springs of Dove ;
A maid whom there were none to praise,
 And very few to love.

" A violet by a mossy stone,
 Half-hidden from the eye !
Fair as a star, when only one
 Is shining in the sky.

" She lived unknown, and few could know
 When Lucy ceased to be ;
But she is in her grave, and oh !
 The difference to me ! "— *William Wordsworth.*

814. " HISTORY OF A LIFE.

" Day dawned ; within a curtained room,
Filled to faintness with perfume,
A lady lay at point of doom.
Day closed ; a child had seen the light,
But, for the lady fair and bright,
She rested in undreaming night.
Spring rose ; the lady's grave was green ;
And near it, oftentimes, was seen
A gentle boy with thoughtful mien.
Years fled ; he wore a manly face,
And struggled in the world's rough race,
And won at last a lofty place.
And then he died !   Behold before ye
Humanity's poor sum and story :
Life—Death—and all that is of Glory."

—Barry Cornwall.

815. Among the ancient classic poems, the " Tristia " of Ovid are the most celebrated elegies ; to these there is nothing superior in their kind among modern lyrics. See in particular book i. 1, 3, 5 ; b. iii. 1, 10, 12, 13; b. iv. 10. With b. iii. 13 compare Job ch. iii. (see Rollin's *Belles-Lettres*, vol. ii.)   Many of the Psalms are elegiac in character ; in particular Ps. vi., xvi., xxi., xxvii., xli., xliii., l., lxxviii., lxxxvii.   Such are also the "Lamentations of Jeremias."   Of most of these pieces there exist poetic translations in English. Ps. cxxxvi., "Super flumina Babylonis," is translated by Mrs. Hemans, Byron, Barrow, Trumbull, Aubrey de Vere, and others. We subjoin a version, never yet published, from the pen of a departed friend, the Rev. L. Heylen, S.J.:

"BY THE WATERS OF BABEL.

" By the waters of Babel in sadness
The lone captives sat silent and wept,
As they mused on the days of their gladness
When their feasts in lost Sion were kept.

> On the willows that shaded the border
>   Our loved harps sad and voiceless were hung—
> Ne'er in chains to the tyrant's proud order
>   Shall the hymns of our freedom be sung.
> May my withered right hand lose its motion,
>   May my tongue to my parched palate cleave,
> If, forgetting my childhood's devotion,
>   I rejoice whilst thou, Sion, shalt grieve !
> Lord, remember the dark desolation
>   Of the city of peace in her fall,
> And the boasting of Edom's fierce nation
>   To leave not a stone of her wall !
> Back upon thee, proud Babylon's daughter,
>   May the woes that afflict us be thrown !
> And thrice blessed be the hands, red with slaughter,
>   That shall dash thy crushed babes on the stone ! "

ARTICLE IV. DRAMATIC POETRY.

816. Dramatic poetry is that in which events instead of being narrated are acted on the stage. It comprises two kinds, tragedy and comedy. *Tragedy* deals with the grave and affecting events of life ; it arouses the more earnest passions, especially pity, terror, and deep admiration for heroic virtue. *Comedy* is employed upon the lighter incidents of life, the humors, follies, and pleasures of men ; it brings into play the gentler passions, especially ridicule.

§ 1. *Tragedy.*

817. Tragedy has passed through great changes of character. We shall first explain **the tragedy of the Greeks. Æschylus** conceived the plan of expressing by dramatic dialogues, interspersed with music, dance, and song, the control of fate and the will of God over the destinies of men. His conceptions are singularly grand, his language highly poetical, and his choruses frequent and magnificent,

but his plans are exceedingly simple. A few bold touches sketch his facts and his characters. A. W. Schlegel's *Lectures on Dramatic Art and Literature* give a clear account of what is called the *trilogy of the Oresteia—i.e.*, the history of Orestes dramatized in three of Æschylus' tragedies, "Agamemnon," "Electra," and "The Furies" (lecture vi.)

818. **Sophocles,** while exhibiting the overruling power of fate, pays more attention to the varied actions and passions of men. His taste in matters of detail is very delicate. See, for instance, his "Œdipus at Colonos" and his "Antigone." (See also Schlegel, lecture vii. on his "Ajax"; and Felton's *Ancient and Modern Greece*, vol. i. course i. c. xii.)

819. **Euripides** has less of ideal elevation, deals much more in human character, passions, and incidents. His "Medea" represents an uncommonly bold and unyielding woman, whose wicked passions, not fate, are the clue of the story.

820. The dramas of the ancients were represented on a scale of magnificence in scenic decorations, costumes, and choruses, and with a concourse of people unrivalled in our day. Athens was then in the zenith of her literary glory. (See Felton, *ib.*, vol. i. course ii. c. xii.)

821. The lectures of A. W. Schlegel treat the entire subject of the dramatic art with great learning and good taste. On the tragedy of the Greeks the most learned work, a rich mine of information, is *Le Théâtre des Grecs*, by P. Brumois, S.J. (1688).

The **Latins** had no great tragedians whatever; they merely translated the Greeks.

822. **French tragedy** arose after the English, but it was modelled on the Greek, and therefore we shall consider it in close connection with the ancient drama. **Corneille** was the Æschylus of France; his "Le Cid" was his first master-

piece: "as beautiful as 'Le Cid'" became a common expression for perfect beauty. He did not court popular favor by flattering the softer passions, but he raised his audience to admire true honor and heroism. His "Horaces" and "Cinna" exalt classical, his "Polyeucte" Christian virtue. His later works are less commendable.

823. **Racine** is refined, like Sophocles. Unlike Corneille, he exhibits the frailties of human character and the play of the more tender passions. His "Andromaque" is a touching picture of maternal love (1667). Next came his "Britannicus," "Bérénice," "Mithridate," "Iphigénie," and "Phèdre." He appears to have been ashamed of the excesses of lawless love as exhibited in this last drama, and for twelve years he abandoned tragedy. He returned to it as a religious poet, and produced his masterpieces, "Esther" and "Athalie," both worthy of careful study; the latter is unsurpassed as a production of classical taste. Voltaire attempted to remodel the French stage. His plays, while they have brilliant scenes at times, are as defective as they are pretentious. (See Schlegel, lect. xx.)

824. The Greek and French tragedians admitted in the course of their dramas no scene which did not affect the final issue of the piece—the **catastrophe**, as it is called: *i.e.*, the overturning of the hero's fortune ($\varkappa\alpha\tau\acute{\alpha}$, $\sigma\tau\rho\acute{\epsilon}\varphi\omega$, to overturn). The exclusion of all foreign matter is called the **unity of action**. The action itself embraced no events but such as might occur in one day; this is **unity of time**. And as the Grecian stage was, as a rule, never deserted during the whole play, every scene was laid on the same spot; this is **unity of place**.

825. The **chorus** consisted of a band of persons who were supposed to have been present at the occurrences represented. They were actors, or rather spoke and sang like one actor in the drama, uttering the voice of

wisdom, counsel, moderation, religion, etc. Their unfailing presence on or near the stage was a source of great
embarrassment to the poet, for it was not probable that
opposing parties should plot in presence of the same witnesses. The chorus was thus an encumbrance as well as
an ornament. From time to time they sang an ode suggested by the play, thus relieving the attention of the spectators. Hence originated the division of a play into **acts**,
usually five in number.

826. **The great French tragedians,** with their natural
love of regularity, were very particular about **the three
unities** just explained. In the course of an act the place,
with them, could not be changed, because the scenes were
all connected with each other, so that the stage was never
vacant except at the close of an act. When a new actor
enters or any one retires they count it another **scene;** and
they require that each scene shall flow naturally from the
preceding, no actor coming or going without apparent reason for so doing. Their tragedies thus exhibit the most
perfect regularity, but the poet is constantly shackled by
such restrictions.

827. Both Greeks and French confine their tragedies to
serious events, to what is grave, terrible, and pathetic;
rigidly excluding all that is comical or too familiar. This
is a leading feature of **classical** as distinct from **romantic**
taste. The English idea of tragedy is very different from
all this. Shakspeare (born 1564) originated it independently of Grecian models. His genius created the romantic
tragedy, which is as different from the classic as a magnificent and wild landscape is from a beautiful and regular
garden.

As in a landscape we may have vast plains, towering
mountains, deep gorges, frightful precipices, interspersed
with delightful vales, clear lakes, and refreshing fountains,

all mixed in wild confusion, so we have in Shakspeare the most varied grandeur mixed with scenes of tender pathos, loud merriment, buffoonery, extravagance, all in endless profusion.

"The ancient art of poetry," says Schlegel, "rigorously separated things which are dissimilar. The romantic delights in indissoluble mixtures and contrarieties; nature and art, poetry and prose, seriousness and mirth, recollection and anticipation, spirituality and sensuality, terrestrial and celestial, life and death, are by it blended together in the most intimate combination" (Lect. xxii.)

828. **Shakspeare** displayed a wonderful fertility of invention. He created highly dramatic scenes, intricate plots full of interest, and characters so grand, so distinct, so varied, so true to nature, and so consistent that no poet has ever surpassed him. His language has a power of its own; every sentence is a coin destined to circulate, and stamped with the mark of his particular mint. He generally observes unity of action, which is the essential unity of dramatic poetry; but he totally disregards the minor unities of time and place. Some of his dramas include the transactions of many years and the scenes of distant lands. He carries this liberty to the extent of license, with no slight detriment to probability and naturalness.

829. **An English play** is divided into acts and scenes, but these terms with us have not the same meaning as with the French. **An act** may consist of detached scenes laid in various lands and at various times; and **a scene** embraces all that is done in close succession at a given place, provided the same leading personages remain on the stage.

830. On one important point classic and romantic poets are agreed, both classes making tragedy the realm, chiefly if not solely, of the powerful passions—of pity and terror, of admiration for exalted virtue and detestation of crime

and villany. In this respect tragedy is **favorable to virtue.** Aristotle says of it that it "purifies the passions of men by means of pity and terror." The pernicious influence which the stage is justly accused of usually exercising results from abuses not essential to it, but unfortunately too common ; the passions, instead of being purified, are perverted by it, especially the passion of love. Beaumont and Fletcher in particular are shockingly immoral. All the old tragedians, Shakspeare included, indulged in gross vulgarity. Modern tragic poets are more polished, but often more corrupting .withal.

831. From a literary point of view Shakspeare is **at times deserving of severe criticism,** his comic wit degenerating into meaningless puns, his serious passions swelling into bombast. Besides, he is exceedingly irregular, and sometimes extravagant ; he so mixes faults with beauties as to be a very unsafe model for imitation.

832. But he superabundantly atones for these defects by **unrivalled excellences,** several of which we have already mentioned. One we must explain more fully, as it is the characteristic perfection of dramatic poetry. It is thus described by Cardinal Wiseman in his last literary effort, a lecture on Shakspeare, intended .to be delivered, by invitation, before the Royal Institution of Great Britain :

" Its essence [that of Shakspeare's dramatic art] consists in what is the very soul of the dramatic idea—the power to throw himself into the situation, the circumstances, the nature, the acquired habits, the feelings, true or fictitious, of every character which he introduces. This forms, in fact, the most perfect of sympathies. We do not, of course, use the word in that more usual sense of harmony of affection or consent of feeling. Shakspeare has sympathy as complete for Shylock or Iago as he has for Arthur or King Lear. For a time he lives in the astute villain as in the innocent child ; he works his entire power of thought into intricacies of the traitor's brain ; he makes his heart beat in concord with the usurer's sanguinary spite, and then, like some beautiful creature in the animal world, draws himself out of the hateful evil, and is himself again, and able, even, often to hold his own noble and gentle qualities as a mirror, or exhibit the loftiest, the most generous and amiable examples of our nature. And this is all done without study, and apparently without effort. His infinitely varied characters come naturally into their places, never for a moment lose their proprieties, their personality, and the exact flexibility which results from the necessary combination in every man of many qualities. From the beginning to the end each one is the same, yet reflecting in himself the lights and shadows which flit around him.

"This extraordinary versatility stands in striking contrast with the dramatic productions of other countries. The Greek tragedian is Greek throughout—his subjects, his mythology, his sentences play wonderfully indeed, but yet restrictedly, within a given sphere."—*Catholic World* for 1865, vol. i. p. 559.

833. There lived in England about the time of Shakspeare a number of brilliant **tragic writers**, such as Marlowe, Webster, Decker, Tourneur, Heywood, Middleton, Chapman, Ben Jonson, Marston, Massinger, Ford, Beaumont and Fletcher. (See a criticism of these in Whipple's *Essays*, vol. ii.)

834. **Spanish tragedy** was created about the same time as the English by two geniuses, Lope de Vega and Calderon, who have supplied their nation with dramatic works of the highest merit and suited to the purer morals of a Catholic people. De Vega resembles Shakspeare. Calderon is more like Racine; his priestly office did not cool his poetic ardor.

835. **To become acquainted with the great tragedians** it would be of little use to study such brief extracts as might here be given. Those who wish to apply themselves to this portion of literature should read a few, at least, of the great masterpieces; for instance, the "Agamemnon," "Electra," and "Eumenides" of Æschylus; the "Œdipus Tyrannus,"

" Antigone," and " Œdipus at Colonos " of Sophocles ; the " Medea " and "Iphigenia in Aulis " of Euripides ; Corneille's " Le Cid," Racine's " Esther " and " Athalie," Shakspeare's " Macbeth," " Hamlet," " Julius Cæsar," and " Coriolanus." Shakspeare's tragedies may be read to advantage with the judicious notes of Hudson or of Rolfe in their school editions, in which the most offensive passages are omitted or toned down. George H. Miles' comments on " Hamlet " find favor with many. But it must be allowed that even in most of the expurgated editions of Shakspeare there is much in plot and scene, if not always in expression, bearing on such vices as the apostle tells us should not even be named among Christians.

Happily we have some beautiful dramas of a very different kind, the reading of which can only benefit the student. Such are " The Hidden Gem " of Cardinal Wiseman ; " The Dumb Orphan," " Sebastian," " The Family of Martyrs," etc.

836. It remains for us to add some further **precepts on the composition of tragedy**:

1. The *story* should be interesting and full of pathos.

2. The *characters* should be distinctly drawn, naturally presented, and made to act and speak consistently throughout the play. They need not be taken from history nor from public life, nor should they all be virtuous ; mixed characters—that is, those partly good and partly bad—are the most natural.

3. The *first act* must make us acquainted with the situation, excite interest, and introduce some of the leading characters. It is desirable that the play should explain itself without needing introduction or comment.

4. In the *second, third, and fourth acts* the plot thickens ; the great point to be aimed at is to keep the passions alive : let there be no languor, no personages but such as are

needed—and these should be put in interesting situations—
no idle declamation. All must be action rather than discourse.

5. The *fifth act* contains the catastrophe, which is the
surest test of the poet's genius. After the suspense has
been carried to a great height in the preceding acts it is
brought to a crisis in the fifth. The catastrophe should be
brought about by natural means, in a plausible though quite
unexpected manner. It should discard long speeches and
idle declamation. It should be so clear as not to check
passion by obscurity, so simple as not to embarrass the
mind by intricacy. The end may be the success of the
innocent, as in Racine's "Athalie"; but usually the impression of virtuous sorrow is left full and strong on the
heart.

6. Throughout the play the greatest *probability* must be
preserved: nothing must appear unaccountable, in order
that curiosity may be fully satisfied.

7. *Poetical justice* requires that the actors meet with their
just deserts, so that the lot of the virtuous appear on the
whole far preferable to that of the wicked.

8. *Unity of action* is essential: it can never be dispensed
with in tragedy, whether classic or romantic. The *unities
of time and place* add to the probability of the story and to
the symmetry of the poetic structure. They are beauties,
but, like rhyme in verse, they may be discarded, provided
they be replaced by greater beauties. Let no one imagine
that irregularity is pleasing in itself to a well-ordered mind,
especially in works of art: irregularity is inartistic.

837. It is a much-debated question **whether the classic or
the romantic drama is to be preferred.** An analogous question would be whether a garden or a grand architectural
structure is more beautiful than a delightful, varied landscape. This is a matter of taste. We appreciate both clas-

sical and romantic art ; preference for the one or the other depends usually on early associations.

838. **Exercise.** Write a criticism of a tragedy. (See b. iv. c. v. art. ii. § 3.) Notice in particular : 1. What is known of its author? 2. Is the subject historical or fictitious? how far historical? 3. Narrate the story briefly. 4. Criticise the poem according to the eight precepts for tragedy just explained.

§ 2. *Comedy.*

839. The **ancient comedy** had not the regularity of the modern ; it formed a complete contrast to the ancient tragedy, of which it was a wild parody. Tragedy delighted in harmonious unity, comedy in chaotic exuberance, seeking out the most motley contrasts and the unceasing play of cross-purposes. The action of an ancient comedy might be as fantastic as possible, if only it could place a series of comic incidents in a glaring light. Man is shown by it, not in all his nobility, but in all his frailties and often in all his baseness. Many consider the old comedy as only a beginning of the comic art ; but Schlegel defends it as distinguished from the later comedy in kind rather than in point of perfection. It was a school of scandal, as is evident from its only representative whose poems are extant, Aristophanes. (See Schlegel, lectures xi., xii.) Felton's *Ancient and Modern Greece* contains an interesting analysis of Aristophanes' "Ecclesiazousæ," or comedy on 'Women's Rights,' the agitation of which question appears to be an old vagary (vol. i. course i. c. xii.)

Later Greek comedy was more like our own ; it was less licentious than earlier comedy, but still very objectionable.

840. **Modern comedy** has a regular plot ; it requires unity of action ; it sometimes observes the minor unities of time

and place and the proper connection of the successive scenes. It requires, above all, great probability in the representation. Unlike tragedy, it requires the scene to be laid in the present time and as much as possible in our own country, "to catch the manners living as they rise." The Latin poets Plautus and Terence, successful in other respects, made the mistake of attempting little more than translating Menander and other Greeks. The reason why we should prefer home scenes is that comedy aims at correcting frailties and follies by ridicule; but there is no advantage to be derived from ridiculing the defects of foreign nations.

841. There are **two kinds of comedy**, that of *character* and that of *intrigue*. In the latter, the plot is more artfully kept up; in the former, character is the chief object of attention. Molière's "Misanthrope" and "Le Bourgeois Gentilhomme" ("The Upstart") are excellent examples of this kind. But the comedy of character should connect its scenes by some kind of plot, and the other species must not neglect the exhibition of characters. It is best to unite both sources of interest in as high a degree as possible. Care should be taken not to exaggerate the peculiarities of character beyond what is natural or at least plausible.

842. The **style** should be pure, elegant, and lively, seldom rising above that of ordinary conversation; never vulgar.

843. Though comedy, like satire, is **intended for the correction** of human frailties, it has been, as a rule, so handled by ancient and modern poets as to be more injurious to the ordinary reader than beneficial. Among the ancients the "Captivi" of Plautus is a piece entirely free from immodesty. His other comedies, as well as those of Terence, are often scandalous. Of Menander we have nothing left except some fragments in Terence's translations.

844. Shakspeare is the pride of our literature in comedy as well as in tragedy. He lived, unfortunately, in an age which was most licentious; and though he is less grossly offensive to modesty than many of his contemporaries, still his pieces would need much purgation before they could be made edifying reading for those not familiar with vice.

ARTICLE V. ACCIDENTAL VARIATIONS OF POETRY

845. Any poetical composition whatever may be classed under one or other of the four species of poetry so far explained. Still, it is usual in rhetorical treatises to take particular notice of some varieties of poetic composition which have peculiar features of their own besides the properties of the species to which they belong. The principal of these varieties are *Pastoral poetry* and the *poetry of the Holy Scriptures.*

§ 1. *Pastoral poetry.*

846. Pastoral poetry is that which is intended to exhibit a life of simple and natural happiness, or, as others express it, the simple happiness of a country life. Poems of this character may be narrative or descriptive, dramatic, lyric, or didactic. Whatever species they belong to, they have certain features of their own to which it is proper to call particular attention.

847. The following are the **principal features of pastorals:**

1. The *emotions* excited are of the gentler kind, such as arise in the beholder from the contemplation of innocence, quiet, candor, and freedom from great anxiety.

2. The *characters* introduced must be amiable in their simplicity; neither too refined nor too rude; of lively

but not excessive sensibility ; possessed of some ambition, and at times of some cunning, but never vicious ; more or less quick of parts, but not too learned. Shepherds and farmers are usually represented, but Theocritus and Moschus introduce also soldiers and inhabitants of cities.

3. The *subjects* are the joys, the cares, the troubles of country life, with its various incidents.

4. The *style* must be sweet and gentle, elegant and melodious. The ornaments must be suitable to the subjects and the characters, and be drawn from the scenes and associations of a country life. Brief and neat descriptions are great ornaments.

848. **Theocritus**, a Sicilian, was the father of pastoral poetry ; his Idyls ($\varepsilon i\delta \acute{v}\lambda\lambda\iota o\nu$, a little picture) are very tender, full of naïveté, and expressed in gently-flowing language. Not all his idyls are pastorals, and not all deserve high commendation. **Virgil** has mostly reproduced the beauties of Theocritus in a Latin version, and often improved on the original. Unlike his Greek model, he never descends to what is low or common. His four books called " Georgics " ($\gamma \varepsilon \omega \rho \gamma \iota \kappa \acute{o}\varsigma$, agricultural) are a didactic treatise on agriculture. His most charming pastorals are his " Eclogues " ($\acute{\varepsilon}\kappa\lambda o\gamma \acute{\eta}$, a choice piece), in particular his first, fourth, fifth, and eleventh.

849. The fourth of Virgil's Eclogues is remarkable for the beauty of its imagery and for the nobility of its thoughts. It describes the expected coming of a Saviour of mankind under the image of a divine child, who is to restore the golden age. Pope has translated this eclogue, blending with it many images taken from the prophecy of Isaias concerning the Messias. It is the most beautiful of Pope's translations, and the grandest pastoral poem in the English language. Shenstone has written a pastoral ballad in four parts, from which we quote a brief passage :

" My banks they are furnished with bees,
    Whose murmur invites one to sleep ;
My grottoes are shaded with trees,
    And my hills are white over with sheep.
I have seldom met with a loss ;
    Such health do my fountains bestow—
My fountains, all bordered with moss,
    Where the harebells and violets grow.

" Not a pine in my grove is there seen
    But with tendrils of woodbine is bound ;
Not a beech is more beautiful green
    But a sweetbriar entwines it around ;
Not my fields in the prime of the year
    More charms than my cattle unfold ;
Not a brook that is limpid and clear
    But it glitters with fishes of gold."

§ 2. *The Holy Scriptures.*

850. We have occasionally in the course of this work referred to passages of **the Sacred Scriptures**, and compared the language of the Holy Spirit with the most perfect productions of human genius. An impression may thus have been produced upon the minds of pupils that there is some kind of equality between the works of God and the works of man. It is proper here to add a word of caution against so erroneous an inference. The beauty and sublimity of Holy Writ are far more elevated above the poems of Homer, Dante, and Shakspeare than the productions of these great geniuses above the daily conversation of ordinary mortals.

851. In all the literary works of men there is a constant effort to rise above the level of common thoughts. The word of God, on the contrary, appears to stoop down in order to bring truths of infinite grandeur within the com-

prehension of our little minds. Hence result two **cha-racteristics of Holy Writ**—*simplicity* and *majesty*.

852. The *thought* is ever **majestic,** and so vast that the more we meditate upon any utterance of God the more meaning we find in it. (See, for an example, Father Coleridge's comments on the " Magnificat," " The Nine Months," c. ix.)

The *expression* in Holy Scripture is usually **simple,** except when God wishes to rebuke the pride of man, or when the prophet or the psalmist labors, as it were, to give utterance to thoughts and sentiments too vast for human language.

853. We shall give a few **examples**:

1. **God rebukes the pride of man** in language full of power and majesty :

" Behold, I come against thee, O Tyre : and I will cause many nations to come up to thee, as the waves of the sea rise up. And they shall break down the walls of Tyre, and destroy the towers thereof : and I will scrape her dust from her, and make her like a smooth rock. She shall be a drying-place for nets in the midst of the sea : because I have spoken, saith the Lord God ; and she shall be a spoil to the nations. Her daughters also that are in the field shall be slain by the sword : and they shall know that I am the Lord " (Ezechiel, xxvi. 3-6).

See also Job, chapters xxxviii. and xxxix., in which God rebukes the arrogance of Job's friends ; these chapters are sublime in thought and language.

854. 2. In the first and second chapters of Genesis God reveals the events of **the Creation** in terms of the utmost simplicity :

" God made two great lights : a great light to rule the day, and a lesser light to rule the night ; and the stars " (i. 16).

Ecclesiasticus, speaking in his own person, though, of

course, under the influence of inspiration, exclaims in terms full of magnificence :

"The firmament on high is His beauty, the beauty of heaven with its glorious show. The sun when he appeareth showing forth at his rising, an admirable instrument, the work of the Most High. At noon he burneth the earth ; and who can abide his burning heat ? As one keeping a furnace in works of heat : the sun three times as much, burneth the mountains, breathing out fiery vapors, and shining with his beams, he blindeth the eyes. Great is the Lord that made him ; and at His words he hath hastened his course. . . . The glory of the stars is the beauty of heaven : the Lord enlighteneth the world on high " (xliii. 1–10).

855. 3. Compare the simple language in which the **passage of the Red Sea,** in Exodus (xiv.), is described by Moses as the historian of the Lord, and the magnificence with which the same facts are set forth in the canticle of Moses (*Ib.* xv.), as also in the Psalm, " Attendite popule meus " (Ps. lxxvii.)

856. 4. Lastly, the history of **Christ's sacred Passion** is told by the Evangelists in language touching, indeed, but exceedingly simple—*e.g. :*

" They crucified Him there ; and the robbers, one on the right hand and the other on the left. And Jesus said : Father, forgive them, for they know not what they do. But dividing His garments, they cast lots " (Luke xxiii. 33, 34).

Now compare with this passage the sublime language of the Prophet Isaias, chapter liii.

857. As might be expected from the preceding reflections, we find that **the poetical portions** of the Holy Scriptures are chiefly the Psalms, the Book of Job, a great portion of the prophetical writings, in particular the " Lamentations of Jeremias," also some passages scattered through the historical books. " The Canticle of Canti-

cles" and the didactic portions of Holy Scripture are likewise full of poetry.

Though not written for the purpose of pleasing literary critics, still our bountiful Lord has scattered through the Sacred Volumes the same profusion of beauty and grandeur which is so conspicuous in all the works of His Omnipotence.

ALPHABETICAL INDEX OF THE PROPER NAMES.

The numbers refer to the paragraphs.

ALPHABETICAL INDEX OF THE PRECEPTS.

The numbers refer to the paragraphs.

www.ingramcontent.com/pod-product-compliance
Lightning Source LLC
Chambersburg PA
CBHW021713110726
47902CB00005B/1172